# Harnessing Value in the Supply Chain

**Wiley Operations Management Series for Professionals**

Other published titles in this series are:

# Harnessing Value in the Supply Chain

## STRATEGIC SOURCING IN ACTION

### Emiko Banfield

*John Wiley & Sons, Inc.*

New York ➤ Chichester ➤ Weinheim ➤ Brisbane ➤ Singapore ➤ Toronto

Published by John Wiley & Sons, Inc.
Published simultaneously in Canada.

This publication is designed to provide accurate and authoritative information
in regard to the subject matter covered. It is sold with the understanding that
the publisher is not engaged in rendering legal, accounting, or other
professional services. If legal advice or other expert assistance is required, the
services of a competent professional person should be sought.

The information and opinions contained in this book are provided by the
author. While the author is an employee of the Southern California Edison
Company, the Southern California Edison Company is not in any way
responsible for the contents of this book and the opinions expressed herein are
not necessarily those of the Southern California Edison Company.

*Library of Congress Cataloging-in-Publication Data:*
Banfield, Emiko, 1946–
    Harnessing value in the supply chain : strategic sourcing in action /
Emiko Banfield.
        p.      cm.
    Includes index.
    ISBN 0-471-34975-5 (cloth : alk. paper)
    1. Business logistics.   2. Strategic planning.   3. Teams in the workplace.
4. Organizational change.   5. Southern California Edison Company.
I. Title.
HD38.5.B36      1999
658.7—dc21                                                      99-17589
                                                                    CIP

Printed in the United States of America.

10 9 8 7 6 5 4 3

# Contents

# Foreword

You are about to read a book that is primarily about people and their relationships—people in the middle of our company, people on the front lines of our services, people we buy from, people inside and outside Southern California Edison whose relationships have set off a phenomenal business revolution.

Those of us in executive leadership can claim only the following credit for this story: We had the good sense to support the bold vision of Emiko Banfield and the hundreds of employees and suppliers who helped her transform a key part of how we do business.

This revolution entails learning to respect our suppliers as much as we respect ourselves, discovering that our vendors sometimes know as much as we know (more, in some situations), and deciding to make relational commitments outside our walls that equal the trust we confer on our own employees.

*Harnessing Value in the Supply Chain* is a business case that has little to do with our specific line of work—energy production, distribution, and related services. It is an enlightening account of how a new approach to corporate procurement changed our company in ways that could benefit nearly every business in America. The originality of this case study is not in the particular concept used—Strategic Sourcing—but in its unique application here at Southern California Edison.

How effective is Strategic Sourcing? When Emiko Banfield proposed this strategy to our executive team, she predicted that it might save us \$100 million a year. She was being conservative. It now saves us \$150 million annually.

John Bryson, Chairman and CEO
Southern California Edison
Rosemead, CA

# Preface

During the writing of this book, the working title was *It's About People and Money*, which aptly identifies the essential elements of the Strategic Sourcing story. As the story began to unfold, we realized it really was a story of organizational transformation achieved during the course of a corporate supply chain cost reduction initiative. The headline for the story might be:

*SCE Set Out to Save $100 Million and along the Way Changed a Culture*

Part One is the story of Strategic Sourcing at Southern California Edison (SCE). It is written to introduce you to the power and possibilities of a new way of doing business. Stories recount the Strategic Sourcing experience at SCE, sharing lessons from the perspectives of the leaders who implemented the strategy and the suppliers who became partners in the change. Part Two deals with the how-to of Strategic Sourcing, providing a step-by-step guide that starts with deciding to act and continues through design, implementation, and reaping the benefits of a successful Strategic Sourcing program in your company. Once Strategic Sourcing is fully implemented, you will have streamlined the supply base and realigned your people, processes, structures, and culture. The net result is a dramatic reduction in total cost and a new way of doing business.

I hope the book enables you to benefit from Strategic Sourcing.

Emiko Banfield, Ph.D.
Vice President, Shared Services
Southern California Edison

# Introduction

*Harnessing Value in the Supply Chain* is designed to provide a strategic view of the supply chain. By taking a strategic view of the supply chain, you can achieve breakthrough results. But breakthrough results require *bold action*. Bold action is born out of a *compelling vision*.

> *Creating a vision is the first step toward results,*
> *but without implementation (action)—the vision is*
> *just words on paper. This book builds a bridge*
> *between vision and action.*

The challenge is to bridge the gap between vision and action. The bridge is Strategic Sourcing. Using the Strategic Sourcing methodology, you can forge the pathway between where you are today and where you need to be tomorrow.

It is becoming increasingly difficult for a company to compete as an isolated entity. Instead, strategically aligned networks of companies, suppliers, distributors, retailers, manufacturers, and other support providers will compete against one another. Corporate boundaries will become less distinct, significantly changing supply chain management as we know it today.

Many companies believe they have already embarked upon Strategic Sourcing; however, certain elements are usually missing from these initiatives. This book is a complete presentation of the necessary components of a successful program.

Ultimately, success occurs when the company and the selected suppliers collaborate within a relationship of mutual benefit and shared responsibility. Together, they plan and design supply chain strategies while measuring and monitoring results.

---

*What is Strategic Sourcing? Strategic Sourcing reorganizes the company's supply base for materials and services to reduce both external expenditures and internal processing costs.*

---

The book is divided into two parts. Part One, "The Voice of Experience," is the story of Strategic Sourcing at Southern California Edison (SCE). It is a real-life story told in the words of people who lived and led Strategic Sourcing over the two years of revolutionary change. Chapter 1, "The SCE Story," describes the who, what, when, where, and why of a major organizational effort to change the way SCE managed the supply chain and made buying decisions. Chapter 2, "The Case for Action—Theory and Practice," establishes the conceptual and practical business foundation for understanding whether Strategic Sourcing is right for you.

Chapter 3, "Suppliers Speak," tells the story from the perspective of the suppliers who, through Strategic Sourcing, became partners in change at SCE. As sourcing partners, they tell how their roles changed, and, as a consequence, how their businesses changed. They also give advice on how to succeed in pursuing Strategic Sourcing relationships, and how to sustain and grow these relationships once you are involved in them.

Chapter 4, "Critical Success Factors in Strategic Sourcing," identifies and explores nine critical factors for implementing a successful program. It describes lessons learned through the SCE experience and provides insights into what worked and what didn't. In Chapter 5, "Suppliers' Critical Success Factors," separate critical success factors are identified by suppliers and discussed from the suppliers' viewpoint.

Part Two, "The Action Guide: Implementing Strategic Sourcing," is a tool for leaders, managers, and teams striving to improve their companies' bottom lines and strengthen their competitive advantage. This part of the book includes a phased methodology for implementing a successful program in your organization. The approach focuses on creating a shared vision throughout the supply chain, systematically and comprehensively addressing external spending and internal processing costs. In addition, this fully integrated framework includes tools useful in change initiatives. All agencies and institutions whose operations include purchasing will benefit from Strategic Sourcing.

> *Strategic Sourcing is a tool to deliver bottom-line results to all types of companies.*

Part Two lays out the complete Strategic Sourcing methodology and is organized into sections that distinguish between corporate and team activity. The phases present a systematic sequence of planning, assessment, design, implementation, continuous improvement, and finally business integration.

To help organize subject matter content, each phase includes the following elements: purpose, expected deliverables, tips, and suggested training. Each phase concludes with a summary of the work accomplished, how it fits into the big picture, and how it relates to the next phase of work.

The activities are arranged in an order that has worked well in a variety of company settings. When you follow this order, the design choices you make in early phases serve as a foundation for decisions in later phases. This is not to say that Strategic Sourcing is a linear process. As you move through the phases, you will perform a number of activities in parallel. The process is flexible and encourages teams to take advantage of new learning throughout.

The book concludes with an epilogue, "Beyond Strategic Sourcing," a discussion on how to institutionalize new ways of doing business created through the Strategic Sourcing effort—how to weave Strategic Sourcing into the fabric of business. It looks forward to the next evolution of supply chain linkages, expanding from a linear value *chain* to a view of the possibilities created by value *networks*.

The book conveys Strategic Sourcing from two distinct perspectives. Part One focuses on a *strategic* look at the business opportunities contained in Strategic Sourcing and the lessons learned from experience. Part Two details the *tactical* implementation of this supply chain initiative. Read together, the two parts are a comprehensive examination of the topic. Depending upon the reader's vantage point and interest, greater attention may be given to the strategic or practical aspects of the story.

## ■ WHO SHOULD READ THIS BOOK?

This book will be useful:

➤ As a tool for **senior executives** who are evaluating strategic options and seeking to understand opportunities in Supply Chain Management.

➤ As a practical guide for **managers** and **procurement professionals.**

➤ As a model for **commodity teams** designing Strategic Sourcing solutions.

➤ As an insight for **suppliers** pursuing Strategic Sourcing relationships.

➤ As a resource to **consultants** helping companies improve competitiveness.

➤ As a case study in organizational change for **teachers** and **students.**

➤ As a best practice for **business professionals.**

# PART ONE

---

# The Voice of Experience

*Lessons and Insights from People Who Experienced Strategic Sourcing at SCE*

## ■ INTRODUCTION

The personal and organizational lessons learned from Southern California Edison's (SCE's) experience with Strategic Sourcing are many. These lessons contribute to an understanding of supply chain management, competitive business performance, leadership, and organizational change. Chapter 1, "The SCE Story," and Chapter 2, "The Case for Action—Theory and Practice," recount observations and insights from the perspective of the leaders who designed the strategy and implemented the program at SCE. In Chapter 4, nine critical success factors are identified in order to focus attention on those elements of the Strategic Sourcing program that proved to be the secrets of our success.

The views of suppliers engaged in Strategic Sourcing with SCE are also included. In Chapter 3, "Suppliers Speak," successful suppliers describe the selection process and the new business relationship created through Strategic Sourcing. Suppliers offer advice on how to succeed in this new supply chain business model. In Chapter 5, "Suppliers' Critical Success Factors," suppliers identify their critical success factors and discuss elements of Strategic Sourcing they experienced as essential.

# The SCE Story

Simply put, Strategic Sourcing is a management process used to systematically assess purchasing requirements across a company and identify opportunities, both internal and external, for total cost reductions. The use of cross-functional sourcing teams achieves a multilevel, multidisciplinary corporate perspective. Specific analytical tools are used to ensure rigor in decision making and accountability for results.

---

*Strategic Sourcing is a structured methodology that utilizes a phased management process, cross-functional teams, and a set of analytical tools.*
*Value is created through better buying decisions.*
*Buying decisions become business decisions.*

---

After two years of Strategic Sourcing at Southern California Edison (SCE), we reduced annual costs by $150 million. Through the experience of Strategic Sourcing, a new SCE culture is taking shape. It is a business culture characterized by new attributes: *collaboration*—a new behavior; *competitive performance*—a new measure; *personal leadership*—a new norm. Still, it is a culture built on an old foundation—operational excellence.

Strategic Sourcing, as a supply chain management strategy, changes thinking about corporate buying decisions. In practice, it is built on the simple premise that the purpose of each buying decision is to create value for the business.

Buying decisions are broadened to encompass the scope of the entire supply chain. Strategic Sourcing uses cross-functional teams to consider and integrate decisions from the corporate perspective. Buying decisions become business decisions.

## ■ A NEW WAY OF DOING BUSINESS

Fundamental change—nothing short of a transformation—has occurred. The result of this transformation is a new way of doing business. Collaboration is the key behavior change. Collaboration across the company creates value through better buying decisions. The initial benefit is $150 million in annual savings for SCE; the long-term advantage is an organizational capacity for building and sustaining relationships and succeeding in a competitive utility world. Quite a claim. How did this change happen?

### ➤ Background

Southern California Edison is an investor-owned electric utility that serves customers across a 50,000-square-mile territory in Southern and Central California. Established in 1886, SCE had grown to be the second largest investor-owned utility in the United States, with over $7 billion in revenue, 4 million customers, and 18,000 employees. For over 100 years, SCE had operated successfully as a traditional regulated utility. It excelled in building and operating a world-class electrical system and providing quality service to customers, managing all of this within an increasingly complex regulatory environment. The utility world was stable and predictable.

> *Strategic Sourcing became proof of SCE's*
> *ability to transform.*
> *SCE had always been recognized*
> *as a best-in-class utility,*
> *but the game was changing.*

Those same 100 years gave rise to a strong and well-defined corporate culture: a culture of operational excellence, top-down authority, strong work ethic, company loyalty, pride, zero defect tolerance, and promotion from within. We were the best and we knew it. Structures supported the culture: distinct organizational boundaries, an inviolate chain of command, a singular operational mission. Internal reward systems all aimed at the operating mission: "keeping the lights on." Zero-based budgeting and the regulatory cycle drove short-term focus. The characteristics of the people at SCE reflected the culture: rugged individualism, command-and-control leadership style, skill at and dedication to their craft, unchallenged respect for authority, an expectation of lifelong employment, belief in the Edison "family."

As SCE entered the 1990s, things couldn't have been better. Of course, prospects for industry deregulation were on the horizon and we began talking in tentative terms about positioning the company for a competitive future. We knew change was coming in the electric utility industry and we believed we had the next decade to prepare. Little did we know. Enter restructuring.

## ➤ What Did Competition Mean?

In April of 1994, the California Public Utilities Commission (CPUC) was the first state commission to issue a comprehensive mandate for competition. The initial proposal to restructure the electric utility industry in California became known at SCE as the "blue book." In the blue book, regulators expressed their belief that opening the business of electricity supply to market forces would ultimately reduce costs of generation and electricity rates for customers.

> *The California Public Utilities Commission was the first state commission to issue a comprehensive mandate for competition in the electric utility sector.*

The regulators' intent was clear, but little else was. How would the industry be restructured to ensure fairness and equity? How would competing jurisdictional issues be resolved? How would benefit be achieved for all stakeholders, today and tomorrow? What had been a stable and predictable world became highly unstable and ambiguous overnight.

The blue book set in motion in the electric utility industry years of rigorous analysis, tough debate, and consensus building among all stakeholders. It also prompted examination of public policy issues potentially affected in a restructured electric utility industry. The ultimate outcome was an industry model for California that could set the standard for the nation. In California, the electric utility industry restructuring became effective in early 1998.

## ➤ A New Method of Ratemaking

Within the same time frame, a new method of ratemaking (determining how to charge customers for electricity) was adopted, changing the way SCE earned money. Under the old model of ratemaking, the utility applied to the CPUC to establish customer billing rates that would recover costs of providing electric service, plus provide the opportunity to earn on invested capital a percentage return also established by the CPUC. The model adopted in the 1996 rate case was called performance-based ratemaking (PBR); under this system the utility is committed to continuously reducing costs through productivity improvements and will earn profits or suffer losses based on specified performance targets.

*Performance-based ratemaking changed
the way utilities earned money.*

These two events—industry restructuring and the switch to PBR—created a different world for electric utilities in California. The economics of the business changed; the ways in which shareholder value was created changed; many rules of the game changed. These sweeping changes necessitated a new way of doing business in the utility. Just as restructuring was driving and shaping fundamental change in the industry, the blue book was to become a driving force behind radical and rapid organizational change at SCE. This included changes in how we thought about buying decisions and supplier relationships.

*Industry restructuring provided the
"burning platform" for change.*

## ➤ Change on All Fronts

Over a period of about three years, SCE was inundated with major organizational changes. The vertically integrated utility structure was replaced with separate business units (BUs) to operate the core utility functions of generation, transmission, distribution, and customer services. A Shared Services organization was created to provide central business services to support BUs, including fleet, procurement and logistics, information technologies, communications, real estate, facilities, and security services. A Corporate Center organization, which included human resources, legal, regulatory, accounting, finance, and strategic planning functions, was established. The Corporate Center assumed primary responsibility for policy, strategy, and fiduciary oversight.

Future changes in our organizational transformation would undoubtedly follow, but the most immediate and obvious imperative was cost reduction. Early on, the simple translation of "get competitive" was "cut costs." Every organization in the company was streamlining operations and reengineering processes in an effort to cut costs. For the first time in the history of the company, employees were laid off. It was in this environment that Strategic Sourcing was launched.

## ■ THE CONTEXT FOR CHANGE

The external expenditure for materials and services at SCE in 1994 was approximately $1 billion. We believed that Strategic Sourcing offered the potential for total cost reductions as great as $150 million per year. Even with such a prospect at hand, the decision to act was complex.

The methodology and tools of Strategic Sourcing are sound. But, even the right methodology and tools, skillfully applied, are not a guarantee of success. One critical consideration in Strategic Sourcing is the company's readiness to undertake such a massive change. Readiness is determined by examining the balance of forces arguing for *change* versus forces arguing for the *status quo* (see Table 1.1). Following is a discussion of the pros and cons of launching Strategic Sourcing at SCE.

| Pro | Con |
|---|---|
| Competitive threat real/large | Competing organizational initiatives |
| Significant cost reduction possible | Strong cultural barriers |
| Urgent, time critical | Resource commitment, cost to implement |
| Easily understood, commonsense strategy | Resistance to sharing power |
| Relatively benign strategy | Fear factor |
| Strong leadership | |

**Table 1.1** Deciding to Act—Force Field Analysis

## ➤ Pro—On the Side of Action

The external environment of industry restructuring that would introduce competition made the competitive threat real. An identified date for implementing industry changes in 1998 made the need for change urgent. Through benchmarking companies that had implemented Strategic Sourcing in other industries, we became confident that significant cost reductions were possible within our business.

> *If you have been to a Price Club or purchased a car, you have experience with the concept of Strategic Sourcing.*

The concept of Strategic Sourcing is easily understood. Everyone who has ever been to a Price Club can relate to the concepts of leverage and volume buying, just as everyone who has bought a car can understand the concept of total supply chain costs. In a speech given by the author, then manager of procurement and material management, to employees in the early days of Strategic Sourcing, she illustrated this point:

> *When you hear that Strategic Sourcing broadens the scope of business decisions across the supply chain, it may or may not mean anything to you. But when you think about the first car you bought, it might become clearer. Remember right after you turned 16 and got your driver's license? You decided you needed a car. Taking the bus was inconvenient, taxis were too expensive, walking or bicycling did not give you enough range. So, you identified the need to buy a car for transportation purposes. The next thing you did was spec your car. Did you need a sports car convertible, a four-wheel drive jeep, an economy car, a station wagon, a van? All could meet the transportation requirement, but each offered something else as well. So you evaluated the value of all those factors against price. There were other considerations. We refer to these as life cycle costs: what were the gas mileage, maintenance costs, insurance rates, and what was the resale value? But, you weren't done yet: new car or used, buy or lease, make payments or pay cash, what car*

*would your friends envy? After considering all these things, you finally decided on a car that made the most sense for you. And, by the way, you made your decision by considering the entire supply chain scope.*

---

*Supply chain scope for buying a car: need–specification–price–life cycle costs–financing costs*

---

Analogies like these help executives and front-line employees alike come to the conclusion that Strategic Sourcing as a corporate purchasing strategy makes sense.

As one cost-cutting strategy in the midst of many, Strategic Sourcing delivers significant bottom-line impact. The impact to employees is relatively benign. In terms of job loss, impact is small relative to overall savings achieved. Also, it is benign in comparison to other initiatives such as reengineering and downsizing.

Strong leadership and the level of executive commitment was an important factor in making the decision. John Bryson, CEO of SCE, provided this leadership, making a personal commitment to the decision and providing visible support throughout the change effort. Other key executives and managers across the company were willing to lead by example.

## ➤ Con—On the Side of the Status Quo

In retrospect, there were several legitimate forces that argued against action. First was the degree and amount of change already taking place. We believed that focus on critical activities was important in a time of change. We were uncertain of when to say, "Enough is enough, we can't take on one more thing." With competing priorities, there is always competition for resources. Strategic Sourcing, because of its reliance on cross-functional teams, would draw resources from every organization in the company. There are only so many people to whom new work can be assigned.

Strategic Sourcing requires fundamental behavioral change in organizations and people. Perhaps the most difficult task was gauging what it would take to successfully overcome strong cultural barriers to the type of change Strategic Sourcing requires.

Determining the cost of implementation required analysis. There were straightforward cost drivers: where and how to use expert consultants; what levels of training would be required to achieve a successful outcome; what infrastructure, including staff support, would be needed to support a project of this size. Other cost drivers were less obvious. For example, identifying total cost and savings opportunity required extensive and reliable information about internal costs, purchasing history, and suppliers. SCE had the necessary information readily available to support the analysis of supplier base and purchasing patterns. But, because cost accounting systems were designed to support regulatory and financial reporting, activity-based cost models had to be developed manually.

One significant outcome of Strategic Sourcing was a shift in power. Cross-functional teams with members from all levels of the company are given the power to make buying decisions traditionally reserved for individuals in positions of power— managers and executives. Line organizations must relinquish the power to make unilateral buying decisions and collaborate with other organizations in the process. When a company spends $1 billion a year for materials and services, the resistance to this basic change may appear insurmountable.

*Employees asked."How will this affect me?"*
*Were the culture barriers to change insurmountable?*

In any major organizational change that touches the lives of so many people, there is a natural human tendency to resist. A fear of the unknown causes personal anxiety. Employees asked, "What will change? How will it affect me or my job?"

### ➤ The Corporate Decision

Ultimately, weighing the reasons to act against the reasons not to act, the decision was made to commit to an aggressive Strategic Sourcing effort.

> *A thoroughly considered decision is the basis for managing expectations.*

A thoroughly considered decision to implement Strategic Sourcing provided an understanding of what it would take to succeed while managing expectations along the way—for employees, executives, and suppliers alike.

## ■ WHAT CHANGES?

Change is described most easily in terms of facts and figures. To illustrate, Table 1.2 depicts changes that occurred in the first two years of Strategic Sourcing at SCE. (Figures represent the first 14 teams that used the Strategic Sourcing methodology.) It is clear these facts represent positive results and imply significant underlying change.

| | Before | After |
|---|---|---|
| Suppliers | 2,763 | 39 |
| Process/activities | | |
| ➤ Invoices | 136,011 | 26,352 |
| ➤ Purchase orders | 9,733 | 196 |
| Inventory ($M) | 39 | 24 |
| WMBE* (%) | 16.87 | 30.56 |

*Women- and minority-owned business enterprise.

**Table 1.2** Sourcing Team Results

➤ **Before and After**

The obvious benefit is cost reduction. However, it is important to recognize the operating benefits that accrued. Streamlining of internal supply chain processes and work flow increased the efficiency of both staff and line organizations. Redundant work was eliminated. Each organization along the supply chain gained clarity about the role it fulfilled and was freed to focus attention and resources on its core work.

*Benefits are gained in operating efficiency and effectiveness, total cost reduction, and supplier diversity.*

The reduction in the number of suppliers with whom the company did business was a key change. Our practice of purchasing from thousands of different suppliers dictated a transaction-based activity. We wrote purchase orders and suppliers filled orders. We were so busy with transactions that we did not have time to be strategic. Consolidation to fewer suppliers—from 2763 to 39 in the experience of the first 14 sourcing teams—accomplished two things.

First, with only 39 suppliers, we were able to replace transactions with strategic relationships. Through greater collaboration with suppliers, we were able to benefit from their expertise and resources to innovate, problem solve, and get smarter about our business. Our ability to align with suppliers created impetus to critically examine the way we did things and challenge ourselves to change. Because we could rely on our suppliers, we were able to reduce inventories and eliminate associated costs.

Second, we aggregated purchases across the company and consolidated those purchases with fewer suppliers. This leveraged our buying power and reduced costs. The savings impact in each area is shown in Figure 1.1.

Lastly, the before and after numbers, reflecting the level of spending with women- and minority-owned business enter-

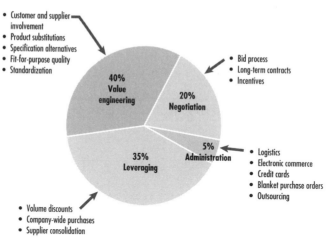

**Figure 1.1** Profile of Savings.

prises (WMBEs), have special meaning. SCE had a long-standing pledge to the community that we would strive to achieve certain levels of spending with WMBE suppliers. We had a proactive supplier diversity program in place and were proud of our progress in this area. When we launched Strategic Sourcing, we wanted to be sure we did not lose sight of our commitment to supplier diversity as we reinvented our purchasing practice. At the outset, there was concern in the supplier community that Strategic Sourcing could only be accomplished by the sacrifice of supplier diversity. Our Strategic Sourcing program included a component to facilitate and support supplier diversity in our sourcing outcomes. The result was that supplier diversity actually increased in those areas where the Strategic Sourcing methodology was applied.

> *The success of Strategic Sourcing depends on an organization's capacity for change.*

One hallmark of Strategic Sourcing is the magnitude of change—systematic, comprehensive change; change on all fronts, at many levels. The success of Strategic Sourcing depends on an organization's capacity for change—not incremental adaptive change, but major transformational change. Strategic Sourcing builds this capacity in every unit of the company, as it introduces a new way of doing business.

As SCE's spending profile changes, we continue to launch new teams. Strategic Sourcing is the new way of doing business. We continue to achieve savings beyond those originally identified. Continuous improvement savings accounted for an additional 6 percent decrease in total costs over the last year, and more improvement opportunities exist.

## ■ WHERE ARE THE SAVINGS?

Strategic Sourcing builds sustainable competitive advantage through working with suppliers to optimize supply chain costs. When Strategic Sourcing is utilized, the total cost savings will far exceed savings achieved through traditional purchasing. Typically, savings are in the range of 15 to 20 percent. A shorthand method of calculating projected savings is to multiply the percentage (15–20 percent) by the company's external expenditures. This number will project total cost savings achieved through both external and internal changes, as well as helping to convey the significant impact Strategic Sourcing offers and giving teams a target to shoot for.

> *Value engineering and leveraging buying power accounted for a majority of the savings.*

Where do the savings come from? Although savings will vary, the areas in which most opportunity arises are fairly consistent. At SCE, the majority of savings were derived from the areas of value engineering (40 percent) and leveraging (35 percent). Value engineering offered opportunities to critically examine our design requirements for construction and equipment and to change specifications. Suppliers offered comparable product substitutions at lower cost, and in many areas we were able to purchase standard, off-the-shelf products and eliminate costly customization.

Leverage buying offered significant savings. Aggregating purchases across the company created volume discounts. Consolidating the supplier base and buying from selected supplier partners had the same effect of increasing volume. Supplier consolidation also enabled the company to focus its attention and build a relationship within which continuous improvement opportunities could be pursued.

Negotiations and process streamlining in all areas of the supply chain represented the remaining 25 percent of total savings at SCE. Figure 1.1 depicts the total cost savings profile at SCE over a two-year period.

Beyond total cost savings, Strategic Sourcing adds value through

➤ Improved quality
➤ Enhanced internal communication and collaboration
➤ Introduction of new suppliers
➤ Simpler business processes
➤ Optimal supplier utilization
➤ Formalized savings tracking systems
➤ Collaborative supplier relationships
➤ Innovation
➤ New competencies
➤ Increased supplier diversity
➤ Improved teamwork
➤ More streamlined and effective procurement

## ■ SUMMARY

Thus far we have touched lightly on why Strategic Sourcing was a key strategy at SCE, and what we learned and accomplished through our experiences. In this chapter we have provided a glimpse into SCE and the business turmoil surrounding the electric utility industry in the United States. We have also introduced a business strategy aimed at creating significant value through the company's supply chain, and have highlighted the results that strategy achieved at SCE.

---

*The strategy and lessons are universally applicable in business.*

---

We have discussed why SCE needed to change and have examined the pros and cons of making the decision to pursue Strategic Sourcing. Although the story of Strategic Sourcing is told as it was lived in a large electric utility, the strategy and lessons are universally applicable. The business forces in play at SCE are not unique: Every company today is grappling with the same pressures. Externally, the forces of competition and globalization exist. Internally, there are demands on every business to be profitable and to be the kind of company where talented people want to work. Strategic Sourcing is a business tool that effectively addresses these common challenges.

This chapter tells the before and after of Strategic Sourcing at SCE. The remainder of the book tells what happened in between. The chapters that follow describe in detail the methodology and critical success factors of implementing Strategic Sourcing. Observations are drawn from direct experiences. Anecdotes illustrate what worked and what didn't. You'll recognize some age-old dilemmas of organizational life and receive some tips for overcoming barriers to change. You'll read about how we learned the important lessons listed in Table 1.3, and more.

---

*If you are interested in transforming an organization, and significantly reducing costs, read on.*

---

Although billed as a supply chain management strategy, Strategic Sourcing is also a strategy for changing organiza-

| | |
|---|---|
| "Ten thousand people really are smarter than 10." | = The power of employee engagement |
| "It's tough running this company from the middle." | = Or is it? |
| "Go for the gold." | = The power of outrageous goals |
| "I'm from Missouri—show me." | = The importance of rigor, facts, and analysis |
| "Changing is an experience, not an intellectual decision." | = The experiential nature of change |
| "Nothing succeeds like success." | = The value of quick wins |
| "Stand up and be counted." | = The power of public commitment |
| "No guts, no glory." | = Someone's got to take a risk |
| "People are more capable of trust than are organizations." | = The personal nature of collaboration |
| "Been there, done that." | = Use pilot teams to show people this is different |
| "Yes, but it will never work here." | = Methodology is flexible and transferrable |

**Table 1.3** Lessons Learned

tional behaviors. The SCE experience with Strategic Sourcing demonstrated the power of working together to accomplish something great. If you are interested in changing an organization, and significantly reducing operating costs along the way, read on.

*Chapter*

# The Case for Action—
# Theory and Practice

Strategic Sourcing is a strategy that is both potent and benign. By concentrating on external material and service expenditures, companies can save money and avoid layoffs. This preserves intellectual capital and employee morale.

To be successful, every company needs a thriving supplier program. In the mid-1980s, the ratio of external expenditures to direct labor was 3 to 1. Over the past 10 years that ratio has increased to 4 to 1.

> *As companies focus on core business,*
> *there is increased reliance on suppliers.*

With the trend toward increased external spending, purchased materials and services represent the single largest expenditure for many companies. As companies focus on their core businesses and assess their critical internal capabilities, often the decision is made to outsource functions that are not core. Suppliers offer a cost-effective alternative to perform the functions. However, the trade-off is that the company must increasingly rely on suppliers. With a greater reliance on suppliers, Strategic Sourcing enables companies to gain and maintain a competitive edge.

## ■ STRATEGIC SOURCING: AN OVERVIEW

Strategic Sourcing is the aligning of a company and its supply base with the ultimate purpose of minimizing the *total cost* across each link in the supply chain for purchased materials and services. Done properly, Strategic Sourcing breaks down the traditional barriers between users, buyers, and suppliers so the company achieves maximum value from its supply chain.

## ■ WHERE STRATEGIES CONVERGE

Strategic Sourcing brings together elements of a number of interventions popular in business today and applies them systematically to reduce overall costs, encompassing many of the tools and processes. This is why Strategic Sourcing can be called a *convergence model* (see Figure 2.1). To illustrate, Strategic Sourcing uses organization development approaches and methods to achieve sustainable culture change; teams and team building are core to the methodology; many processes are reengineered; the cost model builds on activity-based costing; Total Quality Management tools are used in the continuous improvement phase; new technology is often introduced; and supplier alliances and outsourcing are common outcomes of a Strategic Sourcing initiative. Because Strategic Sourcing incorporates various business improvement processes and

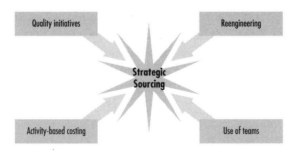

**Figure 2.1** Strategic Sourcing: A Convergence Model.

tools, it is possible to complement and integrate it with existing initiatives.

---

*Strategic Sourcing is where many*
*popular business strategies converge.*

---

Strategic Sourcing, as it was implemented at SCE, was where hard business disciplines such as reengineering, project management, and activity-based costing (ABC) intersected with the softer, culture-based disciplines, such as use of cross-functional teams, change management, and participative decision making. The link that Strategic Sourcing demonstrated between changes in business and culture and bottom-line results became the basis for organizational transformation.

## ➤ Purchasing Comes of Age

Even though many firms spend up to 75 percent of their budgets on purchased materials and services, corporate buying typically was seen as a clerical function. During the inflationary periods of the 1970s and 1980s, negotiation strategies gained importance as a cost control tactic and purchasing departments began to demonstrate their corporate value.

---

*Head count reductions inside companies put*
*pressure on suppliers to offer value-added services.*

---

As companies acknowledged the need to become globally competitive, cost-cutting initiatives became commonplace. Everyone rushed to downsize, rightsize, reengineer, and outsource. At the turn of the decade, one outcome was that many companies began to look to their suppliers for more services. Suppliers, however, were not willing or able to perform these additional services in the context of a business model where corporate purchases were divided among a number of suppliers and the only measurement criterion in place was price.

Divide-and-conquer bid strategies simply did not allow the suppliers to develop long-term relationships to implement value-added services or a large enough incentive to invest in programs. Purchasing departments found themselves in the dilemma of trying to please business units and mollify suppliers. The never-ending spirals that resulted as purchasing tried to please internal customers caused more tension with the suppliers, and in the end drove up the *total costs* in the supply chain.

*Purchasing became the scapegoat for escalating supply chain costs.*

Just as many companies viewed their purchasing departments as clerical functions and judged them on the basis of price/cost, purchasing departments also became the scapegoats for any increases in supply chain costs:

➤ Overly high inventory levels
➤ Excessive amounts of warehouse space
➤ Inordinate numbers of material codes
➤ Large numbers of approved suppliers
➤ Huge numbers of invoices
➤ Obsolete and damaged inventory
➤ Large numbers of checks being cut
➤ Defect/reject rates that were escalating
➤ Too many contracts to negotiate and track
➤ . . . And the list goes on

Progressive purchasing departments recognized that, while many of these problems could be blamed on them, these were just symptoms of a more fundamental problem. What had occurred was a disconnect between company and supplier. Early leaders recognized that all costs in the supply chain are interconnected and that purchasing departments held the key (information) that could pull together the company's efforts to reduce these costs. What was needed was a holistic approach: a procurement strategy that acknowledged that companies and their suppliers were on the same side and could share in the value created by aligned business objectives and a supply chain process that integrated the entire scope of activity and understood total cost.

## ➤ From Backroom to Boardroom

The realization that significant savings opportunities exist in the supply chain elevated the importance of the purchasing function. The increased reliance on suppliers gave emphasis to the importance of quality, on-time delivery, and service levels. The critical link that purchasing provided between those who needed materials or services and those who provided them could no longer be overlooked.

> *From the backroom to the boardroom—*
> *purchasing comes of age.*

It was this insight that has enabled purchasing departments to influence change and to initiate and lead Strategic Sourcing efforts. Often their material management systems house the important price, material, customer, and supplier information. The relationships they have built with suppliers provide them with an understanding of cost drivers that exist in the supply chain. Procurement departments' internal customer relationships provide them with a forum to demonstrate how purchasing savings can have dramatic bottom-line impact for the company. World-class procurement organizations have stepped up to become leaders of Strategic Sourcing. They provide focus and insight to drive out supply chain costs while improving quality and customer satisfaction.

## ■ NEW VALUE IS CREATED IN TWO WAYS

A simple formula for how Strategic Sourcing creates value is *broadest scope + highest level = greatest value.*

---

*Key concepts in Strategic Sourcing are leverage buying and total supply chain cost analysis.*

---

First, considering decisions at the *broadest scope* of the supply chain ensures understanding of what drives costs at every step of the life cycle—from initial identification of need for materials/services and specifications for a purchase, through application and disposition (see Figure 2.2).

Second, setting aside the typical narrow business unit focus allows decisions to be made at the *highest organizational level* of the company and therefore reveals the greatest leverage opportunities (see Figure 2.3). *Making purchasing decisions at the department level is taking full advantage of half an opportunity.* Consolidating and integrating purchasing decisions at the corporate level can double the opportunity for savings.

## ■ STRATEGIC SOURCING MODEL

In the traditional purchasing model, the view of the supply chain is linear (see Figure 2.4). Throughout the supply chain process, each activity is performed in isolation with business units, purchasing departments, and suppliers separated by organizational walls. This is a transaction-based model with little or no relationship existing between buyer and seller.

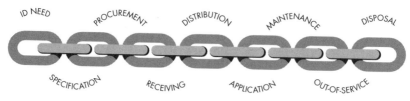

**Figure 2.2** Supply Chain.

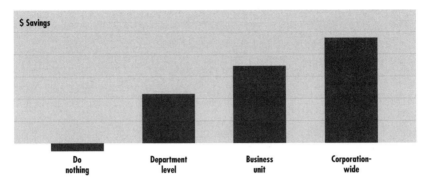

**Figure 2.3** Highest-Level Savings Opportunity.

The traditional purchasing model relies upon specific contractual language to tell the supplier what is required. This traditional contracting does not achieve the interaction necessary to help the buyer and seller to align their interests. Often this results in a win-lose dynamic.

*Strategic Sourcing changes organizational roles and relationships across the entire supply chain.*

The Strategic Sourcing model reorganizes the supply chain into a circle that links business units, purchasing departments, and suppliers together on cross-functional teams (see Figure 2.5). This integrated, holistic view of the supply chain breaks down the walls and helps to align the interests of all parties. The increased interaction, characterized by open communication, reveals opportunities for mutual benefit. This is a relationship-based model. It creates a dynamic in which the

**Figure 2.4** Traditional Purchasing Model.

**Figure 2.5** Strategic Sourcing Model.

expertise and resources of each participant in the supply chain can be optimized. As a result, everyone wins.

## ➤ Strategic Sourcing Applied

### *Roles in the Traditional Procurement Model*

There are three primary players involved in a corporate buying decision. The players remain the same in Strategic Sourcing, but their roles and relationships are very different. In the traditional purchasing model, the business unit (BU) identifies the need to buy materials/services. The procurement organization serves as an administrative link between BU and supplier. The supplier delivers company-identified requirements. In this model, roles are clear, but opportunity for value creation is constrained.

### *Roles in the Strategic Sourcing Model*

Roles in the Strategic Sourcing model are redefined so that each organizational player shares responsibility for creating value throughout the supply chain cycle.

Business units retain the responsibility for identifying a need to buy materials/services, thereby contributing value through their good business judgment. The BUs' ultimate authority is tempered only by a new responsibility to consider the total cost to the company and to leverage opportunities at the corporate level—for example, to aggregate purchases for volume discount.

The procurement organization becomes the steward of the Strategic Sourcing methodology and ensures cross-functional involvement in order to gain corporate advantages. This department retains a linking role between BUs and suppliers, but that role changes from one of *administrator* of contracts to one of *facilitator* of relationships.

The third player, the supplier, has a much greater role in value creation than previously allowed. In Strategic Sourcing, the relationship between company and supplier is one of partners solving business problems, reducing costs, and creating value. It is a relationship built on shared goals, aligned business objectives, mutual respect, and trust. The relationship encourages the company to take full advantage of suppliers' expertise and capabilities.

Having buying decisions considered in the broadest supply chain scope and from a corporate perspective created new value. Working together in the new roles created new sources of value.

## ➤ New Roles Demanded New Behaviors

In implementing Strategic Sourcing at SCE, it became apparent that people needed to learn new behaviors and skills. The critical underpinning of these new roles and relationships was the ability to collaborate—to work together toward shared objectives for mutual benefit. It sounds simple, but it represented a formidable behavior change for many people at SCE. It is understandable that efforts to change a business process that touched so many people were met with a wall of resistance. The first reaction to this change was, "Why me?" The near-term answer to that question for the company was found in the cost savings. For employees, however, the near-term impact was the pain and difficulty of changing long-established practices. Early sourcing teams felt as if the company had everything to gain and the employees had everything to lose. In the long term, both the company and the people won. The outcome of creating a culture of working collaboratively expanded the possibilities for all—employees, company, and suppliers.

---

*The new way of doing business is based on collaboration. What we were really talking about was a behavior change.*

---

The Strategic Sourcing experience taught people how to collaborate. It established as a cultural norm the expectation that organizations and people at all levels align and work together to achieve company goals. At SCE, this meant everyone had something to learn.

### *Business Units*

Line managers, accustomed to having total control of buying decisions and just giving orders, learned to listen and share power and responsibility. Managers traditionally accountable for a narrow operational mission within their business unit learned to apply a corporate perspective and replaced operating decisions with business decisions. Members' participation on cross-functional teams gave them direct hands-on experience in these aspects of collaborative decision making.

---

*Strategic Sourcing taught people how to collaborate. Early on, suppliers became role models for behaviors being learned by company employees.*

---

### *Supply Chain Organization*

The new role of the procurement professional required a great deal of learning and new skills. Experience gained through applying the Strategic Sourcing methodology and utilizing its tools built business strategy and analytical skills. Leading cross-functional sourcing teams and managing new supplier relationships built competency in facilitation, communications, team dynamics, and project management. Every sourcing team was given formal training to support the on-the-job learning.

### *Suppliers*

Suppliers, accustomed to providing materials/services exactly as ordered and engaging in the typical sales activities, also faced a change. The first hurdle was suspending disbelief—acknowledging that the company was changing and that it meant what it said about collaboration and the opportunity to create mutual value. Once that hurdle was crossed, the building and sustaining of a mutually beneficial relationship required honest commitment and active participation in the relationship. For, unlike inside SCE, where training and skill building took place throughout the Strategic Sourcing process, suppliers were selected in part on the basis of their demonstrated ability to work in a collaborative relationship. Early on in the relationship, suppliers actually became role models for employees and accelerated the adoption of collaborative behavior norms.

## ■ STRATEGIC SOURCING GUIDING PRINCIPLES

Three guiding principles underpin the Strategic Sourcing program.

### ➤ Collaboration Is the Behavior That Makes Alliances Possible

➤ Utilize cross-functional teams to identify and pursue opportunities with high potential for benefit from an alliance relationship, and to establish the business relationship between company and supplier. Use a consistent implementation approach that focuses on relationship development, collaboration, and optimal supplier utilization. Working through cross-functional efforts, you reduce internal barriers between the business units and establish the basis for collaboration.

### ➤ Buying Decisions Are Business Decisions

➤ Keep the total cost of the supply chain in clear view when evaluating savings opportunities. Through the use of activity-based costing to understand total cost, you can achieve quantifiable bottom line impact and set a baseline for performance measures. Applying a total supply chain scope will also give visibility to quality and service elements so that these important considerations are not overlooked in the pursuit of cost reductions.

### ➤ Alignment Is a Prerequisite for Success

➤ Develop alignment internally between those who actually use the materials and services (the business units) and those who purchase the materials and services (purchasing, contracts), and externally between the company and its suppliers. Open communication and sharing of goals, strategies, and information are prerequisite to alignment. The better each player understands the others, the better able each is to contribute to shared goals. Across the supply chain process, everyone is on the same side.

## ■ A SYSTEMATIC APPROACH

Strategic Sourcing is systematic and comprehensive. Figure 2.6 depicts the full scope of the methodology identifying sourcing activities in each phase and concurrent change management activities. The Strategic Sourcing methodology includes both a corporate and a team component.

Phases A and B encompass the preparation, design, and corporate analysis activity. The sourcing team activity is con-

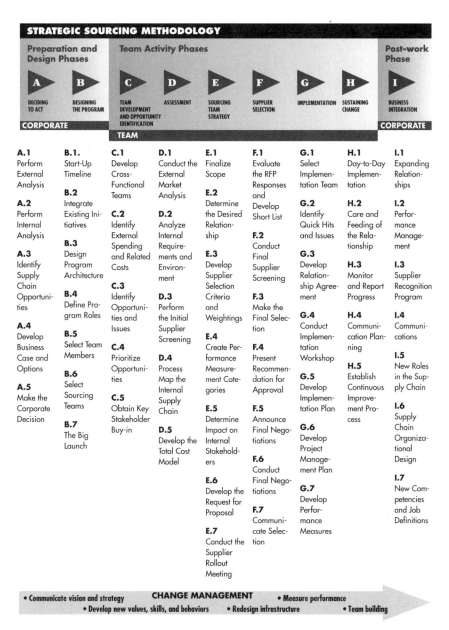

**STRATEGIC SOURCING METHODOLOGY**

**Preparation and Design Phases**

**A** DECIDING TO ACT

**B** DESIGNING THE PROGRAM

**Team Activity Phases**

**C** TEAM DEVELOPMENT AND OPPORTUNITY IDENTIFICATION

**D** ASSESSMENT

**E** SOURCING TEAM STRATEGY

**F** SUPPLIER SELECTION

**G** IMPLEMENTATION

**H** SUSTAINING CHANGE

**Post-work Phase**

**I** BUSINESS INTEGRATION

CORPORATE

TEAM

CORPORATE

**A.1** Perform External Analysis

**A.2** Perform Internal Analysis

**A.3** Identify Supply Chain Opportunities

**A.4** Develop Business Case and Options

**A.5** Make the Corporate Decision

**B.1.** Start-Up Timeline

**B.2** Integrate Existing Initiatives

**B.3** Design Program Architecture

**B.4** Define Program Roles

**B.5** Select Team Members

**B.6** Select Sourcing Teams

**B.7** The Big Launch

**C.1** Develop Cross-Functional Teams

**C.2** Identify External Spending and Related Costs

**C.3** Identify Opportunities and Issues

**C.4** Prioritize Opportunities

**C.5** Obtain Key Stakeholder Buy-in

**D.1** Conduct the External Market Analysis

**D.2** Analyze Internal Requirements and Environment

**D.3** Perform the Initial Supplier Screening

**D.4** Process Map the Internal Supply Chain

**D.5** Develop the Total Cost Model

**E.1** Finalize Scope

**E.2** Determine the Desired Relationship

**E.3** Develop Supplier Selection Criteria and Weightings

**E.4** Create Performance Measurement Categories

**E.5** Determine Impact on Internal Stakeholders

**E.6** Develop the Request for Proposal

**E.7** Conduct the Supplier Rollout Meeting

**F.1** Evaluate the RFP Responses and Develop Short List

**F.2** Conduct Final Supplier Screening

**F.3** Make the Final Selection

**F.4** Present Recommendation for Approval

**F.5** Announce Final Negotiations

**F.6** Conduct Final Negotiations

**F.7** Communicate Selection

**G.1** Select Implementation Team

**G.2** Identify Quick Hits and Issues

**G.3** Develop Relationship Agreement

**G.4** Conduct Implementation Workshop

**G.5** Develop Implementation Plan

**G.6** Develop Project Management Plan

**G.7** Develop Performance Measures

**H.1** Day-to-Day Implementation

**H.2** Care and Feeding of the Relationship

**H.3** Monitor and Report Progress

**H.4** Communication Planning

**H.5** Establish Continuous Improvement Process

**I.1** Expanding Relationships

**I.2** Performance Management

**I.3** Supplier Recognition Program

**I.4** Communications

**I.5** New Roles in the Supply Chain

**I.6** Supply Chain Organizational Design

**I.7** New Competencies and Job Definitions

**CHANGE MANAGEMENT**
- Communicate vision and strategy
- Develop new values, skills, and behaviors
- Redesign infrastructure
- Measure performance
- Team building

**Figure 2.6** Strategic Sourcing Phase Map.

31

centrated in a six-phase methodology (Phases C through H). Corporate follow-up business integration work is described in Phase I. This entire methodology is detailed in Part Two.

Think of the sourcing phases as periods where certain activities are the major focus rather than as sequential events. Each phase of Strategic Sourcing is supported by a change management activity.

## ■ TO WHAT KINDS OF COMPANIES DOES STRATEGIC SOURCING APPLY?

This methodology will be useful whether yours is a large bureaucratic organization looking to reduce costs or a small start-up company seeking to avoid costly bureaucracy in your procurement approach.

*Strategic Sourcing has been applied successfully to companies and institutions of all types, sizes, and ages.*

Strategic Sourcing has been used successfully in companies of all sizes. It has consistently delivered results in a variety of industries, including oil and gas, automotive, manufacturing, healthcare, high-tech, and service firms. For companies in an aggressive growth mode (e.g., high-tech start-ups), Strategic Sourcing is used to structure the supply chain for optimum performance. For companies that have matured (e.g., automotive), Strategic Sourcing methodology streamlines supply chain practices and focuses on core competencies. Companies facing competition or new market forces that create an urgent need to change can achieve significant total cost savings quickly.

## ■ SUMMARY

As companies seek to discover ways to increase overall excellence and competitiveness, a new source of value has emerged—the corporate supply chain. Strategic Sourcing is a proven approach to understanding and delivering significant cost reduction and creating shareholder value through the supply chain.

Strategic Sourcing is where business improvement practices converge, bringing together cost cutting, reengineering, quality, and cross-functional teams in a holistic and integrated supply chain strategy.

Supply chain management practices have come a long way over the past decade. From the starting point of the traditional buy-sell, transaction-based purchasing, the practice has moved through stages of change that redefine most aspects of the business. Today a world-class supply chain practice is radically different. Figure 2.7 identifies the characteristics of each stage in supply chain evolution.

There are several characteristics that define a customer-supplier strategy. These characteristics change at each stage of evolution, with the most dramatic contrast between Stage I, which we label "Commercial Transactions," and Stage IV, labeled "Alliance." Cost focus changes from price to total cost. The expected contract period shifts from the short term (annual) to the long term (continuing for as long as the contract makes sense for both parties). The style of interaction begins as command and control—placing orders in a transaction—but must change to collaborative, with mutual decision making in an alliance. The level of information sharing and communication grows increasingly at each stage. Finally, the performance measures in a transaction are typically specified in the contract terms and conditions, where an alliance establishes mutual two-way performance feedback and measures.

As companies progress through the stages of supply chain excellence, purchasing comes of age—moving from the back-room to the boardroom, bringing a new perspective to corporate decision making. Strategic Sourcing is the key. The methodology presented in Part Two shows you how to achieve this.

At SCE, Strategic Sourcing has delivered significant savings, and these savings continue to grow every year. Taking

| Characteristic | Stage I Buy-Sell Transactions Purchasing | Stage II Traditional Procurement | Stage III Emerging Supply Chain Organization | Stage IV World Class Supply Chain Organization |
|---|---|---|---|---|
| Cost focus | Price | Leveraged price | Total cost | Total cost and value |
| Duration | Annual contracts | 2- to 5-year contracts | 5-year plus contracts | "Evergreen" contracts |
| Style | Command-Control | Command-Control | 2-way interaction | Mutual respect and decision making |
| Communication | Contact after problems | Contact periodic | Contact frequent | Contact continuous |
| Information sharing | Information is proprietary | Need-to-know basis | Supply chain information sharing | Full business information sharing |
| Relationship | "A date" | "A relationship" | "Engaged" | "Married" |
| Metrics | Contract terms and conditions (T&C) | T's and C's | Supplier performance measures | Supplier: Customer two-way performance measures |
| Label | Commercial Transactions | Blanket purchase orders | Partnering | Alliance, aligned business values and goals |

**Figure 2.7** Stages of Supply Chain Excellence.

advantage of another's learning makes good business sense. Failure to take advantage is a missed opportunity. But don't just take my word for it: In the following chapter you will hear directly from suppliers who were part of the Strategic Sourcing process and helped write the SCE story. Read on.

*Chapter*

# Suppliers Speak

In the Strategic Sourcing business model, suppliers play a prominent role in creating value through a company's supply chain. The single most important outcome of the Strategic Sourcing process is the selection of the right supplier partners. Success in identifying and building a relationship with your suppliers is the foundation upon which new value will be built.

> *Lessons from Strategic Sourcing apply universally*
> *to the supplier-customer relationship.*

How suppliers were selected and relationships were built at Southern California Edison (SCE) is the subject of Part Two of this book. In this chapter we will hear the story of Strategic Sourcing at SCE as told by suppliers who were involved directly in the selection and implementation processes.

Executives from eight supplier companies were interviewed in depth to gather real-life experiences and perspectives. Companies that provided input include Asea, Brown, Boveri (ABB); Kuhlman Electric Corporation; McFarland Cascade; Office Depot; S&C Electric; Southwire; Strategic Chemical Management Group (SCMG); and Volt Services Group. These suppliers represent a spectrum of organizational attributes and a rich range of experiences. Included are service companies, manufacturing companies, and distributors with offerings ranging from highly engineered products and systems to low-tech materials. As you read these suppliers' observations, it should become clear that the lessons they learned from Strategic Sourcing apply universally to the supplier-customer relationship without regard to what is supplied. Strategic Sourcing is about how to be a world-class supplier partner. Each company is engaged in a successful Strategic Sourcing relationship with SCE. Each executive interviewed has over two years' personal experience as a Strategic Sourcing partner, and so can speak with the voice of experience.

> *This chapter tells the suppliers' story from the executive level.*

Interviewing executives, and thereby relating the experience from that level, was an intentional choice. Strategic Sourcing is basically a company-to-company strategy. As you will read, building relationships at all levels of the organization is what makes the strategy work. But the prerequisite is a company commitment that starts at the top. Collectively, these interviews speak to the suppliers' experience in Strategic Sourcing at SCE.

Executives telling the suppliers' story include:

Gary Campbell, General Manager, ABB

Lloyd Docter, Vice President, McFarland Cascade

John Estey, President and CEO, S&C Electric

Bill Green, President, SCMG

John Maloney, Executive Vice President of Sales, Office Depot

Steve McLendon, Vice President, Sales & Marketing, Southwire

Brian O'Leary, Vice President, Sales and Marketing, Kuhlman Electric Corporation

Roy Richards, Jr., CEO, Southwire

Jerry Shaw, President, Volt Services Group

This chapter is written as an interview between the author and the suppliers. In their own words, suppliers describe their experiences in Strategic Sourcing and provide a glimpse into how their companies have changed. Suppliers draw on their experience to give advice to companies either pursuing a Strategic Sourcing business strategy or involved in a Strategic Sourcing relationship. These are words of caution and words of encouragement.

*Interview responses provide both collective wisdom and personal observations.*

The chapter is organized in a question and answer format. The responses are written as collective wisdom (a composite response that represents the most frequently repeated observations), and as personal insights (direct quotes from executives that illustrate their experience).

## ■ SUPPLIER INTERVIEW

### Q: How do you define Strategic Sourcing?

**A:** *A cooperative venture where two parties work together to create mutual benefit through the supply chain.*
**Brian O'Leary, Kuhlman Electric**

*A mutually beneficial partnership achieved through business and relationship goals.*
**John Maloney, Office Depot**

*A mind-set where SCE views suppliers as a strategic link in the success of their business.*
**Steve McLendon, Southwire**

*Breaking down the boundaries between two companies: $1 + 1 = 3$.*
**Lloyd Docter, McFarland Cascade**

*A courageous attempt by a group of bright, innovative people to redirect habits of a giant inert bureaucracy and refocus to create supply chain value.*
**Bill Green, SCMG**

*Parties that look at each other as having strategic importance to each company's business.*
**John Estey, S&C Electric**

## Q: What are the basic differences between the traditional way you have done business as a supplier and your experience in Strategic Sourcing at SCE?

**A:** There are three major differences. First, the value proposition for the supplier and the customer changed. Second, the selection process for becoming a Strategic Sourcing partner was different from any other the supplier had experienced. And third, the business relationship between SCE and the supplier became dramatically different. There have been notable changes in every aspect of the business, but among the most pervasive was the effect Strategic Sourcing has on people.

---

*Strategic Sourcing is as much a people process as a business process.*

---

*We have a relationship now. That's different. The relationship changed dramatically, but it didn't change overnight. Because it involves so many people, first we had to figure out that Strategic Sourcing is a people process, not a business process. Sourcing touched people [at SCE] I never would have thought could be touched. Old-line employees whose only goal was to keep their heads down now have new skill sets, new jobs, new security—and they are proud of it.*
**Bill Green, SCMG**

*It is important to view the relationship as a process, not an event. Often people look on these as a one-shot deal and once it's accomplished, things will be wonderful. In truth, it's a process and it requires ongoing commitment. A Strategic Sourcing relationship is only successful because of the people. This isn't an institutional thing. It really is personal.*
**John Estey, S&C Electric**

*The company-to-company relationship really did change and it was characterized by the way in which the SCE team members embraced the change, changed their behavior, and changed their way of doing business with us. It was very much a personal change, a change in the people.*
**Brian O'Leary, Kuhlman Electric**

## Q: How is the value proposition different?

**A:** The scope of the decision SCE was making in the supplier selection process created new opportunity for suppliers to add value and share in the benefit. The Request for Proposal (RFP) was not confined to the usual narrow specified material or piece of equipment. The scope was expanded to include the entire supply chain, which gave suppliers the chance to propose ways to leverage the breadth of their capabilities to create value for SCE.

> *The opportunity for value creation by suppliers was greatly expanded.*

*Traditionally suppliers bid on a package and price was king in the bid evaluation. This time, the team evaluated the supplier to understand the total value they could bring. It gave us a chance to show the whole spectrum of what we were doing in the supply chain. I think the bid package we shipped to SCE weighed about 100 pounds! It was a great opportunity and totally nontraditional.*
**Steve McLendon, Southwire**

The sourcing team at SCE created a total cost model that identified cost drivers along the entire supply chain (for the materials being sourced). The team showed the total cost model concept and challenged suppliers to understand SCE cost drivers and include in the bid suggestions for reducing total costs. The SCE total cost model surfaced redundant activities that could be eliminated in the supply chain to reduce costs either in SCE's operation or the supplier's operation.

*The total cost model that SCE had prepared in advance made it easy for us. All we had to do was fill in the blanks on the creative things that could be done and the potential savings that could be realized. In our proposal we identified activities and probable cost savings that would be derived from changing those activities. We could not have done that with any other company because I don't believe there was another utility company that was prepared to receive that kind of information.*
**Brian O'Leary, Kuhlman Electric**

*Coming up with that cost model and presenting it to us, and asking how much can you take out of this, threw us at first. We can work with it now. But when we initially got it, we didn't understand it. In looking at total costs, yours and ours, we didn't know, where do those lines cross? It was a struggle, but once we knew you were serious, we were serious about it. No company has had the kind of cost information you shared with us.*
**Steve McLendon, Southwire**

---
*Suppliers were invited to bring ideas for innovation.*

---

SCE's approach to encourage innovation with suppliers also expanded the value proposition. In the past, SCE had done all its engineering and design in house and suppliers were expected to provide exactly what was specified with no deviations. In the Strategic Sourcing relationship, SCE invited suppliers to bring ideas for innovation and new ways to create value. When the collaborative approach to continuous improvement results in breakthrough innovation, SCE benefits directly and the supplier can leverage the innovation with other customers.

---
*It is a key leadership decision for a company to rely on its suppliers' expertise.*

---

*SCE recognized that they needed help to reduce total costs in their wire and cable supply chain. That self-awareness and willingness to admit they weren't the experts led to a strategy to rely*

*more on supplier partners. That decision, to go outside to people who were the experts in cable, was a key leadership decision.*
**Roy Richards, Jr., Southwire**

*In the old days there were bid packages [for supplemental personnel]. We would simply submit pricing with a discount for volume. The bids would be evaluated and a winner selected. Contracts usually had a limited term and then suppliers would be required to propose a new bid. All of the responsibility for supplemental personnel usage in the company remained with SCE's HR department.*

*The change we have created is to provide SCE total managed staffing resources. A managed resource bid makes Volt the master vendor, providing a central and customized human resource management system. Clients are able to consolidate their staffing under one full-service vendor. This type of program integrates the recruitment and placement for all requirements, as well as the day-to-day management of contingent staffing functions. Associate vendors are managed by Volt as applicable to the contract, with all processes remaining transparent to SCE.*
**Jerry Shaw, Volt Services Group**

*The supplier benefits because of the relationship. SCE pays closer attention to new products. Decisions to buy are quicker because we have worked together from the identification of need for the product. The relationship opens the door to understand how we can do better and that leads to new product development. We leverage those products with other customers. Increased sales and increased profit are the result.*
**John Estey, S&C Electric**

## Q: How has the company-to-company relationship changed in Strategic Sourcing?

**A:** The fundamental nature of the relationship changes from adversarial and win-lose to aligned and win-win. There is a commitment by both parties to a long-term relationship in pursuit of mutual benefit. Company and suppliers are on an equal footing with shared values and objectives. There is openness and candor. Companies work together collaboratively. This redefinition of the relationship assumes significant underlying shifts in attitude.

---

*The supplier-customer relationship changed dramatically.*

---

*When companies are strategically aligned, the customer's business challenges become the supplier's challenges. You are right there in the trenches together; everyone digs in. This kind of relationship really led to partnering between our companies.*
**Gary Campbell, ABB**

*Strategic Sourcing was a completely different approach. The biggest single thing I see as a failure point in alliances is the inability to relinquish control. If the customer in the partnership continues to express desire to manage wrong parts of the process, you don't go with this. At SCE there was a transition where we assumed more and more of the process and SCE was able to let go of more. It was tough and it took time. We had to build SCE's confidence in us to the point they would rely on us for the service. That is when we really streamlined the supply chain.*
**Bill Green, SCMG**

*Before the relationship had a "mating dance" feel to it, people were guarded and focused on protecting turf. Today we sit down together and people are much more candid and focused on getting results.*
**John Estey, S&C Electric**

*The change was so dramatic, I kept asking, "Can this really be happening?" Prior to Strategic Sourcing, I would say we had an adversarial, judicious type of relationship where no quarter was given. The supplier did everything by the book. No credit was given for successes and penalties were imposed heavily and harshly for failures. Let me give you an example.*

*In a transaction involving eight transformers, we had saved the company $50,000 by designing the units more efficiently. We asked the company if they would be willing to share some of the benefit with us. The company in turn looked at the fine print of the spec and realized that in a different category two other trans-*

formers were slightly less efficient than required. The company refused to pay anything for the benefit gained on the eight transformers, but forced us to pay them for the loss on the other two units or be thrown off the job.

So when SCE announced Strategic Sourcing, we really didn't want the new business, we just wanted to protect our existing business.

In the original meeting the engineers were telling us how things would change; I honestly didn't believe that it would happen. But during the meeting, where we were told that we had been selected, things changed. We were able to put on the table our past difficulties; there were expressions of regret. It was kind of cathartic. And we all realized that we were going to work together as friends. This was different and everyone knew it. And each meeting after that the relationship got better. There was give and take; we were listening to each other. I would ask myself: Is this the same customer, can this really be happening?

You've changed from a company that was tough to do business with to one we love to do business with.

**Brian O'Leary, Kuhlman Electric**

---

*Strategic Sourcing establishes a company-to-company relationship.*

---

The traditional model in the office products business was what I call "good old boy buying." We were one of many suppliers and the degree to which we could build relationships with the purchasing agent determined how much business we got. Strategic Sourcing has established a company-to-company relationship at top levels and leverages the full range of business potential.

**John Maloney, Office Depot**

Successful Strategic Sourcing partners have compulsive behavior patterns and are slightly paranoid. Establishing a Strategic Sourcing relationship is a major business decision. So early in the relationship they want to triple-check every document and overkill on every problem that arises. It is like two Type A personalities trying to be married. You are trying to be too perfect *all the time. For the supplier, it is a very difficult environment. This occurs in part due to the newness of the relationship, the testing that takes place, and the fact that Strategic Sourcing is a more ambiguous way of doing business.*

*As the relationship matures, experience puts things in perspective, priorities become clearer, and the companies learn to work together.*
**Lloyd Docter, McFarland Cascade**

*Strategic Sourcing relationships require a great deal more commitment on the part of both partners. It requires a commitment to spend a lot of time learning about one another's business, what makes a difference in the business, and, particularly from the supplier's side, really understanding what will make the customer, SCE in this case, successful. The neat feature is that they are inherently long-term relationships, so both parties should have all the incentive in the world to make that commitment.*
**John Estey, S&C Electric**

## Q: How is the supplier selection process different?

**A:** It was not the typical supplier selection process. It was more rigorous and challenging. The total cost model challenged suppliers to understand SCE cost drivers in order to identify opportunities for cost reduction. The evaluation of bid proposals by a cross-functional team meant that the total impact of any proposals could be assessed as part of the decision. The short-list evaluation process, interviews, site visits, and creating supplier cost models provided a level of scrutiny that was unique in most suppliers' experience.

> *The rigor and level of scrutiny in the selection process was unique.*
> *Site visits gave suppliers the opportunity to demonstrate what they could do.*

*The requirement to demonstrate what you were proposing took it out of the same "song and dance" presentation into a more inten-*

*sive and comprehensive evaluation. Site visits were the ultimate test of a supplier's ability to deliver on the promises.*

*Where the rubber really hits the road was in the demonstration. We showed how we trip a circuit breaker, and I remember Chuck looking at one of the other guys and saying, "Wow, did you see how fast that happened?" He was really excited, I mean, when he saw how fast it worked. I think when the team left they said, "These people are more than just words, they've got something that actually works." It was the fact that we were able to demonstrate [the equipment]. It was more than just a bunch of overheads and "trust me"; there was some substance there.*
**Gary Campbell, ABB**

*The steps that SCE went through to evaluate the [short-list] suppliers were key to our company winning the business. Through the presentations, interviews, and site visits, we were able to demonstrate the total value we could bring. For the site visit we knew it was a fantastic opportunity for us, so we had the top people from every area—operations, manufacturing, engineering, and shop floor people as well. We had everybody there who could answer any question the team could have and get the true answer. We wanted to make sure that if we lost [the bid] it wasn't because we didn't share or couldn't respond. At our site visit we got to demonstrate innovations and patents we held, technical support on logistics, and electronic commerce capabilities.*
**Steve McLendon, Southwire**

*The difference for us at SCE was that we were encouraged and given the opportunity to really get inside the company and not only hear from you what your needs were, but to identify the problems we could see from our perspective. A significant difference was that SCE didn't have any preconceived notions of what you wanted to see. It was much more open-ended. There was a realization on SCE's part and they said, "We don't have all the answers and we're looking for partners that can help us find the answers." When I first heard that my eyes rolled back in my head and I said to myself, "We'll go into this thing being called strategic partners and we'll end up leaving as vendors!" And instead that didn't happen. During the selection process there was just question after question and very few statements of fact.*

*SCE said, "We think there's a tremendous amount of opportunity here and we just want to listen and we're going to give you open access to help us figure out how to proceed."*
**John Maloney, Office Depot**

## Q: What advice would you give to suppliers going through a Strategic Sourcing selection process?

**A:** The first piece of advice is to understand what Strategic Sourcing is at the strategy level and the implementation level. Strategic Sourcing is not business as usual. There will be demands on the supplier to think and operate in a different way. Ask yourself what the implications are for your company in terms of culture, people, capabilities, and financial performance. Then evaluate whether Strategic Sourcing is the right strategy for your company. Be honest with yourself. To be successful you need to have commitment; you must mean it.

---

*Understand how your company will need to change before pursuing this strategy.*

---

*Both sides need to be open and frank about the deal. If the company says they want to establish a [sourcing] relationship and it's just another word for lowest price, it will fail. And on the flip side, a supplier who proposes to become a partner and really just wants to sell more product will fail. If you are only going into this to get lower prices or sell more product, then it's not going to work. It may work for a short time, but you will miss the essence of the opportunity. If a supplier just wants business as usual it doesn't make sense to do it.*
**Gary Campbell, ABB**

*There are companies who have the buzzword, but not the meaning. If you are going to go down this road, then you better be serious about Strategic Sourcing. It's a lot of time and work, but that is where you will get the value. As a supplier you need to be very serious about making sure you have got all those elements the customer is looking for. If you don't have them, start trying to*

*add them, because over time, from a competitive standpoint, it's where the market will be.*
**Brian O'Leary, Kuhlman Electric**

*A company that is too small on either side of the equation may not be able to commit the resources necessary to make it successful. Or, a supplier may be so large that the business at stake isn't important enough and won't really commit, instead just going through the motions. That level of commitment is one thing a supplier needs to decide and not just jump into these because it's the fad of the week.*
**John Estey, S&C Electric**

*Some companies, when they hear of others' success, it's like a herd mentality. They want to move in that direction, but they don't understand what it means. They will say they are adding Strategic Sourcing but they haven't made a cultural change. They want to do the things that Strategic Sourcing represents but they don't have elements in place to do it or the commitment from management to make change happen. Those are real time-wasting exercises.*
**Steve McLendon, Southwire**

---

### There needs to be a certain compatibility.

---

*To stay a partner in Strategic Sourcing you are going to have to do what is required, in real time, all the time. You are in a long-term deal and you just can't say, "Well, let's not bid on that this week, we're too busy." So there are several things for a supplier to think about before pursuing Strategic Sourcing. Do you really want to change the culture of your company from running at its pace to being hard-linked to another company's pace and rhythm of needs?*

*There will be a constant pressure to perform on both sides. So there needs to be a certain compatibility. There are a lot of companies whose culture is just not oriented to this kind of relationship. Also, I'd say financing should be a real consideration for companies in this because you will have much more responsibility for inventory, reliability, all those sorts of things. In a*

*Strategic Sourcing relationship, you will not have the option of not performing.*

*Every company that looks at Strategic Sourcing has got to ask, "Where are we going with this thing?" "What is it going to do to us?" "How is it going to leverage us?" "Are we compatible with it?" "Is it basically a good business strategy?" My advice is don't play if you are not qualified to win.*
**Lloyd Docter, McFarland Cascade**

*To suppliers I would say, "If you don't have three years, don't bother." I mean this is not a short-term play. I think of the time horizon in terms of managing expectations and understanding what the long haul means, at a minimum.*
**Bill Green, SCMG**

*I would tell someone in my business [supplemental personnel] to make sure their company is well positioned to implement a managed resources program. They are taking on a large respon-sibility for clients that are depending on them to provide not only a qualified workforce, but also efficient process and cost management. They need to be sure they have the expertise, qual-ified team, technology, associate vendor processes, and data management capabilities to serve in this new role and operate a successful program. These contracts are much larger, so the sup-plier must be financially strong. They must have a clear under-standing of what they are capable of. I would advise a smaller company to get on board as an associate vendor and become part of a network.*
**Jerry Shaw, Volt Services Group**

## "Don't get involved in too many."

A second word of advice to suppliers pursuing Strategic Sourc-ing as a business strategy is "Don't get involved in too many."

*It is important the supplier not get overcommitted. Suppliers easily can do that. Don't get involved in too many. These require a big commitment and you really need to live up to your side of the bargain. Be prepared to turn some down. We've turned down*

*more than we've accepted, actually. To companies selecting suppliers, the same caution applies. Be careful to pick ones who are not overcommitted to other things, other relationships, or other businesses even.*
**John Estey, S&C Electric**

*When a supplier receives an RFP for a Strategic Sourcing relationship, there is a definite place for a letter that says, "We very much appreciate this opportunity, let's talk again next time you're looking at this issue. Sorry, we are not able to respond." A supplier needs to use good judgment about the balance the company has between Strategic Sourcing business and the portion of your business that is not tied up in Strategic Sourcing. The non–Strategic Sourcing is a necessary shock absorber for serving your partners. As the business grows you have to be very careful about acquiring new partners, being sure you don't acquire them before you are capable of serving them.*
**Lloyd Docter, McFarland Cascade**

*I want to give a word of advice to companies selecting Strategic Sourcing suppliers: Don't overlook existing suppliers. I think you are ahead of the game if you are fortunate enough to have one of your existing suppliers step up into this new relationship because the learning curve is not as steep. Frankly, I'm not sure that happens very often. Often companies assume that the suppliers in place before Strategic Sourcing will have to go in order for change to take place. Success could include leaving a lot of things in place. You may find that suppliers act like vendors and not strategic partners because that's what the company wants of them. It doesn't mean they aren't capable of doing that. Look for the opportunity to bring existing suppliers into a partnership arrangement. Partnering with progressive companies who can step forward and also have a history with you will greatly hasten the progress.*
**John Maloney, Office Depot**

For suppliers who are pursuing a Strategic Sourcing relationship with a customer, the best advice would be to listen carefully. A Strategic Sourcing RFP likely means that the company has decided to do business in a way that asks suppliers to participate in defining business strategies, not just to respond to customer demands. To win the bid, you will need to understand how this is different and be responsive to the intent of the RFP.

---

*Listen carefully to the customer—*
*it's not one size fits all.*

---

*Going into it, you really need to be prepared to listen a lot and understand. You need to understand what it is the customer is looking to achieve because these Strategic Sourcing arrangements are not "one size fits all." Each organization is different. You need to understand what they're trying to do in order to make a proposal that makes sense and suits what the customer is trying to accomplish.*
**John Estey, S&C Electric**

*At SCE the difference between us and the other suppliers was we listened. We did not respond in the traditional way. We heard what you said and we came back with things [in the RFP] that were more creative, more in line with where you wanted to go. I think some of the other suppliers bid what they thought you wanted to see and it came out very awkward. We listened to understand your company's intent and responded with a proposal for how to get there.*
**John Maloney, Office Depot**

*We listened at the supplier meeting and found you had come to a new way of looking at the world. We had to change our overall goal from one of profitable orders for us to a goal to reduce SCE's costs of providing electricity.*
**Brian O'Leary, Kuhlman Electric**

**Q: The last question dealt with advice to suppliers considering Strategic Sourcing as a strategy or pursuing a Strategic Sourcing relationship. Let's switch gears. What advice would you give to suppliers who are already engaged in a Strategic Sourcing relationship?**

**A:** The overwhelming response is: Deliver on your promise. In Strategic Sourcing each company's success becomes linked with that of the others. The mutual dependence between Strategic Sourcing partners makes it imperative that each company be able to count on its partners to perform.

> *Once you're in a relationship, you must deliver on your promise.*

*This is a no-brainer, but you need to deliver on your promises. Lots don't, unfortunately, and get away with it at least in the short term. But that kind of stuff doesn't work in the long term. You need to say what you'll do and do what you say.*
**John Estey, S&C Electric**

*It's very easy to bid and then not meet the requirements of the bid. I think to be a successful vendor you've got to live up to the elements of the contract and continually offer value-added services.*
**Jerry Shaw, Volt Services Group**

*In Strategic Sourcing what the customer is buying is not the supplier's physical plants or data processing systems or accounting knowledge. What they are buying is the experience of the team. It is much more akin to the hiring process. Suppliers in Strategic Sourcing relationships should think of themselves as employees. As an employee you ought to make sure you are capable of bringing value through your skills and experience. It's your obligation to be competent and perform with extreme consistency. Think in terms of personal accountability for the company delivering on its promise.*
**Lloyd Docter, McFarland Cascade**

> *Take a long-term view.*

Another area of advice is to take a long-term view. Both companies are in this relationship for the long haul and there will be bumps along the way. Some people will fight change. You will need to be patient and persistent to keep progress moving. The relationship and business environment are dynamic. Work to keep it that way. Be alert to opportunity and flexible in your approach.

---

### Keep the progress moving forward.

---

*You better have some patience and flexibility, to keep pushing progress along. It's a willingness to keep talking. This is something you don't just go into, shake hands, and then walk away from. There need to be open channels, and you lean over backward for communications and explanations.*
**Gary Campbell, ABB**

*With time you [SCE] will be able to institutionalize the process. But it takes a long time. You need to have demonstrated success, which is what you're doing. And people need to buy into it. Then the recalcitrant generation has to move out and you'll be there.*

*Once the relationship is off and running, it's really important to get players in both organizations—at middle and lower levels particularly—to brainstorm ways they can help each other. Out of that brainstorming should come a list of projects which have to be prioritized because usually there is enough to choke a horse. Focus hard on real specific projects, the goals, dates, responsibilities, benefits—things that can really focus people's efforts. There should be an accounting for that on two fronts. One, to make sure it happened, and two, to kind of tally up the benefits each party receives. Nothing sells these relationships more than the outputs from successful projects. Once you've generated success everybody gets on board. If you don't believe that, take the attendance statistics for the Chicago Bulls basketball team this past year.*
**John Estey, S&C Electric**

*A big piece of learning from the supplier side of the team was you have to have ongoing and consistent project management. By virtue of doing this we introduced focus.*
**Bill Green, SCMG**

*The thing you've got to do is make a decision and proceed forward. If it's a wrong decision, change it quickly. But to just lose momentum and stop is a disaster. The worst thing in participating in these things is when there is no commitment to change— it's just endless lip service.*

*Our challenge is the tendency of the team to want to run to perfection every scenario. I'd recommend let's do a little triage and narrow the field. Triage, getting it down to the primary battles and then figuring those really thoroughly, would be a big service to SCE in terms of the team's focus. And for the supplier, we would be doing a better job on a smaller number of targets.*

*I think this issue of hand grenade throwers in organizations deserves mention. Any time you are introducing change there will be some hand grenade throwers. The company needs to make it clear: You throw a grenade, you get fired. There needs to be a quick response and it needs to be very aggressive. If people see it as acceptable, suppliers will get very cautious about bringing up ideas. It can be very expensive in terms of lost opportunity. Instead of trying to appease these people, you really just need to tell them to get with the program or get out.*
*Lloyd Docter, McFarland Cascade*

## Q: How has your experience in Strategic Sourcing changed your company?

**A:** All suppliers interviewed reported that their companies had changed as a result of their experience in Strategic Sourcing at SCE. Change was manifested in a variety of ways. The degree of change ranged from complex—creating new business models—to simple—product leverage or process improvement. All companies have stronger and more successful relationships since the advent of Strategic Sourcing. None would return to the old way of doing business.

Suppliers were able to take advantage of Strategic Sourcing on three major fronts. First, in some companies, Strategic Sourcing provided the impetus and model to reinvent a supplier's business and create a new strategic direction. Second, suppliers were able to leverage their Strategic Sourcing experience in creative ways. Third, changes taking place by virtue of the Strategic Sourcing relationship with SCE drove changes in how a company operated internally.

---

*Supplier companies changed in a variety of ways.*

---

## ■ A NEW BUSINESS MODEL

Four companies described how Strategic Sourcing helped them to invent a new business model and strategy. Following is a brief overview of how each company changed.

---

*Office Depot reinvented its delivery strategy
for business customers.*

---

Office Depot reinvented its delivery strategy for business customers as a by-product of its Strategic Sourcing partnership with SCE. (The story as told by John Maloney follows.)

---

### The Office Depot Story

In the Strategic Sourcing process at SCE, using the total cost model to understand existing supply chain practices and cost drivers was a revelation not only to SCE, but to Office Depot as well. Though we were convinced there was value to business customers in a full-service delivery approach, it wasn't until we actually mapped out supply chain processes at SCE that the magnitude of the savings potential became clear.

Because almost every employee uses office products and there are so many choices available, buying office products can quickly become a matter of personal preference. It is easy to rationalize each buying decision because, taken individually, each is immaterial. "A $2 pen or a $3 pen, what's the big deal? It's only a $1 decision in a company that spends millions!" The cross-functional corporate-wide scope of the Strategic Sourcing process revealed that each of those individual $1 decisions at SCE, when aggregated across the company, amounted to more like $14 million worth of decisions each year. The simple acts of elevating visibility of purchases to the corporate level, leveraging buying power, and standardizing on common products reduced external expenditures for office products from $571 per employee per year to $265 per employee per year. Office Depot was able to offer standardization and volume buying by creating a limited SCE online catalog for ordering purposes. The catalog identified those items agreed upon by the Office Products Team and the volume discounted prices. Purchases are authorized automatically through the system and the entire process is paperless. Management reports are generated for purchases made outside the system to give visibility of the cost premium paid.

Aggregating, leveraging, and standardizing on office products created an annual cost savings to SCE of $4 million. Streamlining the supply chain process created an additional million-dollar cost reduction. Creating one common, efficient process for the office products supply chain was a collaborative effort. There were over a dozen different processes in place for ordering, stocking, and paying for office products. Strategic Sourcing brought together all organizations to share their current practices and decide collaboratively on the best process to manage the office products supply chain. Office Depot participated in the evaluation, which mapped various processes, examined systems being used, identified inventory practices, and performed time and motion studies to build an accurate assessment of total costs. The result is a business process model that has reduced SCE's costs by $5 million. SCE also reduced inventory, closed 76 individual supply rooms, and improved the level of ordering response to overnight delivery to most locations. Office Depot has a world-class business model it can leverage in bringing value to other customers.

Today Office Depot and SCE are strategic partners, working collaboratively to pursue continuous improvement in how we do business together, and to discover new ways of creating mutual benefit through the Strategic Sourcing relationship.

---

*In the Volt strategy, competitors became partners.*

Volt Services Group changed from being a supplier of supplemental personnel to a full-service manager of staffing resources. (The story as told by Jerry Shaw follows.)

## The Volt Services Group Story

Volt's partnership with SCE has evolved tremendously over the years. After over 20 years of providing supplemental personnel to SCE, we are at a point today where we provide SCE with total managed staffing resources. By focusing on emerging customer priorities and our corporate goals, Volt expanded its service scope to offer streamlined management programs of this type. Through Strategic Sourcing, Volt became SCE's master vendor, serving as its contact for all staffing and staffing management functions.

Volt's full-service capabilities for temporary/contract staffing services, plus our associate vendor relationships, allow us to fulfill all of SCE's supplemental personnel needs. The program is all-inclusive, incorporating forecasting upcoming staffing requirements, sourcing and screening, customized employee orientation, employee relations, performance measurement, quarterly business reviews, and on-site timecard and payroll services, as well as single-source billing, payment, and management reporting functions.

Staffing programs such as the one Volt has implemented at SCE allow customers to focus on core business functions as a result of the reduced administration activities and reduced customer involvement with supplemental personnel issues.

The Volt program has reduced the number of invoices SCE receives from staffing vendors from 1500 per month to 1. We have further made massive investments in our information systems as a result of the data requirements of managed staffing programs. Volt has installed a data warehouse and systems that can provide regular reports to assist SCE in managing its business. From a sourcing and placement perspective, we have over 375,000 resources in our system.

A unique element of the program at SCE is that we partner extensively with associate vendors to provide SCE with the service package it requires. Over the years, many of our competitors have become our partners through Volt's Associate Vendor Program. Volt has a long-standing commitment to supplier diversity driven by the values of the company. In 1989, we started a comprehensive program to vend out a certain amount of work to minority and/or women-owned vendors. Because of SCE's dedication to an excellent minority vendor program, we thought this participation would be helpful in achieving contract award, while at the same time meeting Volt objectives for minority vendor inclusion. Today the network of vendors serving SCE includes 36 percent minority participation.

---

*Kuhlman crafted a new role in its industry.*

Kuhlman Electric Company reinvented itself, crafting an entirely new role in its industry and redefining how it creates value for its customer. (The story as told by Brian O'Leary follows.)

## The Kuhlman Electric Story

As a result of our experience in Strategic Sourcing with SCE, we have developed a whole new vision of who we are in the marketplace. In the past, we talked about being a competitive and responsive supplier of transformers. Today our company designs, implements, and manages Strategic Sourcing solutions to help utility companies reduce their costs to customers. Through SCE's Strategic Sourcing process, we learned to think in terms of total cost, value, and delivering solutions.

To respond to the RFP, we had to change the way we looked at value. We had to change quickly, be more responsive, set a different goal, change our culture. We started from a strong self-image, we were capable of moving fast, and we were antibureaucratic. We knew we needed to have a comprehensive bid if SCE was going to do business with us. We found a way to joint venture and work cooperatively with other companies. We went out and found a large competitor who did not make our submersible units and didn't make power units, and we brought them in [to the bid]. We went offshore for a large power transformer company in Brazil with which I had some acquaintance. We brought together a comprehensive bid package to SCE. We proved our flexibility in the manner in which we made that happen in a short time.

---

*"We are not interested in
the old way of doing business."*

---

We have experienced such success with our new strategy that we have begun to proactively educate our customer base so it can understand and benefit from the value created and participate meaningfully in this type of supplier relationship. We are not interested in continuing in the old way of doing business. Kuhlman Electric is about a $100 million company. We have made tremendous changes and tremendous improvements in a very short time. The change has been a function of leadership and teamwork. So it's not the size of the company, it's the people in the company.

Based upon what we learned from SCE and what we had seen coming in the marketplace, we have changed. Strategic Sourcing has changed our vision of who we are and helped us realize the gifts that we have and how we can capitalize on them in the marketplace.

---

*A new company was formed that redefined
the supply chain for chemicals.*

---

Using a consortium-building model, a new company was formed to completely redefine the supply chain for chemicals. (The story as told by Bill Green follows.)

---

## The Strategic Chemical Management Group Story

Strategic Chemical Management Group (SCMG) was established as a company specifically to respond to SCE's Strategic Sourcing request for proposal for chemicals. The new company was a consortium of seven companies representing manufacturers and service providers. In the business strategy invented for SCE, we basically took what was a variety of product purchases with extraordinary associated process costs and designed a company to be a full-service supplier of chemicals available for use on site at SCE facilities. Strategic Sourcing was the impetus to create an innovation that turned a product sale into a service sale.

When SCE began talking about making purchasing decisions that considered all the cost drivers along the supply chain, suppliers in the chemicals marketplace knew this would be a significant opportunity to create value. Seven companies, primarily sources of products, linked together to form a full-service chemical supply company. The companies formed a partnership to provide the full range of requirements for SCE. SCE's total cost model gave visibility of all of the process, legal, and regulatory costs associated with chemical purchases. The company understood that for every $10 in product costs, there were $100 in associated cost drivers. This recognition helped us devise strategies to reduce process costs and save the company significant dollars.

The consortium model also created opportunity for small "Ma and Pa" operations to participate in the SCE bid. They were able to focus their businesses to provide products not covered by the major chemical companies. This enabled a full-scope bid to SCE and a growth opportunity for a small local business.

The consortium model links companies together on an equal footing basis and in such a way that each partner company views the world as "Their success is our success, their failure is our failure."

---

After successful implementation at SCE, SCMG was able to apply its business strategy to other customers in the utility and related industries and grow its business. In 1998, three years after Strategic Sourcing at SCE was begun, 40 percent of SCMG was acquired by one of the largest multinational companies in the chemical industry.

## ■ LEVERAGE STRATEGIC SOURCING

Suppliers were able to take what they had learned and accomplished through Strategic Sourcing with SCE and leverage that to create new business opportunities.

*Suppliers leveraged Strategic Sourcing to
create new business opportunities.
A customer problem ultimately became a new product.*

At S&C a new product was created.

*We had a case where you had a big industrial customer, which
kept being shut off. Parts of their processes were being shut off at
different times in the day. The, unfortunately, famous one was a
dog food plant which would have their process shut down at 4:30
every afternoon. You also had a situation where you had a substation you couldn't switch when the space shuttle was in space.
Pre-Strategic Sourcing there were some Edison folks who con-
cluded it was an S&C device that was causing the problem. Under
Strategic Sourcing, we got some people who were understanding of
Strategic Sourcing objectives and how you work with a supplier
you trust to solve a problem. An exhaustive study was performed
and the conclusion was that when they switched a substation
capacitor bank, there were transient voltages being sent out on the
system. Now, that wasn't new. Everybody knew that. But as these
reflected around on the industrial company's system, they
bumped into some capacitors used for power factor correction and
in turn ended up mixing themselves up with the DC bus that led
to the adjustable-speed drives and put the voltage on that bus too
high so the drives would automatically shut off. Well, no one had
ever studied this voltage magnification problem before that. And so
what came out of that study was not only an understanding of the
problem but even better, the solution! Which is a gizmo that ultimately became a product for us as a result of this development
project and, of course, is something that Edison buys many of, and
now you can switch your stations with the space shuttle flying and
they're still making dog food instead of being shut down. So, it's
one of those cases where we actually saw the ugly side of the traditional relationship where people were inclined to fix blame. And
then we saw the good side where in the more enlightened form that
we both operate in today, both parties said, "Whoa! We've got a
problem here, which means we have an opportunity. Let's go get
it." Out of that came a solution which is much more economical for
you, and out of it came a product that we now sell to other people.*
**John Estey, S&C Electric**

At ABB, the partnership with SCE created a growth opportunity.

*We had a technology we were developing that completely spawned a new business for us. The computer capability moved us faster. We experienced phenomenal growth in this area. It was tremendous. We went from $500,000 in 1995 to $6.5 million in 1997.*
**Gary Campbell, ABB**

At Southwire, continuous improvement is a source of new value.

*SCE keeps pushing us to change processes to get to best practices. We do the same thing internally, and we continue to drive our costs down. For example, we are working on a process to make 600-volt cable for you [SCE]. This manufacturing innovation will significantly reduce production costs and we can leverage the new product with our customers.*
**Steve McLendon, Southwire**

Several supplier companies took advantage of a different type of leverage and were able to take what they learned through their experience at SCE and apply the Strategic Sourcing methodology and tools in other business opportunities.

*The Strategic Sourcing experience created a road map for business partnerships.*

At Office Depot the Strategic Sourcing approach was used with other companies.

*Strategic Sourcing at SCE taught us to think differently about our business. The total cost model was the tool that enabled us to see how to create real value for customers beyond low price of office supplies. We have taken what we learned working together in a Strategic Sourcing relationship with SCE, and expanded the philosophy to create a road map for other business partnerships.*
**John Maloney, Office Depot**

> *Suppliers applied lessons to other customers*
> *and to their own suppliers.*

Kuhlman Electric trains other customers in Strategic Sourcing concepts and tools.

> *We realize how important it was for us to be able to pass along the message of SCE to our customers. So we hired a consultant to train us in the whole process of Strategic Sourcing. Being able to understand the concepts of total cost and total value are our competitive edge. We trained not only key management people in sales and marketing, but in production and engineering, and our sales force. That's an uphill battle we have with other customers and the reason we took the training was so we could teach them as we went along. We decided to train our customers to prepare for Strategic Sourcing and work with us to realize the benefits. We have proactively begun to educate our customer base so they could both value and participate meaningfully in the supplier relationship strategy.*
> **Brian O'Leary, Kuhlman Electric**

ABB applies Strategic Sourcing concepts with their suppliers.

> *We are the biggest customer of electrical steel in the world. We work with electrical steel manufacturers around the world. We have a supply management group and they use a lot of the same approaches SCE was using. I, personally, use the Strategic Sourcing concepts in developing my relationships with suppliers in my part of the business.*
> **Gary Campbell, ABB**

## ■ ORGANIZATIONAL EXCELLENCE

Supplier companies applied lessons from Strategic Sourcing to support their own organizational excellence. There were changes in how companies operated internally that were created directly as a result of the experience in the Strategic Sourcing relationship.

Supplier organizations streamlined their operations and created a focus on the customer.

*Southwire sells wire and cable to approximately 100 utilities. SCE was always an important customer, in a group of 25 or so. Entering into a Strategic Sourcing relationship has moved SCE to prominence—to super status as a customer. The focus of Southwire's entire organization is trained on SCE's needs. The value with that kind of link at all levels is phenomenal. By working closely with SCE, Southwire has been able to streamline product scope, standardizing from 100 products to 25 or 30. That takes significant costs out of production and lowers SCE's costs as well.*
**Roy Richards, Jr., Southwire**

*At Kuhlman, we use our relationship with SCE to focus employees on value for customers. When SCE visits, we use those visits to key up the entire workforce toward continuous improvement. We leverage an important visiting customer to generate excitement and change. Employees can hear the customer's appreciation in personal comments, and it really bolsters our morale and responsiveness.*
**Brian O'Leary, Kuhlman Electric**

---

*The sourcing relationship puts a face on the customer that people in the supplier company can relate to.*

---

*Everyone at S&C understands that the relationship with SCE is important and a long-term commitment. I meet three to four times a year with every employee in the S&C family and remind them of who each of our partners is, what we are doing with them, and that our partners' success is important to our success. It is a real advantage to us to help S&C people relate to the customer. When they put a face on the customer, there is tremendous benefit. People perform better when doing something for someone else [SCE] and not just doing a job. As a side benefit, when an SCE order comes through, people pay special attention to it.*
**John Estey, S&C Electric**

*Suppliers' employees gained new skills and
became better businesspeople.*

Suppliers observed that through their companies' participation in Strategic Sourcing, their employees gained new skills and became better businesspeople.

*The Strategic Sourcing alliance with SCE has provided a lot of growth opportunity for Southwire people. We work closely with the engineering and operations people from SCE and that learning has been very beneficial for Southwire employees. As a company, we've got capabilities today that we didn't have when we started with you.*
**Steve McLendon, Southwire**

*The Strategic Sourcing process at SCE challenged us to think about our business. The total cost model forced us to recognize total cost impact and we discovered that the process costs for office supplies could exceed the product costs. We had to understand your business to design ways to take out costs without giving up service. We had to look inside to get more efficient in our operations. In short, we became better businesspeople.*
**John Maloney, Office Depot**

*Strategic Sourcing redefined our business and we recognized that we needed to develop new skills. We created training in Strategic Sourcing concepts and methods and understanding total cost and total value using the total cost model concept. Our workforce is prepared to help the company succeed in our new role.*
**Brian O'Leary, Kuhlman Electric**

## ■ SUMMARY

This chapter presents the voice of experience from suppliers engaged in successful Strategic Sourcing relationships at SCE. Each supplier has been part of shaping SCE's supply chain strategy. Each has personally participated, living through the beginning and evolution of Strategic Sourcing at SCE, and brings a supplier's-eye view of the change. In this chapter, suppliers speak about their experience and share insights. They describe what is different in the Strategic Sourcing business model, recount things they have learned and how their companies have changed, and offer advice to their fellow suppliers. In the next chapter, we turn our attention to the critical success factors necessary for implementing Strategic Sourcing.

# Critical Success Factors in Strategic Sourcing

Learning from the experience of others is a way to gain advantage in most areas of life. At SCE, Strategic Sourcing taught many lessons, large and small. Looking back from the vantage point of experience, it is possible to appreciate which elements of the process at SCE made the difference between success and failure—or at least the difference between incremental results and breakthrough results. We call these factors critical success factors (CSFs).

---

*Critical success factors:*
*Provide governance*
*Provide leadership*
*Use pilot teams*
*Develop a change management strategy*
*Use consultants effectively*
*Utilize the total cost model*
*Develop a comprehensive communication plan*
*Provide training*
*Celebrate success*

---

This chapter identifies nine critical success factors that deserve your attention. We explore each of these facets of a

Strategic Sourcing program to help you understand why each was critical to SCE's success.

Some of the critical success factors are typical project elements we built into the program and in retrospect can appreciate the importance of: establishing formal program governance; leveraging consultant expertise and experience; using pilot teams to show the way. Others are hard-earned insights: the never-ending need for communication; the nature of leadership required to change a culture—visible, accountable, courageous. Still others broke new ground in the practice of Strategic Sourcing: planning and building a solid foundation of change management; using a total cost model to understand and take full advantage of the opportunity; providing training in new skills and behaviors, so every participant could contribute and learn; never missing a chance to cheer and celebrate successes. Thinking through and planning for these critical success factors from the start of a Strategic Sourcing initiative will increase your chances for success.

## ➤ Governance Design

The ability to respond quickly and confidently in decision-making situations depends on the clarity of the decision-making process. In addition, a preestablished protocol is essential to making decisions stick. Keys to eliminating confusion are:

### CRITICAL SUCCESS FACTOR 1:

**Provide Governance**
Before the Strategic Sourcing teams can be launched, the project must have a governance structure and a supporting infrastructure. Clarity regarding authorities and accountability helps ensure appropriate checks and balances and program integrity.

➤ Building shared agreement on how decisions are made

➤ Defining who holds authority at what levels

➤ Deciding upon the protocol for escalating decision conflicts

➤ Communicating the process

One of the early tasks is to create a *decision protocol* for escalating decision conflicts. A decision protocol is a matrix that identifies key stakeholders and their levels of authority. Authorization categories may include *recommend, approve, concur, veto,* and *advise.* An example of a decision protocol can be seen in Table 4.1.

The objective of the decision protocol is to make decisions at the right level, and to ensure that the appropriate people are involved and informed. Decision protocols are particularly helpful in delineating decision paths for the myriad of issues that arise during day-to-day planning and implementation

| | Executive Steering Council | Sourcing Team | Program Management Team | Program Support | Internal Resources |
|---|---|---|---|---|---|
| Communication plan | | Approve | Concur | Advise | |
| Resource allocation | Veto | Recommend | Approve | | |
| Team charter/scope | Concur | Approve | | Advise | Advise |
| Presentation guidelines | | | | Approve | |
| Supplier selection | Approve | Recommend | Concur | | |
| Social responsibility | Veto | | | | Advise |

**Table 4.1** Decision Protocol

activities. Protocols assist in timely resolution of differences and safeguard projects from unwarranted delays.

The authorization matrix will provide an explicit, predetermined, preapproved description of approval, authorizations, and the relative levels of authority by category of participant. Once the decision-making protocol is established and agreed upon, it must be communicated to everyone involved.

## ➤ Governance Structure

The establishment of governance structure helps to ensure leadership and responsible oversight. The two key elements of the governance structure are

➤ The Strategic Sourcing champion
➤ The executive steering council

> *The Strategic Sourcing champion is the keeper of the vision and strategy.*

The Strategic Sourcing champion is the keeper of the vision and strategy. As leader of the executive steering council, the champion shares responsibility for total program implementation and results. In the governance role, the executive steering council sets policies and establishes authority levels, gives approval, and acts on team recommendations. Its members ensure the integrity of the process. They are responsible for applying a corporate perspective in decisions, guarding against silo thinking and suboptimization. The Strategic Sourcing champion typically is responsible for managing the overall resource commitment of the project, including the consultant selection, roles and responsibilities, and contract parameters. The following guidelines are helpful in defining the Strategic Sourcing champion's role.

## *Role of the Strategic Sourcing Champion*

➤ Manages all Strategic Sourcing team strategies and activities from a macro level

➤ Models appropriate change behavior; "walks the talk"

➤ Chairs the executive steering council

➤ Provides active direction to the program management team

➤ Enrolls key stakeholders to support the program

➤ Removes obstacles

➤ Assures overall success of the Strategic Sourcing program, including meeting targeted cost savings and other goals

➤ Assures that adequate resources are committed company-wide and that the program stays within budget

➤ Ensures that communication flows upward and downward

At a minimum, the Strategic Sourcing champion must have a compelling belief in Strategic Sourcing concepts and be in a leadership position within the company. The degree of success experienced will depend upon how influential and credible the Strategic Sourcing champion is within the company.

*With so much at stake, a formal, participative executive steering council is essential.*

With the depth of change and amount of savings at stake in Strategic Sourcing, a formal, participative governance body is essential. The Strategic Sourcing champion works with business leaders to establish an executive steering council to formalize the governance structure. The following guidelines define the responsibilities of the executive steering council.

## ➤ Role of the Executive Steering Council

➤ Approves the team's recommendations

➤ Ensures the alignment of Strategic Sourcing change initiatives with the established vision and strategy

➤ Brings diverse viewpoints and experience to the effort

➤ Commits resources to sourcing teams

➤ Advises how the program can best meet the needs of the business units

➤ Ensures that efficiencies and cost savings are leveraged across the various sourcing teams and the entire company

➤ Keeps the CEO informed

➤ Ensures the integrity of the process through participative oversight

➤ Identifies and resolves issues of significant risk, cost, and impact

➤ Ensures the success of the program in the business units, including the resolution of issues

➤ Ratifies and mandates the implementation of new Strategic Sourcing solutions

➤ Celebrates team accomplishments

Individually, each executive steering council member also has a role.

### Role of the Executive Steering Council Member

➤ Ensures the successful rollout of the program, including communication and training in his or her organization

➤ Demonstrates visible commitment inside and outside the company

➤ Models appropriate change behavior; "walks the talk"

➤ Breaks down barriers to change within his or her business unit and supports innovation

➤ Assures management alignment and support of recommended changes in the business units

➤ Assumes responsibility for implementing the projected changes in his or her organization

Establishing a cross-functional executive steering council creates a powerful dynamic. Each executive, by merit of personal participation on the council, has explicit accountability for the process and for the results. This means that collectively they must live up to the expectations they set for the teams. Specifically, teams are asked to collaborate, to set aside business unit self-interest, and to challenge each other to figure out how to serve the best interests of the company. When the time comes to adopt a team's recommendations, can any different standard apply to the executive steering council?

---

*The executive steering council is not just a rubber stamp.*

---

The executive steering council is not just a rubber stamp. The council charters the teams. There are milestones throughout the process at which teams bring their work to the executive steering council for input and direction. When the time comes to approve a recommendation, the executive steering council understands the rigor and analysis that lie beneath the recommendation. Once the recommendations are adopted, the executive steering council has the confidence and commitment to take action. In actuality, the teams hold the council accountable to do just that.

### Results Management Team

The natural evolution of the process also revealed the need for a new governance body. As 14 of the teams completed their work and cost savings were realized, budgets were reduced. Given the magnitude of the savings, it became clear that an independent body was needed to verify the projections. This was the final test of Strategic Sourcing. Managers said, in essence, "The teams identified $150 million in savings, but since it comes out of my budget, prove it to me." Thus the Results Management Team was formed. It was a cross-functional team generally composed of the financial managers representing each business unit. The managers examined the documentation from each of the sourcing teams to track specific recommendations to where savings were identified. The audit trail created by the use of the total cost model made such a verification possible. The cost model also was used to track the money to the appropriate budget accountability. The Results Management Team reported its findings to the Executive Steering Council, validating projected savings and adjusting business unit and corporate budgets accordingly. The discipline to remove dollars from budgets was what achieved the bottom-line impact at SCE.

> *A cross-functional team audited savings projections*
> *and drove budget reductions.*

## ■ VISIBLE LEADERSHIP

Change and leadership are inseparable. At SCE there was a vision for Strategic Sourcing: SCE would become a world-class customer to world-class suppliers in a way that fostered openness, creativity, and collaboration. Everyone knew this meant SCE was going to change in significant ways. Perhaps the most significant change was the shift from a hierarchical model of

---

### CRITICAL SUCCESS FACTOR 2:

**Provide Visible Leadership**
As Strategic Sourcing unfolds, leadership will emerge from everywhere. As people experience real participation in decision making, problem solving, and changing the business, teams will step up to the demands for leadership. But until that happens, Strategic Sourcing requires strong, visible commitment from the company's leaders.

leadership to a team environment where power and decision making were shared at all levels. That change had to start with the leaders. And it did.

Another shift was from "knowledge is power" to "relationships are power." Cross-functional decision making required that information be shared openly, which eroded the "knowledge is power" hoarding of information. At the same time, participants were learning to collaborate and building new relationships that lasted beyond the team assignment.

> *A major cultural shift occurred as people shared power and leadership at all levels.*

A major cultural shift occurred as people shared power and leadership throughout the company. For sourcing team members to be willing to take the risk to think and act differently, they had to draw confidence from their leaders that the risk taking would be tolerated and the new behavior valued, not punished. Team members had to believe that this was for real, that action would result, and that their contribution was important. In short, participants had to trust their leaders.

Strategic Sourcing did not change the culture at SCE. Rather, it was the venue within which significant cultural change was able to occur. The degree of culture change driven by this approach to Strategic Sourcing validates and underscores the need for change management strategies to support the business change.

## ➤ Leadership Structure

Key players in providing visible leadership early in the Strategic Sourcing program were:

The Executive Steering Council

The Strategic Sourcing Champion

The CEO

The Program Management Team

### *Executive Steering Council*

The Executive Steering Council members were the business leaders with ultimate responsibility for the success of Strategic Sourcing. The members of the Executive Steering Council, more than anyone else, had to "stand up and be counted." Their commitment was tested at every step. Employees watched the interactions among the Executive Steering Council members and between the Executive Steering Council and the teams carefully. Since actions speak louder than words, the tests were less frequent as the Executive Steering Council interacted in a forthright, "give and take" manner with teams throughout the process and acted upon team recommendations.

---

*More than anyone else. the Executive Steering Council had to "stand up and be counted."*

---

Until time allowed for such a demonstration of leadership, a powerful device for communicating the executives' commitment was a visible change in behavior. This took place in two ways.

### *"Walk the Talk"*

From the project launch on, executives publicly expressed their belief in the concepts of Strategic Sourcing and backed up their words with actions. They demonstrated their willingness to collaborate across organizational silos for the corporate good. They were willing to explain their thinking to those below them and to listen to what employees had to say. Because Strategic Sourcing was based on collaborative decision making, that new behavior had to start at the top.

### *A Public Pledge*

The second public commitment took the form of a pledge in which executives documented their collective commitment to team members (see Figure 4.1). In essence, it said, "You can

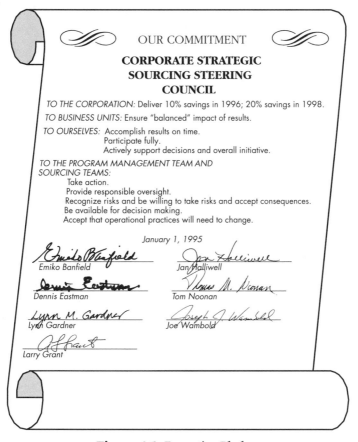

OUR COMMITMENT

**CORPORATE STRATEGIC
SOURCING STEERING
COUNCIL**

*TO THE CORPORATION:* Deliver 10% savings in 1996; 20% savings in 1998.

*TO BUSINESS UNITS:* Ensure "balanced" impact of results.

*TO OURSELVES:* Accomplish results on time.
Participate fully.
Actively support decisions and overall initiative.

*TO THE PROGRAM MANAGEMENT TEAM AND
SOURCING TEAMS:*
Take action.
Provide responsible oversight.
Recognize risks and be willing to take risks and accept consequences.
Be available for decision making.
Accept that operational practices will need to change.

*January 1, 1995*

Emiko Banfield

Jan Halliwell

Dennis Eastman

Tom Noonan

Lynn Gardner

Joe Wambold

Larry Grant

**Figure 4.1** Executive Pledge.

count on us." This pledge was signed by each Executive Steering Council member, made into posters, and displayed everywhere teams gathered.

## ➤ Strategic Sourcing Champion

The Strategic Sourcing champion creates the vision of what can be and communicates it in such a way that others are able to make the leap of faith. The vision is a clear, concise message that embodies both the why and the how of the change, and conveys the belief that Strategic Sourcing will succeed. The Strategic Sourcing champion repeats the message so often it almost becomes a mantra.

At SCE the broad vision of what we could become was "a world-class customer to world-class suppliers." Teams had another vision that focused on the task at hand:

> *By working together, we will reduce total supply chain costs by 30 percent.*

The Strategic Sourcing champion is the keeper and protector of the vision. It was the Strategic Sourcing champion's job to keep the commitment public and to challenge every action that contradicted what we said we would do. Every participant, at all levels, was held publicly accountable to "walk the talk." Constancy of leadership—never losing sight of the goal—provided a touchstone for people as ambiguity or challenges arose along the way.

## ➤ CEO

It may surprise you that the CEO is listed third. Conventional business wisdom has it that a corporate initiative of such magnitude must be mandated from "on high." In fact, many people with experience in implementing Strategic Sourcing insist that to be successful, Strategic Sourcing must be driven from the top down, by the CEO. That was not the case at SCE.

*The CEO provided constant, visible endorsement inside and outside the company.*

John Bryson, CEO, played the role of symbolic champion of Strategic Sourcing, providing visible endorsement and encouragement inside and outside the company. He understood and believed in Strategic Sourcing and was called on to demonstrate his belief. John participated in the launch of each wave of teams and in the celebrations to recognize the accomplishments of employees. There were tests of John's commitment as people were affected by changes being made. Throughout the change, John Bryson never wavered in his public and private commitment to Strategic Sourcing. At every request for John to intervene or countermand a decision made through the Strategic Sourcing process, he deferred to the work of the teams and the actions of the Executive Steering Council.

## ➤ Program Management Team

The dynamic quality and complexity of the change meant that the day-to-day support for the teams had to come from a level of the organization intimately involved with operations. This need was answered by forming the Program Management Team. The leadership responsibility of championing the Strategic Sourcing process and changes to the people in the field fell to the Program Management Team. It took a special leadership quality to build and sustain confidence in the process and the methodology.

*Leading by example made the difference at SCE.*

The leadership challenge is not unique to Strategic Sourcing. Strong, courageous leadership is required to accomplish major organizational change. The structure to provide leadership was important. But when teams had doubts, it was the actions of the leaders at SCE, who stepped up to the need to change and led by example, that made the difference.

## ➤ Pilot Teams Show the Way

Pilot teams are used to refine the methodology and guide implementation. Because there is a learning curve, pilot teams should have a manageable scope and limited exposure. Choose a material/service that is not overly complex or the company's largest area of expenditure.

| CRITICAL SUCCESS FACTOR 3: |
| --- |
| **Use Pilot Teams** Pilot teams serve as a demonstration project to teach people about the methodology and show where value can be found in your company. Therefore, be sure to start with teams where savings opportunities are great and varied. Handpick credible team members in the company who will become champions for change. Also consider the suppliers: Are they ready and able to learn a new way of doing business with you? |

The lessons from pilot teams will be invaluable to the teams that follow. More importantly, pilot team members will become role models for future participants. There will be no greater testimonial to the power and value of Strategic Sourcing than the stories told by team members.

By using pilot teams, each company can amend the sourcing process to meet its own unique requirements. Each sourcing environment has its own supply chain peculiarities, and the pilot teams are likely to surface these. Using pilot teams as an internal warning system to wave red flags can avoid unnecessary effort.

For example, where a team experiences a leadership void, there might be an opportunity to further develop the program architecture. At SCE, when both pilot teams felt their business units at the operational level were not sufficiently informed about the Strategic Sourcing initiative, the Program Management Team members stepped up. They went out to all operational units to communicate the progress of the Strategic Sourcing effort on an ongoing basis.

As pilot teams completed their work, it was helpful to debrief with other teams and stakeholders. Not only did the pilot teams present their work and recommendations, but also the rigor of their work, the options they examined, and the lessons they learned. These sessions included a critical review of the support promised/received from leadership: how cultural assumptions helped their work and hindered it; and what they would do differently if they were to start over.

It is important to disseminate these early lessons widely and often. As other teams complete their work, debriefing allows a company-wide best practice to evolve. A description of the pilot teams at SCE is included in the following pages.

---

*The pilot teams at SCE surfaced most of the variables and issues that Strategic Sourcing would confront. Supplier responses ranged from "It's about time" to "Why didn't you tell me you meant it when you said you were changing?"*

---

Pilot teams prove the methodology works in the company and that people/management are willing to change. Those first actions, particularly if they have previously been tried and failed, will send shock waves through the company and the suppliers.

Nothing succeeds like success. Build on real stories. Personal testimonials from people involved at all levels are a powerful tool for building momentum.

## ■ CHANGE MANAGEMENT

*Organizational change* is a misnomer. Granted there are many things that can be changed in an organization: structures, systems, products. But, fundamentally, organizational change equals individual change multiplied by the number of people in the organization.

### CRITICAL SUCCESS FACTOR 4:

**Develop a Change Management Strategy**
Organizational change is a very personal experience. The experiential nature of learning in Strategic Sourcing was evident in each step along the way.

Change management is the essential ingredient in ensuring that the tenets of Strategic Sourcing are embraced by employees and become a new way of doing business.

## WOOD POLES AND TREE TRIMMING PILOT TEAMS

At SCE, the first teams chartered were to source wood poles and tree trimming. These two teams represented a microcosm of most of the variables and issues that would be confronted in the larger Strategic Sourcing project, and as such, could be used to demonstrate as well as test the methodology.

The pilot teams applied the methodology to both a material (wood poles) and a service (tree trimming) purchase. Both teams had multiple business units—transmission and distribution—as users. As a consequence, cross-functional decision making and collaboration would be put to the test. There was duplication and redundancy between the business units; the opportunity was created to challenge each other. Top leaders of both business units were ready, able, and willing to make changes. Both executives were on the Executive Steering Council.

There were significant internal costs associated with the inventory and distribution of wood poles. SCE kept an inventory of wood poles and related products in its own pole yard. It owned specialty trucks to deliver poles from the pole yard to the job location. There was a staff of seven employees to run the pole yard operation.

Through benchmarking, we knew that tree trimming had been sourced at Ohio Edison with significant cost savings and increased reliability. We were able to draw on Ohio Edison's experience to show the way.

The supplier readiness level was different for each supplier base. Suppliers of wood poles were ready to participate in doing business differently. Over the years, several suppliers had proposed improvements to SCE without much success. Their response when SCE announced the intention to strategically review and source wood poles was, "It's about time!"

The tree trimming contractors were more skeptical. The following anecdote illustrates how many suppliers in the early stages viewed the change:

After the tree trimming team completed the sourcing process and had consolidated the business with four contractors, the selection was announced. This prompted a call to the procurement manager from one of the unsuccessful bidders.

The call came from a contractor who had been doing business with SCE for over 20 years. He said, "Why didn't you tell me you meant it when you said you were going to change the way you work with your suppliers? I would have changed my bid approach. I heard you say it, I just didn't really believe SCE would ever change."

The results of the pilot teams were convincing on several levels. The Wood Pole Team identified a $4 million (67 percent) annual total cost reduction on an external expenditure of $6 million per year. With that percentage reduction, it is obvious that a majority of the savings had to come from areas other than price or margin.

Instead, savings came from partnering with our supplier. The supplier recommended a change in the type of wood we used for poles. We built sufficient confidence in one another to eliminate duplication of work. The suppliers were able to deliver poles and crossarms on a just-in-time basis. The change eliminated redundant cost for inventory, quality control, inspection, delivery, and disposal. SCE was able to close the pole yard, reduce inventory, salvage vehicles, and reduce the internal supply chain costs.

The tree trimming team achieved a more modest savings of $1.2 million annually (12 percent) while maintaining service levels. But, it taught a valuable lesson. The experience of the team became living proof that SCE was willing to listen to and learn from employees in making business changes. As one team member put it: "Over the years I've been on lots of teams. So when I was chosen for this team, my reaction was, 'Why me?' Because in the past we would get assigned to a team, the team would work hard to come up with ideas for improvement, and we'd make our presentation to management. Management would thank us and then it would just die. Nothing ever changed. But, being on this team, actually making recommendations and having management act upon them, has made me feel like I made an important contribution to the company. This is the most exciting thing I've done in the 29 years I've worked for SCE."

*Organizational change is, in reality, personal change times the number of people in an organization.*

## ➤ The Experiential Nature of Change

The experiential nature of change was a lesson that was repeated over and over throughout Strategic Sourcing. After the first wave of teams completed their work, there was a core group of employees experienced in Strategic Sourcing. As new teams were launched, they were made up in part of people who had experience on previous teams, in part of people new to the process. We expected that the experienced members would jump-start the teams and bring the others up to speed instantly. We were wrong. As new participants were introduced into Strategic Sourcing later in the process, it proved impossible to insert them without going back to the basics. We had to allow time for the new members to build some base of personal experience in Strategic Sourcing before they could become believers and full contributors. Group experience and change management support helped to accelerate the transfer of understanding, but personal change required personal experience.

*Some base of personal experience was required for people to become believers*

## ➤ Transferring Experience

The challenge of leadership was to translate the personal experience of participants into organizational learning. The question was how to capture the learning of team members and transfer their experiences to establish institutional knowledge regarding Strategic Sourcing methods and tools.

The answer was a portfolio of corporate Strategic Sourcing management tools.

SCE tool kits were developed that provide general guidance and specific instructions, templates for performing Strategic Sourcing work, and examples to illustrate the methodology and tools of Strategic Sourcing. Tool kits were developed in support of several areas of Strategic Sourcing and related organizational changes. Specific tool kits included the sourcing team tool kit, sourcing team simulation training, the implementation team tool kit, the financial tool kit, and the business integration tool kit. The kits serve as development material for new teams and participants. They have also proven essential in anchoring the strategy in the face of continuous changes in the business and turnover in personnel.

## ➤ The Need for Change Management

A change management strategy is the key to sustaining large-scale change in any company. Before plans for innovation can be realized, people must learn new behaviors, attitudes, and skills. To make change stick, underlying organizational structures and systems must be developed that enable, encourage, and reward new behavior.

Organizations may be adept at analyzing current shortcomings and drafting plans for change; however, many reach an impasse at the implementation stage. To facilitate the process of turning theory into practice, a change management strategy and formally drafted plans for communication, training, organization system redesign, and performance management are needed. The building blocks of the change management program to support Strategic Sourcing at SCE are illustrated in Figure 4.2.

Invariably, companies discover that

➤ It is difficult to make the envisioned changes.

➤ Theory does not get translated into practice.

**Figure 4.2** Change Management Building Blocks.

➤ An organization often prevents change because its members cannot let go of old practices.

➤ Change efforts seem to work in slow motion.

A solution to this organizational dilemma is a comprehensive change management strategy that encompasses people, processes, infrastructure, and culture.

*Program elements to manage change:*
*Align organization*
*Enroll stakeholders*
*Develop teams*
*Communicate*
*Redesign infrastructure*
*Develop skills*
*Develop new values*
*Measure performance*

## ➤ An Approach for Effecting Systemic Change

The elements of change management that address the entire system are described in Table 4.2.

➤ Align the organization around a common vision, strategy, and measurable business goals.
  —All managers, down to first-level supervisors, are clear about the vision, strategy, and business objectives of the Strategic Sourcing program.
  —Program targets, such as percentages of anticipated savings, are clear and agreed upon across all levels of management.

➤ Enroll all stakeholders to participate in the program.
  —Stakeholders are trained in new Strategic Sourcing concepts.
  —Stakeholders understand the benefits of the Strategic Sourcing program to their business unit and the company as a whole.

➤ Develop teams for successful cross-functional work.
  —Teams are established to perform Strategic Sourcing and oversee the program.
  —Team members are trained in Strategic Sourcing concepts and tools.
  —They are provided skill development in team building, collaboration, facilitation, and problem solving.

➤ Communicate strategies and plans across the company.
  —Communicating strategies and plans broadly is a key component of corporate alignment. Communication includes many vehicles, from formal (such as communication forums led by senior management) to informal (such as discussion in the elevator).
  —Communication guidelines—the when, who, and how of communication— are critical to overall program success.

➤ Redesign the infrastructure to match the requirements of redesigned process.
  —Infrastructure includes organization structures, IT system, processes and procedures, and roles and responsibilities required for those new processes. Infrastructure changes may range from company-wide to sourcing team–specific. For example, new IT systems may be required for all Strategic Sourcing activities; however, only a given sourcing team may require a process change.

➤ Develop new technical, organizational, and behavioral skills to support a new way of doing business.
  —Training of team members and stakeholders is an important part of moving an organization to a new way of doing business.
  —Training includes both technical skills (for example, how to develop a cost model or how to negotiate a contract) and behavioral skills (how to develop a trusting relationship with a key supplier or an internal customer).
  —Sourcing team learning must be transferred to the rest of the company to create the foundation for organization change.

**Table 4.2** Elements of a Change Management Strategy

➤ Develop new values to support a transformed culture.
  —Strategic Sourcing values include partnering, openness, trust and entrepreneurial thinking. These values need to become part of the company culture.
  —Living the values—"walking the talk"—is a prerequisite to moving the company in the direction of a collaborative culture.

➤ Measure performance to track progress and success.
  —Performance measures are key indicators of the efficiency or effectiveness of an operation and provide focus and discipline.
  —Performance measures provide visibility of achieved results.
  —Monitoring progress indicates when corrective action is necessary.
  —Performance measures need to be established at both the macro and team levels.

**Table 4.2**  *(Continued)*

All efforts at organizational change will have some short-term impact. However, ignoring this critical success factor will set you up for long-term failure.

## ■ CONSULTANTS

Consultants provide outside perspective, expand the universe of thinking beyond the company, and bring expert knowledge and experience in the Strategic Sourcing methodology. In addition, they provide the objectivity and skills necessary to facilitate the teams.

Experience has shown that the use of external consultants provides the highest probability of success. It is difficult for internal personnel who have never implemented such a program before to overcome the tremendous learning curve.

---

### CRITICAL SUCCESS FACTOR 5:

**Use Consultants Effectively**
Not all consultants are created equal. The responsibility for using consultants wisely is yours. The use of consultants in formulating and initiating Strategic Sourcing will enhance the quality of the output. Consultants challenge parochial thinking and will accelerate change and learning.

External consultants shortcut the learning curve and will bring credibility to the strategy, provided you select professional support that is expert, skilled, and experienced.

The use of seasoned external experts will bolster the momentum of the program and speed delivery of results. The key to applying appropriate external resources is to import expertise that complements internal capabilities. A Strategic Sourcing change effort can benefit from consultant expertise in a variety of areas. The discipline areas represented in a Strategic Sourcing program include Strategic Sourcing methodology, market assessment and analysis, activity-based costing, benchmarking, organizational development, change management, and team building.

---

*Use consultants to provide needed expertise while they build the company's internal capability.*

---

Regardless of the type of consulting support you feel you need, bear in mind that the best type of consultant is one who strengthens the skills of the client organization. Helping the client move toward self-sufficiency is the aim. Transfer specific knowledge and skills into the company by using consultants to teach and coach teams.

The right consultants have a lot to contribute to the success of your Strategic Sourcing program. Be sure to choose and use consultants well.


## ➤ Selecting Consultants

The following section will guide you in your choice and use of consultants to bring value to the Strategic Sourcing process.

Ultimately, Strategic Sourcing is a massive organizational change strategy where experience counts. Strategic Sourcing requires professional support that is seasoned, aggressive, and credible. It requires consultants who understand how to effect change, not just articulate a theory. Your program may be served best through a complement of consulting backgrounds, from industrial engineering to technical engineering, accounting, management, logistics, organizational development, and communications. Strategic Sourcing is rarely served well by freshly minted MBAs who have no practical experience in Strategic Sourcing and business.

Because of the dynamic and hands-on nature of Strategic Sourcing engagements, consultants frequently have to change hats as they shift from one facilitative function to another. Such shifts will be effective only if the consultant is sufficiently experienced to ascertain which role is appropriate for which function, situation, and client.

When interviewing consultants, be certain to ask:

1. Where have you done Strategic Sourcing before?
2. What savings were identified?
3. How were those savings driven to the bottom line?
4. How was change implemented?
5. What implementation structure was utilized?
6. How were suppliers affected?
7. What worked well and what didn't?
8. Who are your references?

---

*Visit companies to see Strategic Sourcing in action.*

---

Regardless of the number of consultants you interview, investigate sites where Strategic Sourcing has been done. Visiting companies with Strategic Sourcing experience is essential to understanding the potential value of Strategic Sourcing to your company. Lessons from those who have gone before will help shape your strategy and strengthen your conviction.

## ➤ Total Cost Perspective

The total cost model provides a structured approach to understanding the total supply chain costs associated with a material/service by using activity-based costing. Because the

CRITICAL SUCCESS
FACTOR 6:

**Utilize the Total Cost Model**
The total cost model is the single most valuable tool for achieving bottom-line impact through Strategic Sourcing. Through the use of this model, the sourcing team can discretely identify specific actions for reducing costs across the supply chain. The total cost model establishes the basis for accountability for budget reductions and provides an audit trail to monitor savings. It also gives the team the necessary data to defend against challenges to cost reduction projections.

total cost model reveals every cost driver, it will be critical in evaluating supplier proposals for adding value and in selecting the right suppliers. It will also guide the pursuit of continuous improvement opportunities throughout implementation.

The *total cost* of materials/services comprises the following key elements:

➤ External spending with suppliers (price paid)

➤ External spending with contractors for services related to the materials and services (e.g., third-party inspection)

➤ Inventory carrying cost, based on inventory value

➤ Internal costs consumed by the internal supply chain activities identified in the process maps

Let's use the analogy of an iceberg (see Figure 4.3). On average, 80 percent of the iceberg is submerged beneath the surface of the water and not visible; the same is true of total supply chain costs. Traditional interaction with suppliers placed a strong emphasis on the price of the materials or service, both because this is easy to quantify and because it is often used to measure a purchasing organization's effectiveness. However, price is the sum of the supplier's costs plus markup and not an indicator of total costs. In our iceberg anal-

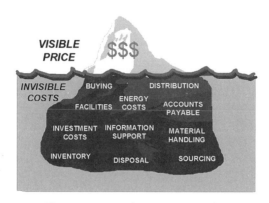

**Figure 4.3** Total Cost Perspective.
(*Source: SCE Program Management Team Communication Package*)

ogy, typically purchase price is the 20 percent visible above the water line. By having a sourcing team focus on the opportunities that may exist across the supply chain, we can expand the opportunities far beyond the supplier's margin or manufacturing costs.

## ➤ Activity-Based Costing (ABC)

Through the use of ABC, you can understand where savings can be achieved at the team level. Once the sourcing teams are under way, it is through the ABC methodology that the total supply chain costs and savings are identified with certainty. Until ABC is used to create a total cost model, savings potential is speculation.

It is the rigor of ABC, as applied at SCE, that allowed the teams to deliver quantifiable bottom-line impact. It is this rigor that quantifies where the savings are identified and creates the ability to drive costs out of the system, with an audit trail of how the savings are achieved.

> *ABC allows a comparison of suppliers' proposals that contain different supply chain elements.*

ABC is a tool used both to identify opportunity and to demonstrate where savings can be derived in the supply chain beyond price savings. Because the total cost model identifies all supply chain cost drivers—quality costs, process costs, specification costs, and operations and maintenance (O&M) costs—it allows suppliers to make proposals for adding value through changes anywhere along the supply chain. The total cost model provides the team with a methodology to compare supplier proposals containing different elements and base its critique on facts and data rather than perception.

Updating the total cost model periodically after implementation is a reliable check on progress made toward the objective of total cost reduction and helps to counter a tendency to revert to simple price comparisons.

## ■ COMMUNICATION

There is a direct link between organizational change and communication. Effective communication creates understanding. Understanding enables change.

A comprehensive communication plan seeks to sustain a level of information sharing that enables interested people, at any point in time, to answer three questions: What is going on? Why are we doing this? How will changes affect me?

---

### CRITICAL SUCCESS FACTOR 7:

**Develop a Comprehensive Communication Plan**
During times of large-scale organizational change, it is critical that open communication occur often and everywhere. Don't let others tell your story. Rumors, speculation, and folklore are naturally occurring phenomena in organizations, and will be created as people observe change happening. If you make sure people are equipped with the facts, they will be able to separate truth from fiction.

---

## ➤ A Communication Plan

Plan the overall communication strategy early in the initiative. This will ensure that the right audiences receive the right messages at the right time—the essence of effective communication.

Effective communication can literally make the difference between success and failure. Altering the direction, processes, or practices of a company requires hundreds of people to understand and support the changes. Planned communications designed to educate everyone on the goals of the initiative and to provide regular updates on progress will help sustain project momentum.

> *Communication is the path to manage expectations as well as responses to change.*

Apathy and resistance are common responses to change initiatives lacking effective communication. People need to see the advantages they will gain when they are asked to change habits, beliefs, and work. Communication is the path to manage expectations as well as responses to change.

## ➤ Systematic Communication

In developing a total systems communication plan, remember to:

1. Prepare a careful audience analysis for each communication. Each stakeholder's preference for amount of detail of message and timing of message differ. A single template approach to communicating with everyone will not work.

2. Define key messages simply. Sometimes less is more. Ensure that key messages are simple, user friendly, and unambiguous.

3. Prepare regular updates. Many communication efforts begin with a big bang and then die. It is important to keep to a regular schedule of periodic communications.

4. Prepare a communication plan at both the program level and team level.

The goal of communication in the Strategic Sourcing program is to influence and move people to change. The greatest degree of enrollment is attained when stakeholders have a positive attitude and make behavior changes willingly. Too often, the communication element is underestimated as a primary means for creating visibility and enrollment.

When used properly, the communications planning process not only helps you decide the best way to deliver the messages, but also builds consensus and buy-in from the key players. A thorough communications planning process ensures that the right messages get to stakeholders at the right time. A template for a communication plan is included in Phase C, *"Team Development and Opportunity Identification."* Consistent and credible communications are vital to the successful implementation of plans and change initiatives.

## ➤ A Comprehensive Approach to Training

Training is an ongoing activity. Training programs for upper management and change leaders begin during the preparation phases and may continue, either formally or informally, through the course of the Strategic Sourcing program. Training for stakeholders across the company can be rolled out in parallel with the flow of the communication program. Training of specific sourcing teams and implementation teams occurs at points along the team activity phases (Phases C through H).

A comprehensive training plan will provide the target audiences the appropriate training at the appropriate time. Develop a training plan that includes:

┌─────────────────────────────────┐
│        CRITICAL SUCCESS         │
│           FACTOR 8:             │
└─────────────────────────────────┘

**Provide Training**
Effective training enables people to participate fully in the change process. Educating people regarding the strategy and underlying concepts helps overcome a natural fear of the unknown. Equipping people with the new skills required for the business change builds acceptance. Training also supports people in moving forward.

➤ Training in Strategic Sourcing concepts and technical skills—identify curriculum

➤ Training in behavioral and organizational skills—identify curriculum

➤ Training matrix—who needs to be trained in what areas

➤ Training calendar—when specific training modules are presented

Examples of each element of the training plan at SCE are shown in Tables 4.3 through 4.5 and Figure 4.4.

For greatest impact, training should happen according to a plan on a just-in-time basis. Training delivered too early to be used, or after the fact, is a lost opportunity to maximize on the training investment. Plan training into the process.

## ■ CELEBRATE SUCCESS

It is true that participation in Strategic Sourcing has its intrinsic rewards. The work is significant. There are frequent opportunities for learning. Teamwork is collaborative and fun. Individuals are a part of making important corporate deci-

| Topic / Example | Company-Wide Training (Change Leader, Key Business Unit Managers/Influencers) | Sourcing Teams and Process Participants | Key Suppliers |
|---|---|---|---|
| Strategic sourcing concepts: General | ▲ Benefits of Strategic Sourcing<br>▲ Understanding the supply chain components<br>▲ How the Strategic Sourcing program uses the supply chain | Same as Company-wide, plus:<br>▲ Characteristics of the supply chain specific to a given sourcing team's materials/services | Same as Company-wide, plus:<br>▲ Emphasis on supplier relationships |
| Total cost | ▲ Understanding total cost<br>▲ How supply chain scope and total cost approach yield savings<br>▲ How to perform value analysis and value engineering | Same as Company-wide, plus:<br>▲ Total cost model specific to a given sourcing team's materials/services<br>▲ What specific value engineering steps can be incorporated | Same as Company-wide |
| Customer focus | ▲ How to identify customer needs<br>▲ How to work backward from customer value | Same as Company-wide, plus:<br>▲ How to do customer surveys | Same as Company-wide |
| New roles | ▲ How the roles of supply management personnel will change<br>▲ How the roles of business units will change<br>▲ How company/supplier relationship roles will change | Same as Company-wide, plus:<br>▲ Specific new role definitions and meanings | Same as Company-wide |
| Supplier relationships | ▲ How to interface with suppliers<br>▲ How to negotiate with suppliers<br>▲ How to establish a WMBE program<br>▲ What and how to outsource | Same as Company-wide, plus:<br>▲ Specifics about designing supplier relationships and negotiating | ▲ How the company/supplier relationships will change |
| Business skills | | ▲ Business skills such as process mapping, establishing performance measures, benchmarking, developing incentives, and establishing a continuous improvement program | |

**Table 4.3** Training in Strategic Sourcing Concepts and Technical Skills

| Topic Example | Company-Wide Training (Change Leader, Key Business Unit Managers/Influencers) | Sourcing Teams and Process Participants |
|---|---|---|
| Leadership | ▶ How to be a customer advocate<br>▶ How to pass the test of leadership<br>▶ How to coach, motivate, and influence others<br>▶ How to be a barrier buster<br>▶ How to provide a living example | For sourcing team leaders, same as company-wide training |
| Teamwork | ▶ Key principles and practices of teamwork<br>▶ How to collaborate successfully across functional boundaries and with suppliers<br>▶ How to develop effective relationships | Same as company-wide training, plus:<br>▶ Team-specific development<br>▶ Specific training on how to practice cooperative behaviors with internal customers and suppliers |
| Communication | ▶ Effective communication<br>▶ Active listening<br>▶ Planning communication events | Same as company-wide training, plus:<br>▶ Specific techniques useful for communicating to team stakeholders |
| Problem solving | ▶ Problem-solving techniques, as needed | Same as company-wide training |
| Decision making | ▶ Decision-making models and techniques | Same as company-wide training |
| Facilitation | ▶ Facilitating meetings | Same as company-wide training |
| Creative thinking | ▶ How to enhance out-of-the-box thinking to foster innovation | Same as company-wide training |
| Organizational skills | Skills needed at both the leadership and team member levels: charter development, effective meetings, consensus building, performing external research, conducting focus groups, stages of transition, interviewing, giving presentations | |

**Table 4.4** Training in Behavioral and Organizational Skills

| Training Topics | Change Leadership | Business Unit Managers | General Stakeholders | Sourcing Team Members | Sourcing Team Stakeholders | Key Suppliers |
|---|---|---|---|---|---|---|
| Strategic sourcing leadership challenges | X | | | X<br>Team leaders | | |
| Strategic sourcing concepts | X | X | X | X | X | X |
| Customer focus | | X | X | X | X | X |
| New roles | X | X | X | X | X | X |
| Supplier relationships | X | | | X | X | X |
| Teamwork | | | | X | X | X |
| Communication | | X | | X | | X |
| Cooperation | | | | X | X | X |
| Problem solving | | | | X | | X |
| Decision making | | | | X | | X |
| Facilitation | | X | | X | | |
| Creative thinking | | | | X | | X |
| Specific strategic sourcing and business skills | | X | | X | | |
| Organizational skills | | | | X | | |

**Table 4.5** Training Matrix

sions. But the employees from all levels of the company who step up to the challenge of making Strategic Sourcing happen have earned more.

## ➤ Celebrations

Celebrations became a regular part of the Strategic Sourcing experience at SCE. Whether sourcing team pizza dinners for 10 or receptions for 200, celebrations provided periodic opportunities to remind everyone that what was being accomplished

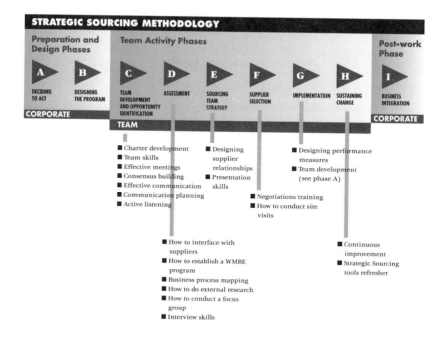

**Figure 4.4** Team Activity Training Calendar.

through Strategic Sourcing was cause to celebrate. Top executives and Executive Steering Council members made special efforts to participate personally in events to acknowledge and congratulate employees. The fun and festivity of these celebrations reinforced the experience that Strategic Sourcing was a different way of work life. The energy that surrounded these events was created by people getting to share their personal sense of accomplishment and see that leaders returned their enthusiasm.

## ➤ Team Rewards and Recognition

Team participation was demanding, intense, and at times grueling. Team members took on the sourcing assignment and continued to perform their regular jobs. This level of effort, commitment, and results deserved special recognition. At the conclusion of the term of each sourcing team, the Executive Steering Council hosted a dinner for team members. Executives joined team members for the express purpose of celebrating. In an atmosphere of fun and relaxation, team members relived the adventures they had been through together. The bonding that had occurred among team members was evident as they told stories about the happiness and hardships, good and bad times. People shared insights and laughed at the absurdities they had encountered.

---

*Team rewards took many forms: celebration dinners,*
*symbolic gifts, cash bonuses.*

---

A unique gift was selected for each team, intended to capture the team's unique identity. The Office Products Team members received personal copies of *Build a Better Life by Stealing Office Supplies—Dogbert's Big Book of Business* autographed by the Executive Steering Council. Each member of the Computer Services Team received a tiny desk clock in the shape of a computer. The Program Management Team members received a ceramic lighthouse representing the way they had helped "light the way" to change. The team sponsors were proud recipients of authentic bull whips for the great job they did in keeping the teams moving along. The team gifts soon became a tradition, and team members displayed their gifts as symbols of their roles in Strategic Sourcing.

Each team member also was given a cash reward in recognition of his or her team's contribution to the company's com-

---

### CRITICAL SUCCESS FACTOR 9:

**Celebrate Success**

For many team participants, Strategic Sourcing was the career event of a lifetime. Their collective participation changed the company profoundly and significantly impacted the bottom line. At SCE, this was cause for celebration!

petitiveness. The special efforts to celebrate and reward teams soon became widely known and generated interest from those who had not participated on teams.

## ➤ Corporate Celebrations

Two major events were held at the conclusion of the first year of Strategic Sourcing that brought everyone together to celebrate the corporate achievement. The first was a reception for the 200 SCE employees who had participated in launching Strategic Sourcing. Display boards were created for each sourcing team with team photos and items identifying team accomplishments. John Bryson, CEO, presented a scroll to each team participant and had his picture taken with teams. Bringing together all the people who had pioneered Strategic Sourcing filled the room with the excitement of being part of something special.

The second corporate event was held a few weeks later. The first Strategic Sourcing supplier partners were invited to celebrate the new relationship we had entered. Approximately 150 executives from suppliers and SCE expressed their commitment to the new way of doing business that was emerging as a result of Strategic Sourcing. Plaques were presented to supplier companies honoring them as "Edison Supply Partners." The networking that took place that evening was the beginning of the company-to-company relationships at the executive level that are an important element in sustaining the change.

## ➤ Publicity

Recognition for accomplishments also came in the form of publicity. News articles were published and video productions circulated telling the Strategic Sourcing story. Strategic Sourcing leaders were invited to speak at conferences across the country.

Celebrations and recognition events touched everyone from the CEO to team members to suppliers, and even those not directly involved in Strategic Sourcing. Celebration reinforced and gave momentum to Strategic Sourcing. It was critical to our success at SCE. You could try Strategic Sourcing without including celebrations and rewards and recognition. But we wouldn't recommend it.

## ■ SUMMARY

This chapter has singled out nine critical success factors based on SCE's Strategic Sourcing experience. While nine may seem like a lot of factors to concentrate on, it reminds us that Strategic Sourcing is a complex and comprehensive undertaking. These critical success factors were what differentiated SCE's Strategic Sourcing success from other initiatives of its kind.

In the next chapter, suppliers identify their critical success factors and discuss Strategic Sourcing from their viewpoint.

Chapter 5

# Suppliers' Critical
# Success Factors

Critical success factors are defined as those elements of the Strategic Sourcing process at SCE that made the difference between incremental change and breakthrough results. Chapter 4, *"Critical Success Factors in Strategic Sourcing,"* identifies and discusses what these factors were from the perspective of leaders of Strategic Sourcing at SCE. The focus from the SCE perspective was on the company's Strategic Sourcing process and methodology up to initial implementation. The suppliers enter that process near the end when they bid to be selected as Strategic Sourcing partners. Their focus would be on the supplier selection process and successful implementation of the relationship. So, to round out the picture, suppliers were asked to identify their critical success factors. Not surprisingly, there was little overlap in the two lists. Of the nine critical success factors identified by suppliers, only one—leadership—also appeared on the company list.

There is, however, strong agreement among the suppliers interviewed. Private interviews were conducted with executives of eight supplier companies. The success factors on the supplier list in this chapter were identified by at least half of the executives as critical in their companies' experience. A synthesis of the most frequent comments is contained in each critical success factor description. The quotes that follow illustrate the points.

---

*Suppliers' critical success factors:*
*Provide leadership/top-level commitment*
*Choose your customers carefully*
*Build trust and openness*
*Build relationships at all levels*
*Select team members carefully*
*Assign point responsibility to manage relationships*
*Create organizational alignment*
*Practice team building*
*Understand value*

---

This chapter highlights nine elements as critical success factors for suppliers involved in Strategic Sourcing. These factors provide sound business advice: Choose customers carefully, and understand how you can create value. Suppliers describe a relationship that must be characterized by leadership and top-level commitment as well as openness and trust between companies. There is also practical advice: Build relationships at all levels, align the company internally, select the right team members, build the team, and assign point responsibility for the relationship. Although the view is that of the suppliers, the insights have meaning for all participants in a Strategic Sourcing relationship.

## SUPPLIERS' CRITICAL SUCCESS FACTOR 1:

**Provide Leadership/Top-Level Commitment**
Strategic Sourcing demands top-level commitment from both partners in the relationship. Executives have a mutual obligation to provide leadership within their respective companies and to build the relationship between the companies. Effective leaders embody the principles of Strategic Sourcing and create a compelling vision for the future.

*We made mutual commitments in the very first [implementation] meeting. SCE had a significant cost reduction plan and the team had requirements from upper management to come up with savings. So everybody [on the team] had a career commitment to making it work. In part, because there was also very strong and visible senior management support, which we've struggled with in other companies, where the team people don't get that support.*

*The number one cause of failure in Strategic Sourcing is the lack of a company vision and leadership in the company that says, "This is the way we will do business in the future." Leadership has to drive it and support it.*

**Brian O'Leary, Kuhlman Electric**

*Strategic Sourcing creates a major change in the buyer-seller relationship and it was different from a management standpoint. Prior to Strategic Sourcing, we did not have our top management, the president, CEO, CFO, actively involved in the sourcing process. They had their jobs and we had ours in sales and marketing. When we saw how SCE was defining Strategic Sourcing at the first [supplier] rollout meeting, we knew top management had to be involved. The stakes were so high, and we felt that if we did not present everything from the right sources, we wouldn't be evaluated properly. Our president and top management were involved from the very beginning, just like SCE top management was—the same way. That is totally different from the traditional way.*

**Steve McLendon, Southwire**

*It is very important to get top-level commitment. One thing that SCE has done better than anybody I've seen is getting top management involvement—the buy-in, the participation, and the contribution from the folks at the top is exceptional.*

**John Estey, S&C Electric**

*Leadership needed to provide a clear and compelling vision of what could be. Strategic Sourcing at SCE was unique in that it was always clear; the train had left the station. The message was this [Strategic Sourcing] is something we're committed to— this was right, needed, and made perfect sense. That was differ-*

*ent here. You were our first customer so we had no comparisons, but as we went on we saw how important that leadership is. So it was, in our opinion, coming right from the top.*
**Bill Green, SCMG**

---

> *Top-level involvement from both companies is needed to drive the strategy.*

---

*A critical success factor in making the relationship successful is top-down commitment. The implementation work is delegated to the team, but it still has to have direction and focus. The team needs to see top-level leadership. Leadership must come from both companies. The Strategic Sourcing relationship must be driven from both companies. You cannot drag a supplier along unless they really want to do it.*
**Roy Richards, Jr., Southwire**

---

## SUPPLIERS' CRITICAL SUCCESS FACTOR 2:

**Choose Your Customers Carefully**
Strategic Sourcing is a relationship between two companies in pursuit of mutual value. Often, what it means to be a Strategic Sourcing partner is in the eye of the beholder. The most important work of the Strategic Sourcing selection process is finding the right supplier partner for the company. It may be just as important for suppliers to find the right customers. Mutual value will be found in the relationship that is built. Be certain there is a basis for a relationship.

---

*I think that it's very important for companies and suppliers to recognize that not all business is good business. Not all customers are good customers. What we have to do as a company is be very careful to select customers who share our vision and to walk away from those that don't. Probably as important a part of our success is not only the business that we do, but the business we don't do.*

*For suppliers pursuing a Strategic Sourcing relationship it is critical to identify not only the intent but the spirit of the relationship. We needed to validate whether there was commitment on the part of SCE to engage in a partnership, was this a serious attempt or just talk. The first step was selecting a customer that had a similar definition of partnership. Once we knew our purposes seemed to be aligned, we were able to validate the process that we felt very definitely would get us there. Sometimes the intent is there but the process is flawed and you're never going to get there.*

*My advice to suppliers: Interview the customers. Recognize that not every customer will have the culture, will make the commitment, will get the support from the top, which is absolutely essential. So, if every customer isn't a candidate [for a Strategic Sourcing relationship], we have to pick our customers carefully. Ask, what is their view of a strategic partnership? What is important to them, their values? If you don't make sure there is a shared understanding of value in the relationship, then you can be awfully frustrated. Partnership is a way overused word and not too many people are doing it right. In selecting SCE as a customer, we validated early on that we both "got it."*

*In the selection process at SCE, we demonstrated we could bring innovation and creative thinking to the business of office products and we presented ideas that were in line with where you wanted to go. And, because we had validated you were the right company to partner with, we could stay true to ourselves and our vision of partnership.*

**John Maloney, Office Depot**

---

## Not all customers are good customers.

---

*Our strategy is to select good customers and train them. We felt we could get ahead of the game and pick off at least the customers who are most inclined to move in that direction [Strategic Sourcing] and work with them to find ways to get them and retain them.*

**Brian O'Leary, Kuhlman Electric**

*Suppliers need to select customers with whom there is a certain compatibility. A supplier needs to think about, "Do you really*

*want to change the culture of your company?" It's a little bit like selling your soul to the customer.*
**Lloyd Docter, McFarland Cascade**

*A critical success factor is to find people you can dance with. Most old-line people cannot see beyond their narrow self-interest. In Strategic Sourcing, you need to look for the ones that really get it when you talk about things like collaboration and mutual benefit—select the right partners.*
**Bill Green, SCMG**

---

### SUPPLIERS' CRITICAL SUCCESS FACTOR 3:

**Build Trust and Openness**
For a Strategic Sourcing relationship to reach its potential, there must be openness and trust established between the companies. Once goals are aligned and everyone has a common objective, barriers come down and trust can begin to build. Trust is earned through personal acquaintance and actions. Frankness and openness in communications is a good starting point.

---

*Once you said, "We are convinced that you understand where we want to go, that we have shared value here, let's join together," the whole relationship changed. From then on the barriers were broken down, we had one common objective. On the team no one felt threatened or suspicious; ideas flowed freely. We threw things out. No idea was a bad idea. We got to know each other. We enjoyed being with each other. We got to trust each other.*
**John Maloney, Office Depot**

*To get the real value from the relationship you must get to the point where the company can say, "I have enough trust in you that I am going to start letting go."*
**Bill Green, SCMG**

*Strategic Sourcing relationships require a great deal of openness and candor. People really have to put it out on the table for the other people to look at if you're both going to benefit from the relationship. You can save a lot of time if people tell you the truth and are candid. This requires that old word, "trust."*

*Some people really need to change their attitudes in order to build that trust. People who are still suspicious of this technique can really ruin things. It's the old expression, "If you have a barrel of sewage and a cup of wine, you have sewage. If you have a barrel of wine and a cup of sewage, you have sewage."*
**John Estey, S&C Electric**

---

## To build trust, let people see for themselves.

---

*One way we built trust was by exchanging visits and letting people see for themselves. Our engineering people began to make trips to your substations. Your [SCE's] engineering people came to our factory and pointed out things we could do to improve quality and service. They also came to assure themselves that we do a good job. So there was mutual trust and trust played a big part in our success.*
**Brian O'Leary, Kuhlman Electric**

*One of the key things I look at is management's attitudes. When you sit down face to face with management, you pick up that sixth sense that these people are honest, they're forthright, and they really want to work with you. That is something an audit can never measure. It's a personal issue of trust that comes forth.*
**Gary Campbell, ABB**

## SUPPLIERS' CRITICAL SUCCESS FACTOR 4:

**Build Relationships at All Levels**
A company-to-company relationship is the basis for doing business in Strategic Sourcing. Although the implementation team has primary responsibility for progress, it is important that relationships be fostered at all levels of the companies—executives to front-line employees. The more closely linked companies are, the greater their degree of motivation to work together collaboratively. This personal acquaintance will build trust and confidence in the partners, gaining acceptance for changes taking place and accelerating progress.

*We must take the initiative to keep in touch at the senior levels. Team members change and the company relationship is reflected at the executive level and gives teams confidence.*
**Brian O'Leary, Kuhlman Electric**

*As we were engineering the new process, we spent a lot of time visiting with people at all levels—clerical all the way up to executive. The team is the primary focus of the relationship ongoing. But at the senior levels we need to review progress, to continue to challenge and adjust the vision if needed.*
**John Maloney, Office Depot**

*One way we stay in touch is to have our Volt representatives located on site at SCE. They are able to manage the staffing requirements for SCE and handle problems as they arise. That representative becomes like an SCE manager and knows what you need and how you operate.*
**Jerry Shaw, Volt Services**

*One of the critical things was you [SCE] were an electronic culture, so we could have e-mail. It sounds like a small thing, but we have customers who don't do e-mail. It's a very important piece. It's how you can stay in touch. It's part of the access and part of the speed.*
**Bill Green, SCMG**

*A big difference in Strategic Sourcing is that really all levels get involved. You need to be interested in and prepared to work more closely with your Strategic Sourcing partners at all levels. In a traditional procurement relationship one or two levels are involved consistently, but not all levels get involved as much as they do in Strategic Sourcing. It's important to have a good method for communication to flow top down and bottom up. People need to understand at all levels in both companies what the objectives are and what's trying to be accomplished. We really all have to be pulling together. If the oars start going in different directions, it's chaos.*
**John Estey, S&C Electric**

*We have built such strong relationships, sometimes the lines blur. As part of working on this project we have several of our technical people colocated with you at an SCE facility in Alhambra [California]. We had a couple of people out there for over a year, and they would answer the phone "ABB West." Even after we were no longer there, they had developed such a team identity that when you would call the SCE number they would answer "ABB West."*

**Gary Campbell, ABB**

---

*"Crew-to-crew visits" built personal acquaintances at the front-line worker level.*

---

*There is a strong senior-level relationship between SCE and Southwire. There are periodic visits to Southwire facilities by senior management people from SCE and regular discussions about how to work together to gain mutual benefit. The implementation team recognized we were overlooking a very valuable resource in our ongoing continuous improvement program. They put in place a program they called "crew-to-crew visits." Teams of front-line workers from SCE visited Southwire's manufacturing plants and saw the operation, talked to workers, and learned what Southwire was about. In turn, teams of shop floor people from Southwire visited SCE and went out on the job with line crews who were installing the products they made. From talking with and observing people actually using the product, they get a better understanding of the work and can devise ways to increase productivity or make a product easier to install. In addition to the improvement ideas generated and relationship established among the visiting teams, there is an added benefit to the companies. When these workers return to their jobs they help to educate others about the sourcing relationship and the partner company.*

**Steve McLendon, Southwire**

| SUPPLIERS' CRITICAL SUCCESS FACTOR 5: |
| --- |

**Select Team Members Carefully**
Implementation team members will be the ones to achieve results and build the basic working relationship between the companies. The team is cross-functional, with representatives from key disciplines from both companies. Choose people who are team players, are credible, and are able to get things done. Effective team members must understand and be committed to a Strategic Sourcing relationship. Your company's success depends on these people.

*The number one critical success factor in making the relationship work is the people. I'm completely convinced of that. In the beginning of the process, there are so many unknowns that you have to have the right amount of organizational experience and integrity, combined with the ability to say, "We're punting on that one." Someone with enough organizational savvy to go around the bumps, so you don't end up seeing the short-term road in front of you so littered with mines and potholes, you say "I'm never going to get there." They have to be implementation driven. A personality match helps. At the end of the day, it's a people deal.*
**Bill Green, SCMG**

"*It isn't an institutional thing—it really is personal.*"

*In truth, the Strategic Sourcing relationship is only successful because of the people. It isn't an institutional thing. It really is personal. The chemistry has to be right. There's a certain sort of personal drive and charisma required to make something new happen.*
**John Estey, S&C Electric**

*When we first selected a team [to prepare a proposal], it was a team that could not only be the architects but could actually*

*build too. While some of us that were more vision/big picture oriented played a more active role initially, we became more the monitors. The people who ended up implementing the process, and still to this day drive the business, are those people who were in there right from the beginning. A very important part of the strategy is pick the team early, get 100 percent buy-in, make sure the implementation team members participate in the vision to start with and they stay in the process. I think the biggest single success factor for us in improving process and relationships is we had full buy-in from the very same people that today, two years later, are living the vision.*
**John Maloney, Office Depot**

*You've got to have good team players that are qualified in their area and will keep the agenda moving. You have to have a good selection process for team members, cross-functional team members. They have to be able to make decisions and make a mistake. You just have to keep juggling until you get the right mix to make it happen, then empower them and support them.*

*If you are going to have to do a lot of process change in the field to get results, it is helpful to have someone who is well respected in the operations side be team leader. The field people can't say, "They're staff people and they don't know what's going on."*
**Steve McLendon, Southwire**

---

## SUPPLIERS' CRITICAL SUCCESS FACTOR 6:

**Assign Point Responsibility to Manage Relationships**
The implementation team needs to strike a balance between cross-functional involvement in decision making and expediting day-to-day progress. The way to accomplish this is to assign a person from each company who acts as the official point person for the relationship. This person must have the authority to speak for his or her company and make decisions that will keep progress moving.

*It is extremely important to have one key person that is viewed as lead for each company. If you have too many people the left hand doesn't know what the right hand is doing. At the beginning everybody talked to everybody and we had a real state of confusion. And then each company said, "Okay, Chuck is the person for SCE and Jim is the person for ABB," and it started to get better. People still tried to go around but we got that under control. It's key to have official representatives, making sure they have the ability to speak for their company.*
**Gary Campbell, ABB**

*Part of the relationship-building strategy [between companies] has been to have a lead person for each company who personifies what Strategic Sourcing means. Jerry was the lead for SCE. His credibility, his expertise, his willingness to share his knowledge in a constructive way, meant a great deal to us. On the other side of the coin, our manufacturing general manager, Paul, is very gifted as a motivational change agent. He uses the SCE relationship to key up the entire workforce to perform better.*
**Brian O'Leary, Kuhlman Electric**

*You need to have one person for each company who is responsible for coordinating the relationship. You need one person everybody can look at who will know it all.*
**John Estey, S&C Electric**

---

### Each company needs an individual who "owns" the relationship.

---

*You get the best continuous improvement progress when someone, an individual, owns the relationship—a focused relationship person. For us, that's Bob. Bob owns the problems and the successes. We're very focused. There's no question who's got the ball. The team needs to get involved with monitoring progress and major issues. But identify a focal point to manage much of the day-to-day stuff. Each side needs someone with clear authority to drive the process and make decisions. That keeps it going.*
**Lloyd Docter, McFarland Cascade**

## SUPPLIERS' CRITICAL SUCCESS FACTOR 7:

### Create Organizational Alignment

Alignment concerning the Strategic Sourcing approach to business is a prerequisite to a successful partnership. Internal alignment within a company is a demonstration that the strategy is understood and supported by the entire company and its separate functions. Because of the interdependence created in a Strategic Sourcing relationship, it is critical that the same alignment be achieved between the partner companies.

*It is impossible for any company to have external alliances without first having internal alliances: marketing/production/ engineering. No alliance happens without the belief and commitment of all leaders in the company. Troops respond to that belief and won't commit to a program du jour.*

*Strategic Sourcing relationships require for success a very strong internal alliance in each organization. You can't have the supplier's salesmen or even sales executive commit to things if the design people and the factory people aren't equally committed. Likewise it doesn't work to have a procurement organization commit to something and then find engineering and operations on a different page. I beat that drum because I've seen it create problems in our company and we're a little company. You really need to have everybody in a given organization on the same page if you want to get both organizations (in the relationship) to end up on the same page.*

**John Estey, S&C Electric**

*Everyone needs to be on the same page.*

*In the end you are looking for strong alignment between partners. On the project we were working on for SCE, your goals became our goals. Your deadlines became our deadlines. That's alignment.*

**Gary Campbell, ABB**

*The vision of Strategic Sourcing needs to be understood and shared from the people on the front lines to management seven layers up. Everyone understood from the very beginning what we were trying to accomplish and they shared the vision. Many times we do a good job in developing vision and forming a partnership at a high level and then we try to cram the concept down somebody's throat and that person has to live with it.*
**John Maloney, Office Depot**

*We create internal alignment around our strategy by training everyone. We built a common base of understanding and skills around Strategic Sourcing.*
**Brian O'Leary, Kuhlman Electric**

*The most important thing I would say is make sure there really is an organization decision. It's not just the guy on top or the people in the middle or the guys from the field. You should really have a consensus [internally] that you want to make this work. The worst thing is to get this whole thing going, spend a lot of time, make a lot of good decisions in the team and then delegate to an operational group that says, "It wasn't my idea, it's not going where I want to go." It just gets ugly.*
**Lloyd Docter, McFarland Cascade**

## SUPPLIERS' CRITICAL SUCCESS FACTOR 8:

**Practice Team Building**
In Strategic Sourcing at SCE, each new supplier relationship began with a three-day team-building meeting to establish the team identity and charter. (This session is described in Part Two, Phase G.) Suppliers agreed that this strategy to solidify the team with a structured team building session was a worthwhile investment of time and energy. It focused the team and modeled a way of working together. Participation by senior levels provided endorsement and visible support. Cross-functional participation ensured that the companies could move forward into implementation with all stakeholders on board.

*At first we just wanted to jump on things and start solving problems and you [SCE] wanted to get acquainted. You planned the team-building time together over a weekend so we could get to know each other. The team created a real bond. We needed to do that. There are some things that you don't realize you need to do but if you're going to do this [Strategic Sourcing] you need to have that relationship. We had some tough decisions, tough things we had to go through, and we needed to have that foundation so we could discuss the issues and still respect the people. It was very meaningful to go through. At the time we didn't realize it. When we got home, we didn't realize it. But in retrospect you can see the value.*
**Steve McLendon, Southwire**

*The three-day meeting to get the [implementation] team started was very effective in jump-starting the relationship. Everyone was personally involved—executives, stakeholders, team members. As we talked through what we were trying to do, how it was different, what the role and commitment of the team would be, everyone at the table was equal. We checked our egos at the door. As a result, people could get creative and everyone was allowed to contribute their ideas. Barriers were broken down, trust developed. Because of that participation process and top-level involvement, the team could demand my full endorsement. It was impossible not to support the team's work. It was stimulating for the team and became the basis for how they worked together.*
**John Maloney, Office Depot**

---

*A common base of experience helps people shift directions as a group.*

---

*When we were invited to the implementation team kickoff meeting for three days, I was not initially a believer and thought it would be a waste of time. I left feeling that it was an extremely important session. The team building helped develop the team's ability to talk and listen to one another. It forced discussion of where we were going and why, and surfaced assumptions and issues. It taught the team how to work toward consensus. The three days were both necessary and useful. People have to create a common experience and shift directions as a group.*
**Lloyd Docter, McFarland Cascade**

> ### SUPPLIERS' CRITICAL SUCCESS FACTOR 9:
>
> **Understand Value**
> The total cost model in Strategic Sourcing became the basis for a shared understanding of costs and value between suppliers and SCE. Once that is established, coupled with a commitment to creating mutual value, a critical piece is in place.
>
> Another critical piece is understanding total value. Mutual value creation is the ongoing work throughout the life of the Strategic Sourcing relationship. It is important that the supplier understand how value can be grown and what the supplier brings to the table in terms of continuous improvement and innovation. In implementation, performance metrics focus the team on value and results.

*Performance metrics—you gotta have 'em! The traditional quantifiable targets—inventory goals, cost reduction, performance improvement. Visibility of what is important and expected in terms of results. To institutionalize the relationship, we need to work together to establish more performance metrics, challenge ourselves to higher levels of performance, and create value.*
**John Estey, S&C Electric**

*In the adversarial days, manufacturers were so gun-shy of not meeting specification for equipment efficiency they would put in—I'll exaggerate here—$5000 worth of material to prevent $500 overage in losses. We have changed completely our view of how to manufacture toward efficiency requirements. With SCE we looked at the simple economics and said we should go for the most efficient manufacturing. We recognized that the smart trade-off would create value for both companies. A secret to our success has been this kind of willingness to look for mutual benefit.*
**Brian O'Leary, Kuhlman Electric**

*A shared understanding of total value is the basis for pursuing mutual benefit.*

*The Strategic Sourcing process allowed us to understand SCE's business drivers and strategies. We shared our strategies with SCE and were able to link much more closely to what was required strategically. We established very close relationships based on a sense of equality and mutual benefit. In supplier-customer relationships, you are always looking for hidden agendas. But this is different. If you asked me what is the hidden agenda for us or SCE, I really can't find one. I don't think there are any hidden agendas.*
**Gary Campbell, ABB**

*The thing that has worked so well at SCE is that after good goals are set, our rep goes out and works directly with a field person. Together they implement some baby step forward, followed by another and another. Things get done very quickly; there are no meetings, you just make some progress. It is a passion for continuous improvement, people willing to make small changes all the time in the process. It avoids the stagnation.*

*Suppliers in Strategic Sourcing relationships are going to tend to price aggressively because of the continuity of business. We designed our business to run very lean to be a good partner. I think every company new in Strategic Sourcing should think hard about how to design the process to be efficient with their partner.*

*Logistics and material management is an area where suppliers can add value. We really do have the tools and system to service the customer. In response to a disaster, we can reschedule a plant, we can flex inventories, we can add distribution resources. Someone on the other end, who is just a customer, never really knows how to outguess the supply side. I would say the best relationships tend to get the customer out of the business of forecasting, warehousing, reshipping, material management. The supplier benefits from higher utilization and the customer manages less and gets better service.*
**Lloyd Docter, McFarland Cascade**

---

*Periodically, the company-supplier team should validate that the relationship continues to be competitive.*

---

*In a perpetual relationship, it's incumbent on the supplier to continue to bring process improvement and additional value to the relationship. This also means taking steps to validate that what we are doing together continues to be competitive. Suppliers can draw on their experience with other customers. Periodically, the team should make a complete review of the relationship, what we are doing and what we are not doing. Ask, if you had your wishes, hopes, and dreams, where would you take this relationship?*

**John Maloney, Office Depot**

*It is important that there is a common understanding of what constitutes value. In a Strategic Sourcing relationship, as the strategy is evolving, you need to learn what is important. Most attempts at performance metrics are all too ambitious. In the beginning start with the three things that are most important to both partners, follow through, and then go to the next three and follow through with those. Then, if you need to, you can get more sophisticated.*

**Bill Green, SCMG**

## ■ SUMMARY

The supplier's view of the essential elements in Strategic Sourcing has been captured in this chapter as critical success factors. It is revealing that of the nine factors identified, five deal specifically with the relationship that must be built between companies.

In this chapter, suppliers have shared their experiences and views about Strategic Sourcing. Theirs is a different perspective than that from which the rest of the book is told. Their words help us to understand the full scope and impact of Strategic Sourcing.

This concludes Part One, *"The Voice of Experience."* In Part One we examined the supply chain strategy at SCE to learn from that company's experience. Lessons and personal insights from the leaders of Strategic Sourcing at SCE were shared. Eight of the supplier companies partnering with SCE related their experiences, providing a different perspective on the strategy and its value. Part One was written to help you decide whether to pursue Strategic Sourcing as a method to harness the tremendous value in your supply chain. Part Two is written to tell you how to design and implement a Strategic Sourcing program. Drawing from the real-life example of the Strategic Sourcing program at SCE, Part Two provides a comprehensive, step-by-step guide to the methodology and tools of this supply chain strategy.

# PART TWO

# The Action Guide

*Implementing Strategic Sourcing*

## ■ INTRODUCTION

This part of the book presents a comprehensive, step-by-step guide to implementing Strategic Sourcing. The methodology is presented in chronological sequence as it took place at SCE, and contains both corporate elements and sourcing team activity phases. The earliest preparation and design phases of the Strategic Sourcing program were performed at the corporate level. These phases discuss making the decision to adopt Strategic Sourcing as a company-wide initiative at SCE and how the corporate program was structured and implemented. The team activity phases apply the sourcing methodology through a series of cross-functional sourcing teams. The final phase identifies several corporate-level initiatives that were undertaken to accomplish full integration of Strategic Sourcing methods and changes into the company business practice. Figure P2.1 depicts the phases and identifies major program elements contained in each phase.

Throughout Part 2, the following icons are included to highlight recurring elements:

**PURPOSE**
Overview of the activity included in the phase and why it is performed.

**DELIVERABLES**
Work products that support and document the process.

**TRAINING**
Recommended training to support each phase. Training content specific to Strategic Sourcing is detailed.

**TIPS**
Advice for leaders and teams based on lessons learned from real-life Strategic Sourcing experiences.

**Figure P2.1** Strategic Sourcing Phase Map.

The phases contain methodology defined at the activity level and present analytical tools. Templates and examples are included to illustrate practical application.

Chapter 6

# Deciding to Act

Before deciding to act, there is some work to be done. Preliminary analysis, assessment, and strategy development will assure that all stakeholders will support Strategic Sourcing as the correct intervention. The high-level storyboard in Figure 6.1 depicts the approach to take to achieve the necessary support.

As shown in the storyboard, the assessment includes an external market analysis and an internal analysis, resulting in a business case with options. The decision to act is made by a cross-functional senior executive group representing major stakeholder organizations. A consensus decision is recommended so that stakeholders will have a shared understanding of the decision and a clear plan for future supply chain activities with Strategic Sourcing at the center.

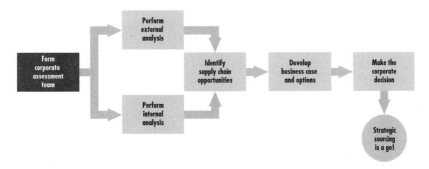

**Figure 6.1** Storyboard—Deciding to Act.

### PURPOSE

The purpose of this phase is to determine whether Strategic Sourcing is the right strategy to pursue at this time. This requires in-depth research of both the internal and external environments and sufficient levels of executive alignment around the decision to utilize Strategic Sourcing.

### DELIVERABLES

Performing the steps in Phase A will lead to the development of the following work products:

➤ External analysis

➤ Internal analysis

➤ Business case and options

➤ Executive presentation

### TRAINING

➤ Benchmarking

➤ Change management (SCE executives attended GE's Change Acceleration Program)

What follows is a description of a suggested process (see Figure 6.2) that will help to identify the magnitude of opportunity as well as to support decision making. The resulting business case will be presented to executive stakeholders for buy-in. The following section describes the process steps in detail.

## A.1 PERFORM EXTERNAL ANALYSIS

The external market analysis covers all the areas to be considered in order to develop a complete picture of the company's

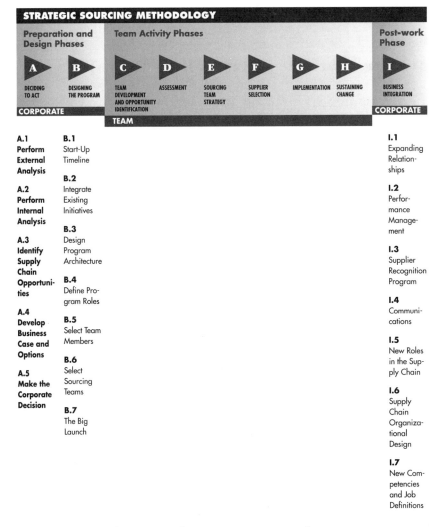

**STRATEGIC SOURCING METHODOLOGY**

**Preparation and Design Phases**

**A** DECIDING TO ACT

**B** DESIGNING THE PROGRAM

CORPORATE

**Team Activity Phases**

**C** TEAM DEVELOPMENT AND OPPORTUNITY IDENTIFICATION

**D** ASSESSMENT

**E** SOURCING TEAM STRATEGY

**F** SUPPLIER SELECTION

**G** IMPLEMENTATION

**H** SUSTAINING CHANGE

TEAM

**Post-work Phase**

**I** BUSINESS INTEGRATION

CORPORATE

**A.1**
Perform External Analysis

**A.2**
Perform Internal Analysis

**A.3**
Identify Supply Chain Opportunities

**A.4**
Develop Business Case and Options

**A.5**
Make the Corporate Decision

**B.1**
Start-Up Timeline

**B.2**
Integrate Existing Initiatives

**B.3**
Design Program Architecture

**B.4**
Define Program Roles

**B.5**
Select Team Members

**B.6**
Select Sourcing Teams

**B.7**
The Big Launch

**I.1**
Expanding Relationships

**I.2**
Performance Management

**I.3**
Supplier Recognition Program

**I.4**
Communications

**I.5**
New Roles in the Supply Chain

**I.6**
Supply Chain Organizational Design

**I.7**
New Competencies and Job Definitions

**Figure 6.2** Phase Map—Corporate Phases.

133

opportunities as well as the potential risks. Figure 6.3 illustrates different elements of the external analysis.

A method to examine each element of the external analysis is described in the following text.

## Industry Assessment (Competitive Forces)

➤ Conduct research on what suppliers in your industry are doing to meet their customers' demands in terms of quality, cost, delivery, and service.

➤ Seek information about what your competitors and their Strategic Sourcing processes are doing to drive competitive advantage.

➤ Conduct research on cost trends in Strategic Sourcing programs. *How are suppliers' costs being affected? Are they going down? Up? Why?*

## Best Practice Identification

➤ Contact best-in-class companies inside and outside your industry to determine current practices. *What approaches are these companies taking that could be incorporated into your company?*

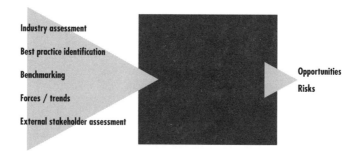

**Figure 6.3** External Analysis.

➤ Talk to both existing and new suppliers to find out what's happening externally. *What different approaches are these suppliers taking with other customers that might be beneficial to you?*

## Benchmarking

➤ Contact companies inside and outside your industry to compare and measure your performance against other companies' supply chain practices. For example:

|  | Company A | World-Class |
|---|---|---|
| Supplier lead times | 35 days | 8 days |
| Order input time | 6 min | 0 min |
| Late deliveries | 33% | <1% |
| Shortages/year | 400 | 4 |
| Suppliers/buyer | 34 | 5.3 |
| Rejection rate | 4% | 0.01% |
| Supplier lead times | 35 days | 8 days |

## Forces/Trends

➤ Research political, economic, social, technological, legal, and demographic trends relevant to your business.

*For example, are there changes in technology in your industry that will affect the type of materials/services needed in the future? Will this change affect the types of suppliers needed?*

*A current example in the political arena is the impact of deregulation and privatization affecting industries worldwide.*

## External Stakeholder Assessment

➤ Identify key external stakeholders.

➤ Contact those key stakeholders to learn their primary objectives.

*How do those stakeholder objectives align with the objectives of Strategic Sourcing?*

The purpose of the external stakeholder assessment is to enable you to evaluate potential options through this stakeholder lens.

## TIPS

➤ The scope of Strategic Sourcing is company-wide: Opportunity will be found in all aspects of the business. Therefore, to understand the extent of the opportunity, it is important that a company-wide perspective be present during the analysis.

➤ Selecting the right people to perform the assessment is key. The work of this team will position the company to undertake a major step. Take care to identify people with the pertinent knowledge, necessary skills, and positive attitude.

## A.2 PERFORM INTERNAL ANALYSIS

The internal analysis provides the picture of the company's business requirements both now and in the future. Understanding the current state of the company will allow you to formulate a strategy that delivers realistic expectations and opportunities. Understanding the long-range direction of the company will support a strategy that delivers sustainable value. Figure 6.4 illustrates the different elements of internal analysis.

A method to examine each element of the internal analysis is described in the following text.

### Related Company Initiatives

➤ Identify all ongoing initiatives in the business units or other organizations. *Are these initiatives in competition with or complementary to Strategic Sourcing?* For example:

**Figure 6.4** Internal Analysis.

—Reengineering
—Cost cutting
—Automation
—Mergers
—Downsizing
—Divestiture
—Organizational change
—Acquisitions

## Purchasing History and Practices

➤ Identify historical spending patterns and the level of overall external purchases within departments.

➤ Identify the number of suppliers with whom you have done business in the last 12 months.

➤ Assess the variety and complexity of materials and services purchased.

➤ Identify the extent of purchases outside the formal procurement process.

➤ Review recent audit findings related to purchasing practices.

### Internal Stakeholders

➤ Identify your internal stakeholders and their primary business objectives.

### Procurement and Material Management Organization

➤ State the present procurement strategy and practice.

➤ Identify existing systems and structures to support the supply chain.

➤ Document organizational performance. *What criteria are used to assess organizational performance?*

➤ Assess organizational capabilities and competencies—knowledge, skills, and abilities.

➤ Determine the availability of data on supplier history, spending patterns, and inventory levels to support decision making.

### Internal Culture

➤ Describe the culture and attitudes of employees/leadership within the company.

➤ Summarize previous change initiatives in order to understand critical success factors and sources of resistance to change. *Were these initiatives successful or were they binders on the shelf?*

➤ Define your company's capacity to deploy technology.

### Internal Forces

➤ Identify forces that may impact future intervention strategies:

—Union relations
—Social responsibility
—Changing demographics of workforce
—Supplier diversity
—Company values

The purpose of the external and internal assessment is to guide you in developing your strategy in a way that serves the needs of stakeholders and ensures buy-in.

**TIP**

Think broadly and for the long term. In both the internal and external analyses, don't underestimate the need to understand the company's business requirements and desired direction. This is the basis for determining the extent of the opportunity offered by Strategic Sourcing and for establishing program goals and objectives.

## A.3 IDENTIFY SUPPLY CHAIN OPPORTUNITIES

Utilizing the internal/external analysis you performed on your company, review the Strategic Sourcing savings profile (see Figure 6.5) to determine whether you have significant opportunities, and if so, where. If you determine that substantial opportunities exist, you can now go on to the readiness assessment.

**TIP**

Avoid "not invented here" thinking. Your company isn't unique. If your business includes purchasing, these areas of supply chain savings likely apply to you.

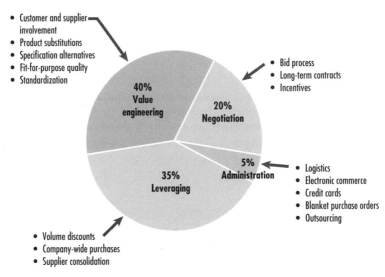

**Figure 6.5** Profile of Savings.

# A.4 DEVELOP BUSINESS CASE AND OPTIONS

This step translates concepts and gathered data into implementable strategies and actions to aid in developing a business case.

Strategic business planning encompasses analyzing the business and its environment as they are *today* in order to create a formal program for guiding development and success *tomorrow*. This analysis identifies the variables that must be considered in order to implement Strategic Sourcing. Each business case is unique. Designing the program to maximize the value will require that you tailor your analysis to your company's particular business environment and circumstances.

### Is the Time Right?

While developing a recommendation to pursue Strategic Sourcing as a key company-wide program, you have done your homework. The external and internal analyses support your conclusion that Strategic Sourcing has the potential to deliver high value in a reasonable period of time—months, not years. It is the right intervention for your company.

Before putting your judgment to a public test, ask one final screening question: "Is the time right for this to happen?" The corporate world is a world of scarce resources, competing priorities, and constantly changing dynamics and players. Focus is important. Is the company ready to take advantage of Strategic Sourcing? The company readiness assessment in Table 6.1 will help you decide.

If you answered "no" to half or more of the questions in Table 6.1, it simply may be the wrong time for Strategic Sourcing in your company. Wait six months and ask these questions again. Strategic Sourcing is an idea whose time will come. If you answered "yes" to four or more questions, it is time to present your idea and business case to the CEO.

| | Y | N |
|---|---|---|
| 1. Is there a "burning platform," a compelling need to reduce costs, a competitive threat? | | |
| 2. Does Strategic Sourcing offer equal or greater opportunity for value compared with existing company initiatives? | | |
| 3. Is there leadership talent available to lead Strategic Sourcing? | | |
| 4. Is the internal political climate neutral or positive? | | |
| 5. Is the supplier base ready? | | |
| 6. Are there adequate employee resources to support Strategic Sourcing? | | |
| 7. Will the company's culture tolerate learning a new way of doing business? | | |
| 8. Are the stakes high enough to warrant company attention and resources? | | |

**Table 6.1** Company Readiness Assessment

| EXECUTIVE PRESENTATION |
| WITH SPEAKER NOTES* |

**Strategic Sourcing**

A new perspective on procurement

➤ Good Morning. I am here to propose that we take a fresh look at how we buy things in the company in order to understand and take advantage of untapped value in the supply chain. At the conclusion of my presentation, I will ask your approval to launch a major company-wide supply chain change initiative. A little background: I have researched the concepts that are the basis of the sourcing methodology I am proposing. More importantly, I have seen sourcing in action at companies in our industry and other industries with similar purchasing characteristics—petrochemical and pipeline companies—as examples. When I apply what I have learned to our company, I am convinced that what I am calling *Strategic Sourcing* has the potential for tremendous cost reductions across our business. Let me tell you why.

**What Is It?**

➤ Strategic Sourcing is a method to analyze corporate expenditures, identify cost drivers, and develop strategies to reduce life cycle costs.

➤ The change our industry is undergoing, from regulation to competition, fundamentally changes the way in which the company creates shareholder value. Because in a restructured utility industry our business drivers are different, we must rethink how we analyze and make business decisions. This slide defines a different way of thinking about purchasing decisions. There is one element in the definition of Strategic Sourcing that represents a distinct change in how we have traditionally approached procurement.

➤ That is "identify cost drivers." Traditionally, regulatory accounting requirements have driven accounting and cost systems that serve the reporting purpose well but do not provide discrete visibility of costs of doing business at the level needed for Strategic Sourcing. This element of Strategic Sourcing will require a considerable investment of time and effort to develop activity-based costing (ABC) and total cost models to understand everything that drives costs in the supply chain process.

*Speaker notes from presentation made by Emiko Banfield to the SCE Senior Executive Team.

**Why Do It?**

➤ To achieve results that are
  —Potent
  —Safe
  —Benign

➤ We know that we must reduce costs. Not just with incremental cost reductions, but major cost reductions. Every organization is working on ways to do just that. I believe Strategic Sourcing should become a priority cost reduction strategy because it offers a way to reduce costs that is potent, safe, and benign.

**Specifically . . .**

➤ Potent:
  $100 million in 1996
  $200 million by 1998
➤ Safe:
  Manageable risk levels
➤ Benign:
  80% nonlabor
  20% labor

➤ Potent—We spend approximately $1 billion per year on goods and services. The experience of companies implementing the Strategic Sourcing methodology has been a total cost reduction of 15 to 20 percent of external expenditures. We can match that in 3 years' time, which would mean total cost reduction of $100 million in 1996, growing to $200 million by 1998. This is an annual reduction that carves out costs across the supply chain permanently.

➤ Safe—Strategic Sourcing is safe. By that I mean there are manageable risk levels. There will be some new risk involved in selecting supply partners and increasing our reliance on them. Streamlining processes may create some risk exposure as redundancy is eliminated. But these are manageable, particularly if we recognize them from the start.

➤ Benign—For the first time in our company's history, we are faced with the possibilities of labor cuts as the only remaining area for cost reduction. I call Strategic Sourcing benign because it has a relatively low impact on labor. Typically, 80 percent of cost reductions identified in Strategic Sourcing are in nonlabor areas.

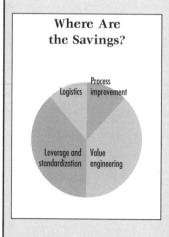

**Where Are the Savings?**

➤ The shorthand way of calculating savings potential is 15 to 20 percent of external spending. This does not mean that we reduce expenditures to our suppliers by 15 to 20 percent. The savings come from four primary areas:

➤ Value engineering has to do with what we buy. Because of business drivers that existed in the traditional ratemaking model, over the years we have built an electrical system that is top of the line, with redundancy and custom-engineered equipment. That practice served shareholders and customers alike. It drove high costs, but shareholders benefited from return on rate base and customers benefited from a highly reliable supply of high-quality power. With the emphasis on cost reduction and efficiencies created by restructuring, there are major opportunities to rationalize what we buy—to examine specifications and requirements, to value engineer. Opportunities also exist to examine standard, off-the-shelf products in place of Edison customization.

➤ Leverage/standardization: Today we have 34,000 suppliers in our supplier base; we have done business with 12,000 in the past year. Decisions about what to buy are made at the level of the local work unit, sometimes the individual. It is a costly way to run a business. Standardizing on common products and leveraging our purchasing power across the company will make a major contribution to our cost reduction target for Strategic Sourcing.

➤ The remaining areas of process improvement and logistics are what I talked about earlier as understanding how we do our work at the activity level using ABC to understand the total costs involved in our supply chain and find ways to become more efficient.

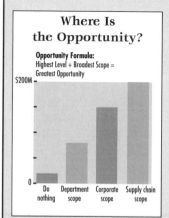

**Where Is the Opportunity?**

Opportunity Formula:
Highest Level + Broadest Scope = Greatest Opportunity

➤ This formula captures where the greatest opportunity can be found in Strategic Sourcing—keeping the perspective of buying decisions at the highest level and expanding the consideration to the full extent of the supply chain.

➤ (First bar) This was never an option.

➤ (Second bar) Today we are here in each department working diligently to find ways to reduce costs within each respective silo. With regard to the supply chain opportunity, I describe this as working diligently to take full advantage of half an opportunity.

➤ (Third bar) This represents where Strategic Sourcing can take us. Full-scope buying decisions made by cross-functional teams that collaborate to make the best decisions for the company will take us halfway to our target.

➤ (Fourth bar) This represents the full supply chain opportunity. By being willing to examine our practices along the entire supply chain and challenge ourselves and our suppliers to think differently, I believe we can achieve the kind of cost reductions I talked about earlier.

---

**What Do I Want from You?**

➤ Make it possible
— Adopt Strategic Sourcing methodology
— Collaborate
➤ Make it happen
— Participate
— Support
— Drive results to the bottom line

---

➤ So, the big question is, "What do I want from you?"

➤ First, I want you to make Strategic Sourcing possible.

➤ Up front, there are two things you need: (1) An executive decision to adopt the Strategic Sourcing methodology at SCE; (2) A key behavior change in Strategic Sourcing—business decision making that sets aside organizational silos and requires collaboration across the company. When we sign up for Strategic Sourcing, we are signing up for that change. The senior executive team has the opportunity to lead by example.

➤ Second, if we move forward I need you to help me make it happen.

➤ Three things are needed: (1) Your organizations will be asked to share in the leadership of this initiative and to participate on teams. The plan is to run multiple teams concurrently. There is a direct relationship between the resources we commit and the results we achieve. (2) As changes are made, your people will look to you to see if we mean what we say—your visible support of Strategic Sourcing process and changes is critical. (3) To benefit from what Strategic Sourcing has to offer, we all need the resolve to take action on what teams recommend and drive results to the bottom line.

## ▧ MAKE THE CORPORATE DECISION

The information generated through this comprehensive analysis convinced us that Strategic Sourcing could provide substantial cost reduction to SCE. This analysis resulted in the preceding presentation to SCE executives with a recommendation to adopt Strategic Sourcing.

Although the Strategic Sourcing project will be led by a team of executives on a cross-functional, collaborative basis, it is imperative to establish a shared understanding of and commitment to the decision to act at the highest level of the company (see Figure 6.6). In the case of SCE, this was the Senior Executive Team. The recommendation to embark on Strategic Sourcing was made and approved in a presentation to CEO John Bryson and his direct reports. The presentation and discussion that followed provided the basis for the decision to pursue Strategic Sourcing at SCE and established the top-level commitment that was essential to launch the program.

The company has made the decision to implement a corporate-wide program of Strategic Sourcing. At the highest levels, we have established two things: a commitment to

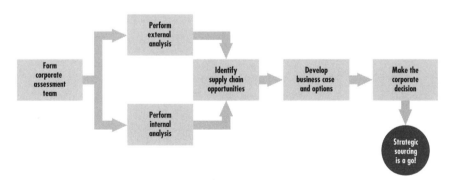

**Figure 6.6** Storyboard—Deciding to Act.

actively support Strategic Sourcing and an expectation that Strategic Sourcing will result in significant cost reduction. Now the task is to design and implement a Strategic Sourcing program that will live up to that expectation.

*Chapter*

7

# Designing the Program

**Preparation and Design Phases**

A lot of preparation has been done to bring us to this point (see Figure 7.1). The decision to act has been made; the analysis tells us where opportunities are greatest; we know what it will take to make Strategic Sourcing happen.

Many executives claim a bias for action but actually have a bias for execution. The difference is important. Take-charge action always has an effect, but that effect may not predictably contribute to the desired outcome. *Execution* is performance in a manner that ensures the actions contribute to the desired outcome.

Executives require sufficient preparation for intelligent, purposeful action. In the case of implementing Strategic Sourcing, "sufficient" preparation is defined in this book. If you are keen on the prospects of Strategic Sourcing and want to "just do it," be patient for the sake of those with a process prejudice. The stakes are high. Allow time to execute the plan—don't rush to act. The time you invest will pay big dividends.

## PURPOSE

In this phase, the decision to engage in Strategic Sourcing will be put into action. Roles will be developed for key players, the program architecture will be designed, and the initial teams will be launched.

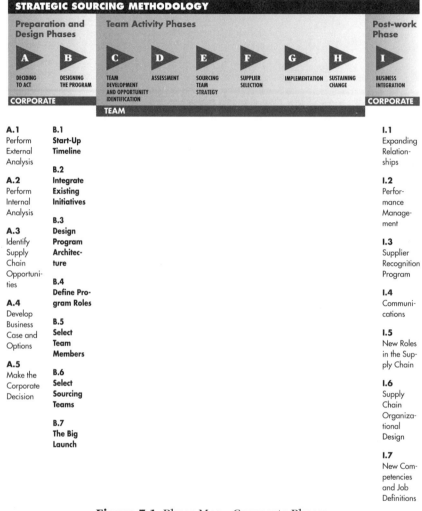

**Figure 7.1** Phase Map—Corporate Phases.

 ## DELIVERABLES

The work performed in Phase B will deliver the following work products:

➤ Launch agenda

➤ Team launch strategy

➤ Change management strategy

**TRAINING**

➤ Team building

➤ Teamwork training

➤ Team sponsor training

➤ Change management

➤ Strategic sourcing principles/processes

➤ Project management

➤ Communication training

## B.1 START UP TIMELINE

Before talking about program design elements, it may be helpful to put all the preceding activity in the context of time and resources required. Table 7.1 is a timeline of preparation activity for the development and launching of Strategic Sourcing at SCE. Four program activities identified on the timeline are discussed in Part One as critical success factors: pilot teams, total cost model, communication plan, and change management plan.

## B.2 INTEGRATE EXISTING INITIATIVES (JUNE)

Preparing the organization to focus on Strategic Sourcing means bringing closure to other directly related initiatives in the supply chain process. At SCE there were 27 such ad hoc initiatives in place in the Procurement and Material Management Department. These were sorted into *strategic* and *tactical* change initiatives, and fell into three categories:

1. Those changes that were complementary to Strategic Sourcing and could be incorporated into the program— for example, electronic commerce.

2. Those that were contradictory to the Strategic Sourcing goal and should be abandoned—for example, a material

| | June | August | October | November | January | February |
|---|---|---|---|---|---|---|
| | Begin research and benchmarking | Select Strategic Sourcing leadership team and support | Senior Executive Team adopts Strategic Sourcing | Launch 2 pilot teams | Adopt pilot team recommendation | |
| | | | | Establish program architecture | | Select new suppliers (pilot teams) |
| | Interview 6 consulting firms | | Convene Executive Steering Council | | Pilot supplier rollout meeting | |
| | Integrate existing procurement/material management initiatives | Develop business case for corporate program | | Present total cost model | | |
| | | | | Develop communication plan | Develop change management plan | |
| | | | | | Select first wave of teams | Big Launch |
| **Resources** | | | | | | |
| | 8–10 participants from procurement; 2–3 consultants | 20–25 participants from procurement; 10–12 from BUs; 3–5 consultants | 30–35 participants from procurement; 20–25 from BUs; 7 consultants | | 40+ participants from procurement; 50+ from BUs; 10–12 consultants | |

Resources represent the number of different participants at various stages of start-up activity. In the first 2 years of Strategic Sourcing at SCE, a total of 14 sourcing teams and 2 redesign teams completed work, involving a total of approximately 200 SCE employees and 12 consultants from several areas of expertise.

**Table 7.1** Strategic Sourcing Preparation Timeline

management system development project built on processes that would change.

3. Those that stood alone and either (1) had value—just do it; or (2) made work—just dump it.

In addition, clearing the slate to concentrate fully on Strategic Sourcing conveyed to the organization that changes would be made, and that Strategic Sourcing had priority status.

**TIP**

Don't assume that Strategic Sourcing is additive to the company's workload. Scrutinize existing efforts to determine what can be incorporated into the sourcing plan and what can be eliminated. Initially, members of the procurement organization will see this change as a significant impact on their time, but they will see the advantage when other efforts are eliminated or incorporated into sourcing.

## B.3 DESIGN PROGRAM ARCHITECTURE (NOVEMBER-FEBRUARY)

The Strategic Sourcing program will require coordination, facilitation, guidance, and expertise to ensure that it is successfully developed, rolled out, and implemented. Internal resources are essential to manage the program and staff teams, develop business strategies, and implement solutions.

The overall program architecture should be in place before the first sourcing teams are launched. Creative collaboration among all parts of the system needs to take place, and the architecture serves to support this. Functional areas in the company that had a link to specific aspects of the supply chain process were identified as resources and called upon on an as-needed basis. The commitment of people for Strategic Sourcing at SCE—where they were drawn from and how they were deployed—is depicted in Figure 7.2.

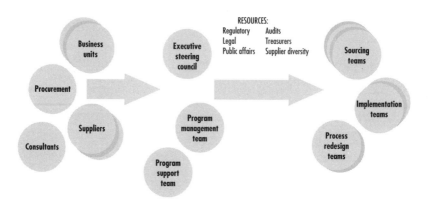

**Figure 7.2** Program Architecture.

The Executive Steering Council and Program Management Team were permanent assignments, generally requiring two days per month for the Executive Steering Council (seven people) and one to two days per week for the Program Management Team (nine people). The program support team was composed of three to four full-time people. Sourcing team assignments were for the duration of the team's work to select supplier partners. Teams were cross-functional, with membership drawn from organizations across the company. Depending upon the area being sourced, the team size ranged from 5 to 10 members, with assignment duration lasting from 4 to 12 months and requiring team members time to commit 2 to 4 days per week depending upon the phase of team activity. Overall, during the first 24 months of Strategic Sourcing at SCE, approximately 200 employees participated directly on a total of 16 teams. It was through their collective efforts that $150 million in savings was achieved.

**TIP**

Knowledge is a social activity. The program was organized so that lessons learned by each component of the system would be shared with other components. Before launching a total systems change effort, it is important to consider how the change will be managed, how the leadership levels will relate to one another, and how learning will be shared.

## B.4 DEFINE PROGRAM ROLES

Internal resources are required to staff ad hoc Strategic Sourcing teams as well as an ongoing program infrastructure. The first piece of the infrastructure is a cross-functional program management team. The executive steering council establishes and defines the role of the program management team, which is drawn from middle manager ranks, typically involved in the day-to-day operating of business units. These are the managers who will have responsibility for implementing change. The following guidelines help define the responsibilities:

### Role of Program Management Team

➤ Acts as sponsor for assigned sourcing teams

➤ Coordinates the work of the various sourcing teams, scheduling cross-team activities as needed

➤ Helps sourcing teams with analysis of market characteristics and customer requirements

➤ Assists sourcing teams to secure financial and operational support as needed

➤ Identifies sourcing team members

➤ Provides detailed data from sourcing team activity to the executive steering council

➤ Serves as liaison between sourcing teams and executive steering council

➤ Acts as communication link among sourcing teams sharing learnings and best practices

The final element of the infrastructure is the program support team. Unlike the executive steering council and program management team, which must have cross-functional representation, the program support team may be staffed within the sponsoring organization.

## Role of Program Support Team

➤ Supports the executive steering council, the program management team, and the sourcing teams in their efforts to plan and implement a Strategic Sourcing program

➤ Maintains a master calendar of all change initiatives

➤ Coordinates activities that involve multiple sourcing teams

➤ Develops and maintains reporting formats and schedules, decision processes, and issue resolution tracking methodologies

➤ Designs, develops, and maintains repositories of data, tools, techniques, and guides related to Strategic Sourcing

➤ Maintains a repository of documents relating to cross-sourcing team processes, such as agendas, communication materials, and team charters

➤ Coordinates communication and training company-wide

## TIPS

➤ It is critical to the project that adequate resources be committed. This entails securing both the people needed to staff the various teams and support activities, as well as the financial resources required.

➤ Don't make the mistake of assigning whoever is available to the Strategic Sourcing effort. Sourcing teams are making big corporate decisions—invest your best talent to get the best results.

## B.5 SELECT TEAM MEMBERS

The Strategic Sourcing assignments will draw employees from throughout the company. There will be people from line functions and staff representing every perspective of the business. There will be people from all levels—front-line workers to senior managers. This diversity of participation in the process contributes greatly to achieving success.

In the first 2 years, approximately 200 employees participated directly on teams. More important than how many people participate in the Strategic Sourcing program is who is selected to participate.

To accomplish appropriate cross-functionality, all teams will need representatives from specific discipline/activity areas in line and staff units. This approach limits the pools from which participants can be selected, but assures that all pertinent perspectives are present in decision making. It also assures that those ultimately responsible for implementing changes are represented.

Selecting members who are credible with their peers and trusted by their executives is important. The decisions these people recommend will change the way the company does business. Choose people based on their knowledge, credibility, and willingness to try something new.

## TIPS

➤ Internal resources are essential to manage the program and staff teams, develop business strategies, and implement solutions. The speed with which you achieve results is directly related to the resource commitment.

➤ Utilizing a cross-functional approach means that a resource commitment will be required from every organization within the company. In order for success to be achieved, there must be a commitment to providing internal resources. Internal resources will become the pacing item in achieving results. Apply the resources and you'll get the results.

## B.6 SELECT SOURCING TEAMS

By January, we were ready to identify where we would apply Strategic Sourcing first.

## Where Do You Start?

Initial investigation will suggest numerous opportunities. You may find yourself on information overload. The first step is to understand where opportunity is greatest in your company.

## The Macro-opportunity

As part of the internal analysis, you have developed a summary of expenditures for materials and services. It is now time to revisit that analysis to determine the approach for the Strategic Sourcing program. The responsibility for assessing opportunities and identifying priorities is that of the program management team.

The business unit spending matrix (see Table 7.2) is a tool that helps identify which sourcing teams to select. Utilizing the data already gathered on company expenditures, you can analyze where the dollars are spent both by material/service

| Commodity | BU 1 | BU 2 | BU 3 | Corporate | Total |
|---|---|---|---|---|---|
| Supplemental personnel | 12.3 | 3.4 | 1.3 | 22.6 | 39.6 |
| Maintenance | 25.8 | 1.3 | 3.5 | 0.6 | 31.2 |
| MRO | 6.5 | 12.2 | 7.0 | 0.2 | 25.9 |
| Computers | 2.8 | 6.5 | 3.1 | 12.2 | 24.6 |
| Construction | 3.7 | 9.4 | 7.0 | 0.6 | 20.7 |
| Transformers | 0.8 | 14.9 | 0.0 | 0.0 | 15.7 |
| Tree trimming | 0.0 | 14.5 | 0.0 | 0.0 | 14.5 |
| Fleet services | 0.6 | 9.6 | 0.7 | 0.0 | 10.9 |
| Wire and cable | 0.1 | 9.3 | 0.0 | 0.0 | 9.4 |
| Telecommunication | 0.2 | 3.9 | 0.0 | 2.4 | 6.5 |
| Office products | 1.7 | 3.2 | 0.3 | 0.5 | 5.7 |
| Radiological | 5.0 | 0.0 | 0.0 | 0.0 | 5.0 |
| Chemicals and gases | 1.3 | 0.3 | 0.9 | 0.0 | 2.5 |
| Poles/towers | 0.0 | 2.3 | 0.0 | 0.0 | 2.3 |
| Total | 60.8 | 90.8 | 23.8 | 39.1 | 214.5 |

**Table 7.2** Business Unit Spending Matrix (Annual $M)—Sample

grouping and by business unit. Observations can then be made from the data that will lead to decision making.

Spending patterns are only part of the opportunity picture. To help identify which materials/services are viable for Strategic Sourcing, a list of selection criteria follows.

Here is a brief explanation of each of the suggested criteria:

1. **High potential for savings**—The amount of external expenditure is large, the material/service itself can have a big impact on reducing costs, or internal duplication exists.
2. **High probability of success**—Based on knowledge of results from other companies.
3. **Speed of implementation**—How quickly implementation could occur, resulting in near-term savings.
4. **Business unit enthusiasm**—Business unit's desire to make changes in how business is conducted with the specific material/service.
5. **Resource availability**—People are available to staff sourcing team with necessary expertise.
6. **Company-wide impact**—The material/service is used throughout the company.

Once the criteria are set, the individual material/service categories can be mapped against the criteria to decide which warrant sourcing teams, and in which order to roll teams out. Table 7.3 shows the start of a sample matrix. Based on this matrix, computers would be the first priority for a sourcing team. Supplemental personnel would be second, based on the availability of resources needed to convene a team at this time.

Drawing from and refining the original opportunity analysis, the Program Management Team selected specific areas of greatest opportunity and identified initial scope for six sourcing teams. The selection was influenced by lessons learned from the pilot teams and practical operating considerations, such as timing and available resources of expertise.

| Material/ Service | Savings Potential | Probability of Success | Speed of Implementation | Customer Enthusiasm | Available Resources | Company-wide Impact |
|---|---|---|---|---|---|---|
| Supplemental personnel | x | | | | x | x |
| Maintenance | x | | | | x | |
| MRO | x | x | | x | | |
| Computers | x | x | x | x | | x |
| Etc. | | | | | | |

**Table 7.3** Sample Matrix

The Program Management Team then staffed teams with the appropriate mix of expertise, operating knowledge, and procurement/logistics experience. Each new team member was personally invited to participate by the Executive Steering Council. These six teams were invited to the Big Launch.

## TIPS

➤ Where possible, pilot team members were selected to participate in this initial wave of teams to give the new team members the benefit of their experience.

➤ A dedicated consultant resource was assigned to the team to teach the methodology, provide an outside perspective, and facilitate team activity.

## B.7 THE BIG LAUNCH

As you can see from the SCE timeline, the Big Launch came approximately seven months into the process. It was the company-wide announcement of the Strategic Sourcing program and was presented with the rollout of the first wave of six sourcing teams. The Big Launch was where strategy and expectations, CEO commitment, and Executive Steering Council leadership were publicly declared, and where project structure, methodology, and tools were introduced. Strategic Sourcing now entered into the corporate spotlight.

| STRATEGIC SOURCING LAUNCH AGENDA | | |
|---|---|---|
| 7:30 A.M. | Continental Breakfast | |
| 8:00 A.M. | Strategic Sourcing Overview | Emiko Banfield |
| 8:30 A.M. | The Case for Change | John Bryson |
| 9:00 A.M. | Leadership Commitment/ Executive Steering Council | Dennis Eastman |
| 9:30 A.M. | Program Architecture and Oversight | Larry Grant |
| 10:00 A.M. | Business Unit Commitment | Joe Wambold |
| 10:30 A.M. | Strategic Sourcing Methodology and Tools Overview | |
| 11:00 A.M. | Wood Poles and Tree Trimming Pilot Teams—Q&A | |
| 12:00 P.M. | Lunch | |
| 1:00 P.M. | Strategic Sourcing Methodology Training | |
| 3:30 P.M. | Overview of Three-day Off-site at Aliso Creek | |
| 3:45 P.M. | Questions and Answers | |
| 4:15 P.M. | Adjourn | |

See you all at Aliso Creek tonight for a reception!

The Big Launch was held in corporate headquarters. Approximately 180 people attended, including sourcing team members and their immediate supervisors, the Executive Steering Council, Program Management Team members, and SCE executives.

The following is an annotated agenda of the Big Launch meeting at SCE.

## Morning Session

Purpose: to launch corporate Strategic Sourcing and share strategy and goals; to introduce program elements, methodology, approach, and timeline; to provide visible executive endorsement and commitment to Strategic Sourcing.

## ANNOTATED AGENDA

8:00 A.M.   Strategic           Emiko Banfield,
Sourcing          Manager of Procurement
Overview         and Material Management,
Strategic Sourcing Champion

Provided background on development and design of Strategic Sourcing program for SCE. Presented benchmarking comparisons, project design, pilot teams, and major concepts of Strategic Sourcing. Identified six teams by commodity, service, and reason for selection. Established stretch goal for every team—30 percent reduction of total costs as measured against external spending.

8:30 A.M.   Case for Change     John Bryson, CEO

Described new business drivers created by industry changes and affirmed cost reduction imperative. Committed top-level executive support for Strategic Sourcing and conveyed high expectations of what Strategic Sourcing could deliver. Expressed personal endorsement of Strategic Sourcing and confidence in team members and program leaders.

9:00 A.M.   Executive Steering   Dennis Eastman,
Council Leadership  Vice President,
Commitment       Distribution Business
Line, Executive
Steering Council

Introduced members of Executive Steering Council. Presentation of ESC pledge to teams with signed document displayed. How this pledge to employees from the executives was different behavior, evidence of new way of doing business.

9:30 A.M.   Program           Larry Grant, Manager,
Architecture       Transmission/Substation,
and Oversight     Executive Steering Council

Introduced governance structure: Executive Steering Council, Program Management Team, and resources and consultants to support sourcing teams and redesign teams. Introduced Program Management Team members. Resources group identified as representing stakeholders with potential interest in outcome of sourcing teams' work and available to provide perspective and support whenever needed.

| | | |
|---|---|---|
| 10:00 A.M. | Business Unit Commitment | Joe Wambold, Manager, Business Strategy, Generation Business Unit, Executive Steering Council |

Presented BU commitment to work cross-functionally for corporate benefit, how the sourcing project complemented cost reduction initiatives in progress in BU, and why change is important to BUs.

| | | |
|---|---|---|
| 10:30 A.M. | Strategic Sourcing Methodology and Tool Overview | Consultants |

Introduced guiding principles of Strategic Sourcing; key concepts: supply chain, sourcing square, total cost; previewed tools (total cost model, ABC, six-phase methodology).

| | | |
|---|---|---|
| 11:00 A.M. | Pilot Team Lessons Learned Concurrent Breakout Sessions for Team Members' Managers/Supervisors | Q&A |

Members from pilot teams shared their experiences and lessons with new team members.

The immediate supervisors of the people on the sourcing teams were also invited to attend the launch meeting until 11:00 A.M. and were then asked to adjourn to another meeting room. The purpose of this breakout was to provide more detail regarding the program, answer any questions or concerns, and share Strategic Sourcing successes from other companies to build confidence in the methodology.

Additionally, the breakout meeting was designed to provide a more in-depth debrief of what was going to be expected of the team members and an appeal to clear any roadblocks that may impede the team members from participating fully.

Morning attendees: CEO, Executive Steering Council, Program Management Team, executives, managers/supervisors, team members, consultants

## Afternoon Session

Purpose: to build common base of understanding of program elements and team assignments; to begin team building and training.

Afternoon attendees: team members, consultants, Program Management Team

From the Big Launch, the team members reconvened that evening to begin a three-day planning off-site and officially embark on Phase C, the first of six team activity phases. This activity completes the corporate preparation phases.

| | |
|---|---|
| 12:00 P.M. | Working Lunch (Seating by Teams) |
| 1:00 P.M. | Strategic Sourcing Methodology and Tools     Program Management Team/Consultants |
| | Detailed introduction to phased methodology and analytical tools including team members' role in process. |
| 3:30 P.M. | Three-day Off-site |
| | Preview of project planning and team-building activities to be accomplished at team off-site to begin that evening. |
| 3:45 P.M. | Q&A |

**TIP**
The widespread publicity and participation in the corporate kickoff meeting created a shared accountability for moving forward. Everyone, from executives to team members, heard the plan and corporate commitment at the same time, which reinforced the message that we were all in this together.

## Preview of Team Activity Phases

The corporate preparation and program design work is now completed. Corporate expenditures have been analyzed and there is a good understanding of where the greatest opportunity exists. A plan is in place to pursue Strategic Sourcing. The emphasis now shifts to sourcing team activity, which involves analyzing opportunities and devising a sourcing strategy for the major areas of expenditure.

The team activity phases (see Table 7.4) teach methodology and analytical tools and apply them to help in selecting a

| Month 1 | Month 2 | Month 3 | Month 4 | Month 5 | Month 6 | Month 7 | Month 8 |
|---------|---------|---------|---------|---------|---------|---------|---------|
| Sourcing team launch | Supplier survey | RFP rollout meeting | | Evaluate RFP | | Recommendation to council | Relationship agreement signed |
| Opportunity ID | | | | Develop short list | Final supplier selection | | Implementation Team launch |
| | Cost model development | | | Supplier site visits | Contract signed | | |

Time from launch to implementation: 8–10 months.

**Table 7.4** Sample Team Activity Timeline

| | |
|---|---|
| Sourcing teams completed | 14 |
| Companies benchmarked | 173 |
| Process map interviews completed | 786 |
| Process maps generated | 92 |
| Initial supplier screenings completed | 4181 |
| RFPs evaluated | 615 |
| Supplier site visits completed | 124 |
| Suppliers selected | 33 |

**Table 7.5** Team Activity

sourcing strategy and suppliers. Table 7.5 illustrates the level of rigor and analysis that goes into the final supplier selection process. The chart represents the actual activities of the first 14 sourcing teams at SCE.

Read on to learn about how to begin team development and opportunity identification.

# Chapter 8

# Team Development and Opportunity Identification

**Preparation and Design Phases**

**Team Activity Phases**

A    B    C

The sourcing teams have been formed and the governance structure established. It is time to dispatch the first wave of teams.

As part of the corporate preparation and design (Phases A and B), the opportunity for savings utilizing Strategic Sourcing has been confirmed. The Program Management Team evaluated the macro-opportunity to target top priorities and identified the first six sourcing teams. The Big Launch presented the Strategic Sourcing program and methodology to the company and introduced the sourcing teams to their assignment. The goal identified for each team was clear: reduce supply chain costs by 30 percent.

The importance of establishing a stretch goal cannot be overstated. A 30 percent reduction could not be achieved without significant rethinking of our supply chain practices. The stretch goal both set the expectation and gave permission to the sourcing teams to be creative and challenge all existing practices. The power of outrageous goals proved itself time and again as teams forced themselves to think beyond the typical incremental 5 to 7 percent improvements.

Phase C (see Figure 8.1) is the beginning of the sourcing team activity that will ultimately determine the company's strategy and select supplier partners to achieve the strategy. The teams will apply the methodology and tools of Strategic Sourcing to analyze the micro-opportunity specific to the scope of materials/services the team defines.

---

*Activity in this module:*
*Launch teams, conduct team training, develop team charter, identify external spending and related costs, identify and prioritize opportunities, engage stakeholders*

---

The first order of business is team development to create a collaborative, effective cross-functional team, and opportunity identification specific to the sourcing team's scope of work.

### PURPOSE

The objective of the first team phase is to assemble data pertaining to the targeted scope of materials/services in order to identify opportunities and priorities. It also brings the cross-functional team together and begins developing their ability to work collaboratively.

### DELIVERABLES

By performing the steps in Phase C, the sourcing team will develop the following work products:

➤ Overview of the company's external spending and related internal costs

➤ Identification of specific opportunities and issues

➤ Prioritization of opportunities

➤ Achievement of stakeholder buy-in to pursue the opportunities selected

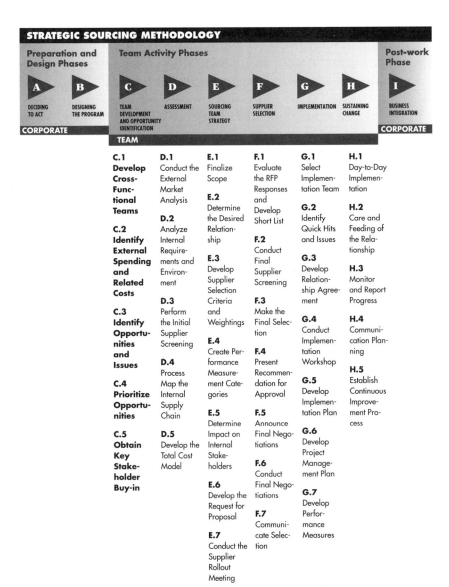

**STRATEGIC SOURCING METHODOLOGY**

| Preparation and Design Phases | | Team Activity Phases | | | | | | Post-work Phase |
|---|---|---|---|---|---|---|---|---|
| **A** DECIDING TO ACT | **B** DESIGNING THE PROGRAM | **C** TEAM DEVELOPMENT AND OPPORTUNITY IDENTIFICATION | **D** ASSESSMENT | **E** SOURCING TEAM STRATEGY | **F** SUPPLIER SELECTION | **G** IMPLEMENTATION | **H** SUSTAINING CHANGE | **I** BUSINESS INTEGRATION |
| CORPORATE | | TEAM | | | | | | CORPORATE |

| C.1 | D.1 | E.1 | F.1 | G.1 | H.1 |
|---|---|---|---|---|---|
| **Develop Cross-Functional Teams** | Conduct the External Market Analysis | Finalize Scope | Evaluate the RFP Responses and Develop Short List | Select Implementation Team | Day-to-Day Implementation |
| **C.2 Identify External Spending and Related Costs** | D.2 Analyze Internal Requirements and Environment | E.2 Determine the Desired Relationship | F.2 Conduct Final Supplier Screening | G.2 Identify Quick Hits and Issues | H.2 Care and Feeding of the Relationship |
| **C.3 Identify Opportunities and Issues** | D.3 Perform the Initial Supplier Screening | E.3 Develop Supplier Selection Criteria and Weightings | F.3 Make the Final Selection | G.3 Develop Relationship Agreement | H.3 Monitor and Report Progress |
| **C.4 Prioritize Opportunities** | D.4 Process Map the Internal Supply Chain | E.4 Create Performance Measurement Categories | F.4 Present Recommendation for Approval | G.4 Conduct Implementation Workshop | H.4 Communication Planning |
| **C.5 Obtain Key Stakeholder Buy-in** | D.5 Develop the Total Cost Model | E.5 Determine Impact on Internal Stakeholders | F.5 Announce Final Negotiations | G.5 Develop Implementation Plan | H.5 Establish Continuous Improvement Process |
| | | E.6 Develop the Request for Proposal | F.6 Conduct Final Negotiations | G.6 Develop Project Management Plan | |
| | | E.7 Conduct the Supplier Rollout Meeting | F.7 Communicate Selection | G.7 Develop Performance Measures | |

**Figure 8.1** Phase Map—Team Activity Phases.

169

## Ⓖ1 DEVELOP CROSS-FUNCTIONAL TEAMS

A three-day development off-site provides each team the necessary training in teamwork and Strategic Sourcing principles. Executive steering council participation at the beginning of the off-site provides visible endorsement of the team's assignment. It also provides a business unit perspective of program goals and expectations. The session concludes with a presentation of the team's charter and work plan to the executive steering council and the program management team. During the three days, the teams perform the various aspects of charter development, determining the specifics of *who, what, how,* and *when.*

 ### TRAINING

Training provides a common language and grounding in specific methodology and tools. The training is applied by the teams, which will result in a work product. This serves as the first test of how the teams and team members will function together as decision makers. Specific team development training includes:

➤ Charter development

➤ Effective meeting management

➤ Communication planning

Other related training subjects will include active listening, skillful decision making, and team development.

### Charter Development

Charters are created by the sourcing teams to gain understanding and agreement on what needs to be done as well as who needs to be involved and in what way. In addition, a charter is a helpful vehicle for getting the team started, keeping its efforts on track, and working in harmony with other groups/stakeholders. The template in Table 8.1 guides the

Charter For: *Office Products* Sourcing Team Example

| | **Direction** |
|---|---|
| **Background** | ➤ Why the team formed |
| | ➤ Overall vision for corporate Strategic Sourcing initiative and the case for change |
| | ➤ Other information that helps explain the need for our team's existence and the central issues we will be dealing with |
| Example | The company spends over $26 million annually on office products. Spending decisions are typically made at the department level. By utilizing the Strategic Sourcing methodology and a cross-functional approach, significant supply chain cost savings may be achieved. |
| **Mission** | ➤ The special assignment of our sourcing team—short statement of purpose |
| Example | Reduce the total supply chain costs associated with office products by 30% of projected purchases while meeting the quality of service needed by the company. |
| **Scope and business impact** | ➤ Scope and boundaries of our assignment |
| | ➤ Areas of the business that will be included in our assessment and recommendations |
| | ➤ What is off limits |
| | ➤ What we heard from our key clients about our assignment |
| Example | The original scope for the office products profile was $26 million. The external spending for the current scope is $28 million ($25 million through purchase orders, plus an estimated $3 million through credit cards and cash vouchers), and includes the following: |
| | ➤ Office machines    ➤ Printing services |
| | ➤ Photo products and services    ➤ Stationery supplies |
| | ➤ Paper    ➤ Kitchen equipment and appliances |
| | ➤ Mailing equipment and services    ➤ Audio/visual equipment and services |
| | ➤ Library products and services such as subscriptions |
| **Goals and objectives** | ➤ Specific goals and objectives of our team process—what we are trying to accomplish |
| | ➤ Targets—what we are aiming for |
| Example | Analyze company expenditures on office products, identify cost drivers, and develop strategies to reduce the total supply chain costs. |
| **Deliverables** | ➤ Specific work products expected from our team |
| | ➤ What our clients and sponsors expect to see |
| | ➤ Milestones and deliverables |

**Table 8.1** Sourcing Team Charter Template

| Direction | | |
|---|---|---|
| Example | ➤ Total cost model that clearly quantifies the current and proposed costs<br>➤ Recommendations that will result in 30 percent lower costs, including recommended suppliers, new practices, and processes<br>➤ Identification of risks and assumptions<br>➤ Delivery of an implementation plan, including timing, key activities, process for continuous improvement, and a list of people that need to be involved | |
| Strategic sourcing process timeline | ➤ Phase 1: Team development and opportunity ID<br>➤ Phase 2: Assessment<br>➤ Phase 3: Sourcing team strategy<br>➤ Phase 4: Supplier selection<br>➤ Phase 5: Implementation<br>➤ Phase 6: Monitoring and continuous improvement | Dates (from > to) |
| Example | ➤ Phase 1: Team development and opportunity ID<br>➤ Phase 2: Assessment<br>➤ Phase 3: Strategy development<br>➤ Phase 4: Supplier selection<br>➤ Phase 5: Implementation<br>➤ Phase 6: Monitoring and continuous improvement | January 1995<br>February–March 1995<br>March–May 1995<br>May–June 1995<br>June–July 1995 |
| Authority level | ➤ Areas of direct control by our team<br>➤ Actions and decisions for which we need approval<br>➤ Decision-making process for our recommendations | |
| Example | The following are actions and decisions for which we need approval:<br>➤ Labor relations issues<br>➤ Legal issues<br>➤ Corporate accounting issues<br>➤ Steering council milestones<br>➤ Benchmarking and supplier visitation trips (budget implications) | |

| Membership | | |
|---|---|---|
| Stakeholders | ➤ Our client groups and key client contacts<br>➤ People who use the materials/services<br>➤ People impacted by the recommendations we will make<br>➤ Our suppliers<br>➤ People whose buy-in or approval is needed<br>➤ People who have influence over the decisions to be made | |
| Example | ➤ Employees<br>➤ Suppliers | ➤ Customer solutions<br>➤ Supply clerks |

**Table 8.1** *(Continued)*

## Membership

| | | |
|---|---|---|
| | ➤ Payroll clerks<br>➤ Payment approvers<br>➤ Procurement agents<br>➤ Accounts payable | ➤ Payroll distribution accountant<br>➤ Mailing<br>➤ Display |
| **Team member roles** | ➤ Core team members and the initial roles we will play | |
| Example | Each core team member will:<br>➤ Show up at meetings<br>➤ Complete team assignments<br>➤ Support ground rules<br>➤ Actively participate<br>➤ Keep an open mind to the "new way"<br>➤ Maximize the collective and individual expertise of the group | ➤ Partner with and support other team members<br>➤ Give and receive feedback<br>➤ Listen<br>➤ Help negotiate and support consensus decisions<br>➤ Remember the corporate focus |
| **Team sponsor roles** | ➤ Commitments from our team sponsor<br>➤ What we need of our team sponsor | |
| Example | ➤ Remove barriers as they apply to time constraints<br>➤ Intervene and clear roadblocks as needed with business units—help sell recommendations if accepted<br>➤ Forward relevant e-mails to team leader<br>➤ Meet with team leader every week<br>➤ Meet with team every two weeks | |
| **Resources** | ➤ Areas of expertise, experience, and influence that we need but do not have on our team<br>➤ Other people who are available to us for special expertise, advice, or assistance | |
| Example | ➤ Materials and equipment (M&E) sales<br>➤ Supplier diversity<br>➤ Labor | ➤ Law<br>➤ Librarian<br>➤ Accounts payable |

## Team Management

| | |
|---|---|
| **Project management and integration** | ➤ Responsibilities that we have as a team for the integration of our activities with those of other teams<br>➤ Integration and information that we will need from other teams<br>➤ Reporting and communication responsibilities |

**Table 8.1** *(Continued)*

173

| | |
|---|---|
| | ➤ Expectations of steering council and team sponsor |
| Example | ➤ Biweekly team report |
| | ➤ Share all teams' biweekly reports |
| | ➤ Benchmarking strategies; integrate |
| **Team logistics** | ➤ Where and when we will meet |
| | ➤ Coordination within our team |
| | ➤ Time commitment from team members |
| Example | We will meet every Thursday 7:30 to 4:30 at GO3, Room 395, unless other arrangements are made. Additionally, the following administrative responsibilities have been assigned: |

➤ Minutes (Tom)
➤ Meeting notices (Ken)
➤ Meeting logistics (Terry)
➤ Room setup/breakdown (Tom)
➤ Copying (Terry)
➤ Update project plan (Tom)
➤ Point person (late, absences) (Ken)

➤ Travel arrangements (Team)
➤ Research (off-line) (Team)
➤ Master binder (Carol)
➤ Data analysis (Team)
➤ Office services requests (Jim)

The time commitment from each core team member is two to three days per week, including one full-day meeting per week.

| | |
|---|---|
| **Ground rules** | ➤ Things that will help us be effective as a team |
| Example | ➤ If you know you will be late or absent, contact the team leader |
| | ➤ Don't interrupt when others are talking; no side conversations |
| | ➤ Interrupt only for process checks |
| | ➤ Clean up your own mess after meetings |
| | ➤ Don't criticize others' ideas; be open to brainstorming |
| | ➤ Make decisions by consensus |
| | ➤ Follow through with deliverables and commitments; if you can't follow through, seek support from the team |
| | ➤ Be courteous; respect each other; pagers on vibrate |
| | ➤ Keep an open mind |
| | ➤ Treat suppliers' data with confidentiality |
| | ➤ Support team decisions |
| | ➤ Bring structure to meetings when in conflict |
| | ➤ Keep "bin list" in process |
| | ➤ Establish times for the agenda |
| | ➤ If you agree, be quiet; if you don't agree, speak up |
| | ➤ Evaluate meetings prior to ending each meeting |
| **Measures of our success** | ➤ How we will measure our success as a team |
| Example | ➤ Identify and recommend cost savings opportunities |
| | ➤ Meeting team schedule |

**Table 8.1** *(Continued)*

| Team Management |
| --- |
| ➤ Executive council accepts and implements our recommendations<br>➤ Achieve buy-in from stakeholders<br>➤ Continuous improvement mechanism in place<br>➤ Had the guts to look at all opportunities<br>➤ We achieved our deliverables |

**Table 8.1** *(Continued)*

sourcing teams in developing the charter. An example from the Office Products Strategic Sourcing team at SCE is included here to illustrate each component.

## Team Roles and Responsibilities

The team has been assembled that represents areas of expertise from line and pertinent corporate functions, i.e., purchasing, finance.

Team members will work together to develop Strategic Sourcing recommendations and select suppliers. The team will select a leader from among team members. The leader is assigned the role of project manager and team coach. Team members are expected to actively participate and attend all team meetings. The sourcing team members will be faced with competing demands and should consider their participation as a priority responsibility, not an intrusion on their "real jobs." Collectively, the team shares responsibility and accountability for outcomes. One specialized team role is that of recorder—the person who documents the team's work.

For each sourcing team, one member of the program management team will be assigned as sponsor. The sponsor serves as a liaison between the team and the executive steering council and other sourcing teams. The sponsor is a resource for guidance and help.

## TIPS

➤ Since members' team assignments will constitute a major portion of their jobs, team members should have their assignments incorporated into their annual performance appraisals and receive credit for their contributions. Conducting and recording peer appraisal of the team is a valuable form of performance feedback.

➤ As you read the roles and responsibilities of sourcing team members, it should become apparent that the attributes and skills that make a good sourcing team candidate also make a good employee and leader. Sourcing offers a tremendous opportunity to discover and develop hidden talents in individuals that will benefit the company.

## Team Documentation

Keeping accurate notes on decisions and issues discussed at each meeting prevents needless rehashing of issues. Agendas, minutes, actions, and open items are all maintained by the recorder. Use the template on the following page for creating a meeting record tailored to your team.

## Importance of Documentation

A crucial element of effective meetings and successful projects is maintaining complete project documentation. Good records are helpful for several reasons:

➤ Sourcing teams may last up to 12 months, and may experience turnover in members. Detailed records document the thought process behind decisions and help new members get up to speed quickly.

➤ Records that document the thought process behind decisions help educate people in the organization and win their support.

---

**Meeting Number**      **Date**      **Location**
1. Project Name
2. Mission Statement:
3. ✓ To indicate "present"
   Member
   Member
   Etc. . . .
4. Agenda: Enter key words indicating the agenda topics. Check off an item when it is completed. Items you do not complete should be carried over to the next meeting.
5. Summary of topics, discussions, decisions, and next steps
6. Open Items List: Items for future consideration but not for the next meeting
7. Meeting Evaluation: Things that went well and things that need improvement ("+", "−")

**Next Meeting:**
Date      Time      Location
Agenda:
Recorder:

---

➤ Team learning is experiential. Anecdotes help tell the story and bridge gaps in knowledge for people who have not participated on the team. Include them.

➤ Frequently, presentations are made to the team sponsor and/or executive steering council. Up-to-date records make presentation preparation easier.

➤ As the project progresses, the team may have to retrace its steps to track problems or errors. Good records provide an audit trail.

Record keeping should begin at the earliest stage. The team should think ahead to the deliverables and discuss what sort of documentation is likely to be needed further down the road. Create a plan to maintain these records as work is accomplished.

## Effective Meeting Management

Though individual team members carry out assignments between meetings, much of the team's work is accomplished in a meeting setting. Many people dislike meetings, but this needn't be. As with other processes, the meeting dynamic can be studied and improved.

Effective meeting management can be learned. One way to have productive meetings is to learn new ways of working together. Some principles of meeting management are listed here:

### *Use Agendas*

Each meeting must have an agenda, preferably one drafted at the previous meeting and developed in detail by one or two members prior to the current meeting. If possible, the agenda should be sent to participants in advance. (If an agenda has not been published before a meeting, spend the first 5 or 10 minutes developing an agenda on a flip chart.) Elements include topic, tool, time allotted, and template.

### *Have a Facilitator*

Each meeting should have a facilitator who is responsible for keeping the meeting focused and productive. The facilitator

---

**GENERAL MEETING DEVICES**

✓ Use agendas
✓ Have a facilitator
✓ Take minutes
✓ Draft next agenda
✓ Evaluate the meeting
✓ Adhere to the "100-mile rule"
✓ Establish ground rules

helps to ensure clarity and completeness in team discussions; summarizes key discussion points; helps to bring discussions to a close; and tests for consensus. The facilitator intervenes if the discussion fragments into multiple conversations and works to prevent any team member from dominating discussions.

### Take Minutes

Each meeting should also have a recorder who registers key subjects and main points, decisions, and items that the group has agreed to address later—in this meeting or in the future. The role may be rotated among the team members.

### Draft the Next Agenda

At the end of the meeting, draft an agenda for the next meeting.

### Evaluate the Meeting

Always review and evaluate each meeting. The evaluation should include decisions to improve the next meeting and helpful feedback on the facilitator's performance.

### Adhere to the "100-Mile Rule"

Once a meeting begins, everyone is expected to give it full attention. No one should be called from the meeting unless it is so important that the disruption would occur even if the meeting was 100 miles away.

### Establish Ground Rules

Ground rules are set by the team and govern interaction. Sample ground rules are included in the sourcing team charter example.

**TIP**
Consensus decision making helps to increase involvement while equalizing the distribution of power within the group. An extensive consensus-seeking exercise also facilitates the critical examination of a variety of alternatives and thus improves the quality of decisions made. Consensus approaches also assist in changing attitudes and behaviors.

## Communication Planning

Creating a *sourcing team communication plan* for what to say, to whom, when, and through what method, should be a collaborative effort initiated early in the process and carried on for the duration of the project. Timely and relevant information is a major need at all levels of the organization during times of transition. When communications are neglected or done at the last minute, they tend to be poorly conceived and poorly delivered. When used properly, the communications planning process can not only help you decide the best way to deliver the message, it can also help build consensus and gain buy-in from the stakeholders.

Although communication is dynamic by nature, it is possible to anticipate some logical communication points in a proactive manner and build them into the team process. Creating a formal sourcing team communication plan leverages these points and allows leaders to manage communication to the right audiences at the right time. Table 8.2 illustrates the components of a team communication plan.

Activities in Phase C.1, "Developing Cross-Functional Teams," have included creating a team charter, identifying and assigning team roles and responsibilities, learning techniques for conducting effective meetings, and planning for communications. Relationships are forming among team members. The sourcing team has mapped out its direction and project plan. At the conclusion of the off-site, members of the execu-

| Kinds of Messages | When | How | Who |
|---|---|---|---|
| A—Charter | A—Now | A—Memo | A—Team |
| B—Detailed status information | B—Monthly C—As necessary | B—E-mail C—Eyeball | B—Individual C—Subteam |
| C—General status information | D—Quarterly | D—Phone E—Staff meetings | |

| Stakeholder | Kinds of Messages | When | How | Who |
|---|---|---|---|---|
| Direct supervisor | B | C | C | B |
| Steering council | B | D | C | A |
| DCM managers (C/S) Etc. | B | D | E | C |

**Table 8.2** Stakeholder Communication Plan

tive steering council come to hear the team's presentation of its work, offer feedback/assistance, and participate in the launch celebration.

## C.2 IDENTIFY EXTERNAL SPENDING AND RELATED COSTS

### Description

Expand data collection to refine external spending estimates provided during team start-up and validate initial scope. Identify related cost drivers.

### Method

For each category within the targeted materials and services, obtain a three-year history of the following data:

> ➤ Annual spending (in total, by supplier, by geographic location, by material type)

➤ Supplier price data

➤ Listing of current suppliers

➤ Number of commodity codes

➤ On-hand inventory value (in total and by location)

➤ Number and average dollar amount of purchase orders processed

➤ Number of invoices processed and/or checks issued

➤ Percentage of dollars spent with women- and minority-owned business enterprise (WMBE) suppliers

➤ Historic usage by company, business unit, and/or cost center

➤ Forecasted usage by company, business unit, and/or cost center

➤ Cost of quality, including internal detection costs, failure costs, and warranty costs

➤ Supplier performance regarding

— Delivery (percentage on time)

— Lead time (number of days)

— Fill rate

— Quality (reject rate)

— Service

— Internal customer service

➤ Supplier certification information

## TIPS

➤ Data, in the form needed to develop this analysis, is often not readily available. The team will need to be creative in its efforts to gather information. The information will come in a variety of forms: formal and informal, systematized and manual, internal and external. Potential sources include departmental expense reports, accounts payable, purchase orders, invoices, general ledger, departmental management reports, inventory reports, supplier-provided sales reports, customer/user interviews, and others.

➤ It is easy to get into "analysis paralysis" during this phase. Rely on the 80/20 rule. Remember that the major purpose of the exercise is to get a feel for the magnitude of spending and the corresponding opportunities so that specific materials/services can be prioritized. It is acceptable to use best judgement and make assumptions if they are documented.

➤ Achieving cost reduction and quality are not mutually exclusive. The work done in this phase—that is, determination of cost of quality and evaluation of supplier performance—is the basis for understanding total cost and keeping the quality component visible.

## ▐C.3▌ IDENTIFY OPPORTUNITIES AND ISSUES

### Description

Expand the thinking about supply chain possibilities. Analyze initial data to identify potential opportunities and surface issues. Work done in this step will help team members understand the valuable impact of the new supply chain practices.

### Method

#### *Step 1*

Review the data collected in Phase A to identify opportunity indicators:

➤ Categories with relatively high levels of external spending within the targeted materials/services

➤ External spending spread over a large number of suppliers

➤ External spending consisting of a large number of low-dollar-value transactions

➤ High number of specifications and material codes

➤ High level of inventory

➤ Low inventory turn ratio

➤ Inventory spread over a large number of locations

## Step 2

Qualitative information obtained from team members and from users of the materials/services may also indicate opportunities or issues to be considered. These indicators may include:

➤ Frustration with the performance of the materials/services or the associated process

➤ Improvement ideas generated by users

➤ Departmental initiatives planned or under way

➤ Changes in the underlying business, creating a different user requirement for materials/services

➤ Impact of poor quality on support operations in returns, processing paperwork for defective material, and expediting replacement material

## Step 3

Ultimately, the scope is a negotiated outcome between a team and its sponsor. The team analyzes the data from Steps 1 and 2 to develop a revised scope. As a rule of thumb, the sourcing team's objective is to develop the largest manageable scope for each sourcing opportunity. The sourcing team may be constrained only by technical boundaries and natural divisions in marketplace conditions. The team presents its recommendation to the sponsor. The role of the sponsor is to challenge the team to define its scope broadly.

**TIPS**

➤ Identify and candidly discuss all opportunities and issues associated with the materials/services, considering the political as well as the operating environment.

➤ Avoid the "not invented here" syndrome. Plenty of good ideas are available; the opportunity is in identifying them and making them work for you.

➤ Consultants add particular value in providing best practices from other companies and industries and reminding team members, "It's a big world out there."

## C.4 PRIORITIZE OPPORTUNITIES

### Description

Apply Strategic Sourcing concepts to the defined scope of materials or services in order to understand and focus on areas of greatest potential value. Establish priorities for activities in Phase D.

### Method

The basic elements for cost reduction in the Strategic Sourcing model are value engineering (product substitution, standardization, specifications), leveraging (volume discounts, supplier consolidation), and process improvement (logistics, electronic commerce, bid process). Test each area in your scope against these strategies to understand where the greatest opportunities exist.

Develop a prioritization matrix with input from the team sponsor. Base it on criteria developed by the team. The matrix is a useful tool for determining the relative values of various opportunities in the materials/services being sourced. Score each opportunity relative to these criteria and arrive at an overall rating for comparative purposes by multiplying across the columns.

A qualitative method for prioritizing opportunities will be useful when certain intangibles exist that could have a serious impact on the company. The potential loss or gain of significant market share is one example.

Using this method, apply consensus-building techniques to arrive at the prioritization of opportunities within the scope of materials/services. Use discussion to consolidate the list of potential opportunities. Then narrow the list to include only the most likely candidates.

 **TIPS**

➤ Involve the team sponsor early. He or she may have access to information not readily available to the team.

➤ When prioritizing, consider the impact on internal resources.

➤ Scope is a work in progress. As the team continues its evaluation, scope may grow or shrink.

## C.5 OBTAIN KEY STAKEHOLDER BUY-IN

### Description

Gain stakeholder support for the team's activities.

This step is a preliminary stakeholder enrollment activity. The main stakeholder enrollment activity is carried out in the communication planning activity described in Phase C.1.

### Method

Develop a key stakeholder list for the categories of materials/services the team will address.

Identify each stakeholder's key concerns.

Meet with key stakeholders (via the communication plan) to explain fully the team's objectives and process, time frames, and impact on resources.

 **TIPS**

➤ Think through to implementation—the end users are the ultimate stakeholders.

➤ Involve the team sponsor in both identifying stakeholders and gaining their buy-in.

➤ Surface stakeholder concerns now rather than later. Do not avoid or circumvent stakeholders who have negative feelings toward the project. Their issues will only come up again later, when the team has already committed significant time and effort.

➤ Leverage what the company already has in place. The Strategic Sourcing tools can be used in conjunction with many well-established organization tools. At SCE, the sourcing teams were launched by using the team development, project planning, and meeting management tools used throughout the company.

During this phase, individuals with an assignment have become a team with a mission. The team building that takes place during this activity will help see the team through the demanding work ahead. The team has identified the initial scope of work and has developed a road map to guide its efforts. At the close of the intense three-day workshop, team members will return to the workplace and begin the task of assessment.

# Chapter

# Assessment

Preparation and
Design Phases

**Team Activity
Phases**

A B C D

The goal of Strategic Sourcing is to realign people and processes while satisfying customer requirements at significantly reduced costs. The assessment phase broadens the examination of people and processes within the supply chain. The work of Phase D—external market analysis, identification of internal requirements, supplier screening, process mapping, and total cost model development (see Figure 9.1)—requires substantial research and analysis. Assessment of the external marketplace, the supplier community, and the company's internal supply chain will help determine where cost reduction opportunities exist. All this assessment ultimately will be used to select a sourcing strategy for the sourcing team's scope of work.

---

*Activity in this module:*
*Conduct external market analysis, determine internal requirements, conduct initial supplier screening, perform process mapping, develop total cost model*

---

Rich organizational learning results from the completed work of this phase. Often for the first time, teams will be able to calculate the total cost of materials and services and to doc-

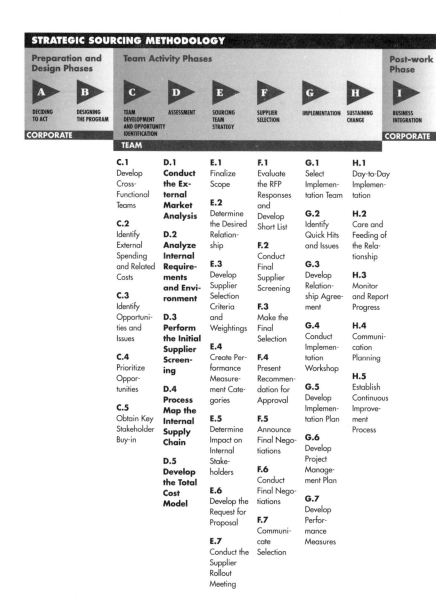

**Figure 9.1** Phase Map—Team Activity Phases.

ument where the redundant and/or non-value-added activities exist. The teams will have both the knowledge and the tools to evaluate where suppliers can add value and reduce the total cost of the supply chain. The knowledge learned in this phase is the basis on which the team will move toward making decisions for the overall corporate good.

The development of a cost model to document the supply chain processes associated with a material or service is critical to the rigor of the process. Through the use of activity-based costing, the team will create a cost planning system designed to support the implementation of savings opportunities that can be tracked directly to budgets and removed from the bottom line of the company.

 **PURPOSE**

The objective of the second team phase is to analyze the details of the materials and services under review by the team. Insights gained in Phase D will be the basis for development of the relationship sought with suppliers.

 **DELIVERABLES**

By performing the steps within Phase D, the sourcing team will develop the following work products:

➤ List of the company's internal expectations regarding future supplier relationships

➤ List of pertinent successful practices being used outside of the company

➤ List of current and future internal materials/services requirements

➤ Initial supplier screening that begins the supplier selection process

➤ Detailed process map of the internal supply chain process

➤ Total cost analysis of current supply chain

➤ Initial supplier assessment

**TRAINING**
Plan and implement the following training workshops for sourcing team members, as appropriate
during Phase D:

➤ Process mapping

➤ Conducting a focus group

➤ Performing external research

➤ Establishing a supplier diversity program

➤ Creating rules of supplier engagement

➤ Implementing Total Quality Management

➤ Interviewing skills

➤ Benchmarking practices

## D.1 CONDUCT THE EXTERNAL MARKET ANALYSIS

### Description

Two main categories are analyzed when conducting an assessment of materials and services:

➤ Suppliers and their respective processes

   —Current suppliers of the materials/services

   —New suppliers

➤ Other companies utilizing the materials/services, both
within the relevant industry and from other industries

The external market analysis should be comprehensive
enough to assist in development of an understanding of the
current state of the material/service supplier base as well as
an indication of how the material/service is evolving. It also
covers an investigation into potential suppliers, as well as
what is currently being done in other leading companies and
the results they are experiencing.

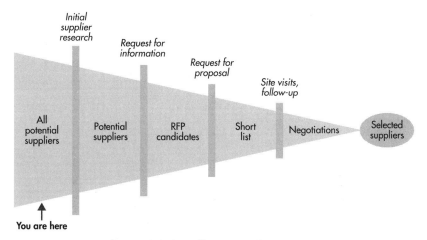

**Figure 9.2** Supplier Screening Process.

Figure 9.2 illustrates the supplier selection process, which is initiated in this phase and continues through Phase F. Potential suppliers identified in this phase must pass through several screens before the supplier recommendation is made.

## Method

### *Step 1*

Develop a list of the supplier community that may be able to supply the material/service.

➤ Identify current suppliers used over the past one to two years for the materials/services.

➤ Identify potential new suppliers that may not have been used by the company before but might be able to add value based on your new objectives. Include foreign suppliers, if appropriate.

Examples of sources for identifying potential suppliers include:

—Existing supplier network

—The Yellow Pages

—*The Thomas Register*

—Buyer's guides

—Trade journals and trade association member directories

—National Association of Purchasing Management (NAPM) network

—Professional networks

—Part drawings

—The Internet

—Consultants

—Women and minority business associations

### Step 2

Analyze the external market to identify new business practices and process improvements.

➤ Scan the external market specific to the scope of the team's work. Extensive assessment of the external market was performed by the company when making the decision to adopt Strategic Sourcing. This work should be shared with the team for applicability to the team's specific area.

➤ Benchmark best practices outside the company. Benchmarking is a rigorous process to improve one company's performance by observing, studying, and internalizing the better practices of other organizations (see Table 9.1). Benchmarking intelligence may be drawn from a number of sources. Company visits, literature searches, or professional associations are often excellent sources of market information.

At the specific material/service level, the team should answer the following questions when benchmarking:

### Planning

A.  Determine the key business issues to be examined; decide the key functions to benchmark and the supporting rationale for how these functions impact the business issue under study. Remember to benchmark those functions that represent a large portion of your total cost chain.
B.  Select performance measures. Don't be afraid to define unusual measures and include qualitative as well as quantitative measures.
C.  Develop a list of benchmarking partners and rationale for their selection.

### Data Gathering

A.  Perform a thorough literature search. Often 15–20% of the needed data comes from published sources.
B.  Cast a wide net—talk to as many industry insiders as possible. Ironically, for preliminary data gathering, in-person interviews are less effective than telephone interviews.
C.  If you develop a written survey, be certain to include open-ended questions.

### Analysis

A.  A benchmarking project is only as strong as the accompanying data analysis. The objective of this data analysis is to explain what drives the difference in performance between you and your benchmarking partner.
B.  Utilizing a standard analytical tool will help create comparisons.

### Action

A.  Convert all the analysis into performance improvements; this is possible once the underlying causes of the performance gap are understood.
B.  Each action item needs to be accompanied by an improvement target and a timetable for implementation.
C.  Upon completion, convert the team learning into communication tools to share your understanding of the marketplace.

**Table 9.1** The Four Phases of Benchmarking

1. What are the current and projected trends in technology relevant to the materials/services? *Is anything technologically changing about your materials/services that will affect the type needed in the future? Will this change affect the types of suppliers needed?*

2. What are suppliers doing to meet their customers' demands in terms of quality, cost, delivery, and service?

3. What changes have your competitors made with regard to their traditional sourcing of the materials/services under review? *Seek to understand the strategic implication of the changes they may be adopting.*

4. How are cost trends, raw material availability, and competition affecting potential suppliers? *How are suppliers' costs being affected? Are they going down? Up? Why?*

5. What are new and existing suppliers predicting about changes to their materials/services? *What different approaches are they taking with their other customers that might be beneficial to our company?*

6. What are the current trends outside the industry with regard to the material/service? *What approaches are others taking that could be incorporated at our company?*

7. What other similar or related materials/services could the supplier possibly provide, thus broadening the scope of its offering and obtaining greater leverage?

8. Are there naturally occurring fluctuations or cycles in market size, prices, or activity (for example, seasonality, year-end clearances, coincidence with labor contract renewals)?

Members of the Information Technology Sourcing Team at SCE used the diagrams shown in Figures 9.3 and 9.4 to communicate the lessons they learned from their external assessment benchmarking activities. These two illustrations demonstrate how to capture and communicate the results of the benchmarking activities.

These two illustrations were part of a larger communication package that the Corporate Technology Sourcing Team

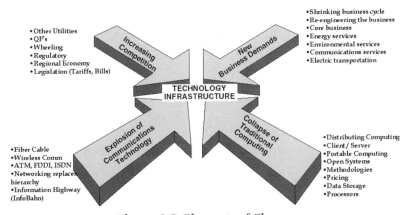

**Figure 9.3** Elements of Change.
*(Source: SCE Information Technology Sourcing Team)*

prepared to keep its stakeholders informed about the current changes taking place in technology outside of SCE.

### Step 3

Refine the supplier list to reflect those suppliers that meet the initial level of expectation based upon the benchmarking.

Based on the research and market analysis, a first cut of the potential supplier base may be indicated. There is typically a minimum level of expected capabilities that is agreed upon by

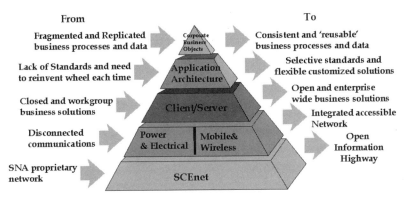

**Figure 9.4** Transition to a New Technology Infrastructure.
*(Source: SCE Information Technology Sourcing Team)*

the team due to its assessment. A written or telephone survey with suppliers can augment this research for a preliminary, high-level assessment of capabilities.

### TIPS

➤ Consider attending relevant industry conferences. Also consider obtaining an associate membership in trade associations to obtain names of potential suppliers and materials/services information.

➤ The supplier world is changing at a rapid pace; don't eliminate a supplier or assume you know a supplier's capability until you have done some investigation.

➤ Include new suppliers in the process whenever possible. New suppliers can offer new ideas and often are more open in sharing their opinions than current suppliers.

## D.2 ANALYZE INTERNAL AND ENVIRONMENTAL REQUIREMENTS

### Description

Examine internal and environmental requirements so that the team has the full internal picture of the company's demands for materials and services, both now and in the future.

This phase includes an investigation into customer expectations, both internal and external; current and future demand forecasts; service needs; technology needs; quality and testing requirements; political/environmental issues; and product specifications.

### Method

#### Step 1

Explore customer expectations and requirements, including current needs and desires for future improvements, to fully understand the requirements and expectations. Moving down the supply chain to your customer's external customer can provide valuable information and feedback.

### Step 2

Develop material/service usage forecasts for the next three to five years to determine the entire scope of materials/services that may be included in a potential future contract.

Forecasts are never 100 percent accurate, but it is important to know at least generally the amount of materials/services needed in the future. *Are requirements going up? Down? Staying the same?*

### Step 3

Define the technical and operational service requirements expected from a future supplier. *What are the specific requirements of the materials/services from a technical and operational perspective, and what technical services (for example maintenance) are required of the supplier?* User surveys may be needed to develop these, as well as other requirements.

### Step 4

Determine the required service levels expected from a future supplier. *What response times, hours of operation, availability, and emergency response capabilities are required of the supplier?*

### Step 5

Define the technology requirements of a future supplier relationship. *What current and future technological capabilities are required of the supplier, in terms of material/service technology, based on your internal requirements?* Look into the future to predict the types of business and applied technology requirements that the company might be using.

## Step 6

Define the levels of acceptable/unacceptable quality. *What supplier quality programs are required? Do you currently inspect your products? Would you like to eliminate the need for inspection? Do you require your suppliers to meet quality standards certification?*

## Step 7

Define key material/service specifications. Start differentiating between required product specifications and "nice to have" product specifications.

## Step 8

Explore supplier diversity practices. *What is the company's current supplier base? What is the company's current level of spending?*

## Step 9

Identify bargaining limits with union employees. *What's open for discussion? What's off limits?*

## TIPS

➤ Don't underestimate the need to understand fully the company's requirements and desired changes, which are the basis for establishing the team's goals and objectives.

➤ Assess the company's commitment to/philosophy for establishing a supplier diversity program.

➤ In assessing requirements, start with the customer value and work back. Challenge every requirement by asking, "How does this add value to customers?" and "Should customers pay more for this?"

➤ As you document the internal expectations, it is important to establish the baseline levels of cost, quality, and service. Understanding the baseline will aid in establishing realistic performance targets and understanding levels of improvement.

## D.3 PERFORM THE INITIAL SUPPLIER SCREENING

### Description

This phase represents the second screen applied in the supplier screening process, as shown in Figure 9.5. This step relies on the use of the Request for Information (RFI), which is submitted to suppliers and evaluated by the team. The results of the RFI evaluation will tell the team whether and how to move forward with the Strategic Sourcing methodology. If the search for suppliers yields only a small number of suppliers, the sourcing team may decide to skip this screen.

An RFI is a formal request submitted to suppliers that asks suppliers to provide information about their companies, including a company's background and its materials and services. It is not an offer to purchase.

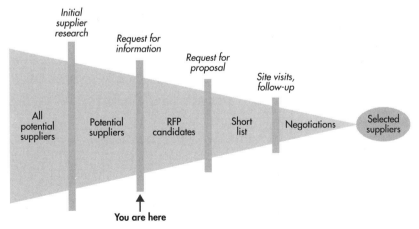

**Figure 9.5** Supplier Screening Process.

Typically, specific prices are not asked for in an RFI. The intent of the RFI is to get further information about a supplier's capabilities and strengths. It is designed to give the team a clearer view of what is possible from its potential suppliers, and to further screen suppliers prior to asking for specific ideas, prices, and terms. It is important to keep in mind that RFI responses will provide a basis for the negotiation process. Use this opportunity to convey your company's vision of the future relationship and performance expectations.

## Method

### *Step 1*

Frame the RFI. Drawing from the results of the external and internal assessment, the sourcing team prepares a summary of where opportunity for cost savings may exist. Determine the specific information to be sought through the RFI. To determine the scope of this information, the team should ask questions in the following categories:

➤ Background
➤ Operational capabilities
➤ Cost management and financial information
➤ Customer service
➤ Subsuppliers/subcontractors
➤ Quality assurance
➤ Technology
➤ Materials management

These categories will be used in developing the supplier capability matrix in *Step 4*.

A team at SCE determined that there were many areas regarding specifications that may yield savings and presented

# SPECIFICATION CHANGES

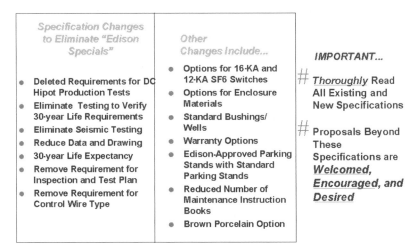

**Figure 9.6** Specification Changes. *(Source: SCE Switchgear Sourcing Team)*

the information shown in Figure 9.6 to suppliers asked to respond to the RFI. Areas that suppliers were encouraged to explore are shown in Figure 9.7.

## Step 2

Determine the evaluation criteria that will be used to assess the RFIs once they are returned. Developing the evaluation criteria before finalizing the RFI helps the sourcing team to word the questions so that meaningful and comparable answers are submitted.

## Step 3

Finalize and send the RFI to those suppliers on the list generated in the external assessment. Allow sufficient time for the suppliers to respond.

## OPPORTUNITIES EXIST!!

Reduce Edison Specials

Systems Design

Direct Jobsite Delivery

Joint R&D / Design

Bundling of Spare parts

Continuous Replenishment

Eliminate Redundant testing

Consignment Inventory

EDI / EFT

Warranty Terms

Training Opportunities

Guaranteed Lead-times

Supplier Managed Inventory

QA Reduce Inspection Needs

Limit Number of Suppliers

Future Automation

Improved Forecasting

Supplier Teaming

Lease vs Buy

Aggregate Product Purchases

Simplify Specifications

Salvage Practice

Pricing Incentives

*... Plus Many More Ideas!!*

**Figure 9.7** Opportunities Exist. *(Source: SCE Switchgear Sourcing Team)*

## Step 4

Once the RFIs have been returned, review and assess them, utilizing the evaluation criteria created by the sourcing team. In addition, it is helpful to develop a supplier capability matrix (see Table 9.2) to visually display the suppliers' capabilities, including their product or service offerings, geographical capabilities, and value-added services.

## Step 5

Sort the population of suppliers to identify those that should be considered for more detailed analysis during the Request for Proposal to be discussed in Phase E.

➤ Suppliers are in a competitive selection process with each other until implementation begins, so it is also important to keep a level playing field and share all relevant information with all suppliers.

| Criteria | Vendors | | |
|---|---|---|---|
| | A | B | C |
| **Background** | | | |
| Corporate direction | ■ | ● | ▲ |
| Product service offerings | | | |
| Financial strength | | | |
| Supplier diversity | | | |
| Labor relations | | | |
| **Operational Capabilities** | | | |
| Operational capabilities and capacity | | | |
| Equipment infrastructure | | | |
| Secondary processing | | | |
| Disposal | | | |
| Training | | | |
| **Cost Management and Financial Information** | | | |
| Etc. (*see step 1*) | | | |

| LEGEND | High | Med | Low |
|---|---|---|---|
| | ■ | ● | ▲ |

**Table 9.2** Supplier Capability Matrix

➤ It is important for the team to agree on and communicate what type of information gained through the RFI may be incorporated into the RFP and shared with all suppliers.

## D.4 PROCESS MAP THE INTERNAL SUPPLY CHAIN

### Description

Create process maps to account for the various processes that take place within the company as they relate to the materials and services being reviewed by the sourcing team. The process maps will serve as the basis for development of the activity-based cost model of current processes.

Creating a process map of supply chain processes provides a cross-functional understanding of how work is performed and how materials/services are being acquired, distributed, utilized, and taken out of service in a company. Process mapping and the resulting cost model create the visualization, documentation, and establishment of common language for supply chain processes. Process maps also provide a useful communication tool for involving people throughout the company in the identification of opportunities for process improvement and cost reduction.

Some necessary definitions follow:

**Activities**—An integrated collection of tasks that an individual or group performs on a routinized basis in daily, weekly, monthly, and annual work toward achieving a discrete product, service, or outcome.

**Tasks**—Steps taken to perform activities.

**Process**—A repetitive and systematic series of activities or operations used to achieve an outcome, which is a product or the accomplishment of a defined goal.

**Process map**—A map that shows how the activities are sequenced from step to step in order to produce an output or outcome. The process map is intended to offer a visual representation of the various activities that take place within your supply chain. It is used to help identify where potential redundancies are found within the system, where the most effort takes place, and where the most people get involved.

**Activity dictionary**—A tool that keeps track of all activities and provides a consistent definition when activities are discussed or tracked. An excerpt from the substation automation activity dictionary at SCE follows:

> **Analysis** Process report, looking at annual allocation and progress reports
>
> **As-builts** Revised final drawings depicting field adjustments, final field adjustments, job logs, and material sheets
>
> **Bid evaluation** Bids received from contractors are analyzed to determine recommendation for successful contractor

**Design drafting** Define conductor loading, weight, angles, pole locations, substructure locations, and foundation dimensions

**Pick, stage, and load** Fill order, stage for loading, and put order on truck to be shipped to user location/job site

**Receive and put away** Monitor freight shipments. Receive truck and/or rail car. Offload and store product. Complete notice of receipt or transfer document.

There are two types of process maps: *High-level* process maps and *detailed* process maps.

➤ *High-level* process maps describe the major activities within a process or even whole processes. They contain limited detail. The goal is to get a picture of the forest before charting out the trees. For example:

—Receiving

—Accounts payable

—Inventory management

➤ Detailed process maps describe each major activity of a process, including documents and decision points. They are used to break down subprocesses and general activities into their specific component steps. For example:

—Enter receipt transaction into system

—Review invoice

—Check stock

## Method

Standard flowcharting symbols are recommended to represent graphically the types of activities and their interrelationships. The sourcing team should start its process mapping with the identification of a need for a material/service and end with the usage and/or disposal of the material/service.

### *Step 1*

Begin with a high-level process map and work with the group to get agreement on the scope and level of detail to be mapped. The initial process map should provide an outline of the supply chain for the materials/services from each business unit's perspective. The high-level maps should also indicate where/ when each business unit is either handed a process or hands off a process to another business unit.

### *Step 2*

Describe each activity distinctly and record it in the sourcing team's activity dictionary. Indicate:

➤ A brief description of the activity

➤ Who or what machine performs the activity, makes the decision, provides the documentation

➤ Who receives the activity, decision, documentation, or output

### *Step 3*

Validate the information. Reduce the time and effort involved in validation by including in the creation of the process maps the people who actually perform the activities, not just the people responsible for the results.

### *Step 4*

Follow up the process map creation by further validating the maps. Ask representatives of each of the mapped areas to review the process flows, decisions, inputs, outputs, and activities as these apply to their areas. Emphasize the point that these are maps of the as-is state rather than the should-be processes. However, as should-be ideas are mentioned, the sourcing team should note them for future savings opportunities.

Things to remember when process mapping: It is important to identify all the major activities that contribute to the
supply chain—that is, those activities that impact the cost of
materials or services or that represent a cost to the company as
part of the total supply chain cost. Also look for cost drivers for
items like facilities and dedicated equipment while creating
the process maps.

It is also important to identify those activities whose costs
vary significantly depending on conditions such as project
complexity, material type, product requirements, customer,
and supplier. For these types of activities, you may need to go
to an additional level of detail and build a subprocess map to
get a full understanding of your supply chain. Include in each
process map the added steps that are required due to poor-
quality performance or mistakes.

Figure 9.8 shows an example of a high-level process map
for a sourcing team at SCE. Each numbered item on the high-
level map is matched to a more detailed map of the process.
Note that the map demonstrates the areas that are unique to a

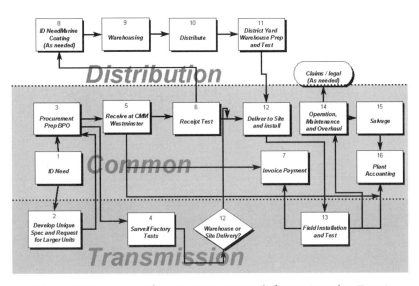

**Figure 9.8** Process Flow. (*Source: SCE Switchgear Sourcing Team*)

business unit (distribution, transmission) and the areas where there is overlap or redundancy (common).

## TIPS

➤ A challenge when process mapping is to account for a sufficient level of data while at the same time not overanalyzing the process.

➤ The process map is a tool that will lend itself to identifying areas of possible improvement as well as the first step in developing the activity-based cost model. Additionally, the process maps will be used for continuous improvement sessions during implementation with the supplier.

➤ When you are process mapping at the activity level, any areas that diverge onto different paths should be enlarged with more detail. This perspective will enable you to reflect accurately the nuances of your supply chain and will ensure that you include all costs in your model.

## D.5 DEVELOP THE TOTAL COST MODEL

### Description

The cost model provides a structured approach to understanding the total supply chain costs associated with a material/service by using activity-based costing. The total cost analysis provides direction for sourcing strategies and focuses the sourcing teams on areas that will yield the largest opportunity for cost savings.

By identifying the costs of activities associated with a material/service, a sourcing team is able to focus on what triggers the activities, how customers consume the activities, and how much it costs to perform the activities. This information is then used by the sourcing team to develop a Request for Proposal that invites the supplier's ideas to affect these areas. It also provides a reliable basis to quantify supplier's ideas for additional cost savings opportunities.

The total cost model is a tool that:

➤ Focuses team efforts on areas of greatest opportunity

➤ Creates a structure for cost data collection and analysis

➤ Directs decisions based on facts and data

➤ Highlights areas of redundancy for process improvements

➤ Provides negotiations insight to the team

➤ Provides a base for measuring supplier performance

The use of activity-based costing to develop a total cost model is the single most important element in understanding opportunity across the supply chain. From it, suppliers can develop quantifiable recommendations. Sourcing teams depend on the cost model to compare the value of supplier proposals. The cost model will not only serve in the bid evaluation process, but will provide the basis for contract negotiations, performance measures, and setting baseline performance.

## Activity-Based Costing versus Traditional Accounting

To contrast activity-based costing from traditional accounting is to look at how costs are tracked. In activity-based costing, costs are tracked by activity rather than accounting codes. For example, a traditional system may have a category entitled *Warehouse Payroll* in which all warehouse employees' salary expenses are tracked. Activity-based costing would seek to portray this same amount of money as a series of activities, or work, performed by the people who are on the Warehouse Payroll. For example, the warehouse employees may perform the following activities: (1) receive materials, (2) put materials away, (3) restock shelves, (4) take inventory, (5) rotate inventory, (6) pull material, (7) prepare shipping documents, (8) package, (9) ship.

By determining how much the underlying activities cost, both within a single warehouse and cross-functionally throughout the company, a sourcing team can arm itself with tremendous information. The sourcing team can determine where the largest costs are, what triggers the need for this activity, how much redundancy is in the system, and the impact the suppliers have on streamlining the process.

## Method

Three steps are involved in developing the internal cost of Strategic Sourcing activities. Figure 9.9 illustrates these steps.

### *Step 1*

Identify people, equipment, and property involved in the process.

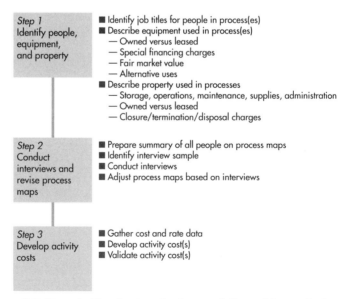

**Figure 9.9** Steps in Developing the Internal Cost of Strategic Sourcing Activities.

➤ After preparing process maps, list the various people who perform the activities listed on the maps. This identification generally takes place in the team through brainstorming.

➤ If the persons noted as performing an activity are union employees, list the first-level managers who supervise their activity. Do not plan on interviewing union-represented employees without approval.

➤ From the process map, note any point in the process where equipment is being used. Determine whether this equipment is owned or leased, whether it has special financing charges, its fair market value, and any alternative uses.

➤ From the process map, also note any facility space utilized in the supply chain process. This property includes relevant office space where employees work, as well as storage areas used to house materials.

### Step 2

Conduct interviews and revise process maps.

➤ Cost data gathering involves conducting interviews of key people within the company whose work function is impacted by the suppliers, services, materials, or any part of the supply chain processes. The purpose of conducting interviews is to develop a picture of the way the work is currently being performed.

➤ The aim of the interview is to identify major activities performed by the interviewee and to develop costs associated with each activity. Additionally, the interview is used to surface additional people performing the activities.

In reviewing the supply chain costs from beginning to end, there are a significant number of items to consider. The total cost checklist in Table 9.3 will help the team determine the right people to talk to and what questions to ask.

| Cost of What You Buy |
| --- |

1. Price of the materials
2. Cost to maintain the materials
3. Operating cost of materials
4. Costs incurred due to supplier selection

| Transportation/Distribution |
| --- |

1. Cost to maintain fleet
2. Labor time to transport and distribute material to job sites
3. Supervisory cost of transportation
4. Depreciation of fleet

| Cost of Acquisition |
| --- |

1. Cost of labor to type, disburse, and file purchase reports
2. Computer/IT costs to prepare, track, and verify orders and shipment information
3. Cost of labor to expedite late deliveries
4. Cost of buildings and office space
5. Supervisory cost of purchasing process
6. Cost of labor and time to interview suppliers
7. Cost of labor and time to prepare and process multiple bids on items

| Cost of Application |
| --- |

1. Cost of labor and time to engineer and specify products for new applications
2. Cost of labor and time to upgrade products for a more efficient operation
3. Cost of downtime due to wrong products
4. Cost of training personnel in use of products
5. Cost of maintaining multiple/like-kind products
6. Cost of inspecting

| Cost of Possession |
| --- |

1. Cost of building space
2. Heat and other utilities
3. Depreciation on entire structure used to house inventory

**Table 9.3** Total Cost Checklist

| Cost of Possession |
| --- |

4. Janitorial and guard personnel
5. Routine and special building maintenance and repair
6. Cost of all supplies, contract work, and so on, needed to run the facility
7. Liability insurance on the facility
8. Estimated loss of return on capital tied up in inventory
9. Tax on inventory
10. Insurance on inventory
11. Yearly interest on loans made to purchase inventory items
12. Taxes on land and building
13. Average cost of in-facility damage or deterioration
14. Cost of labor to receive, stock, identify, move, and maintain material
15. Supervisory cost of inventory
16. Average loss from materials obsolescence and pilferage

| Cost of Disposal |
| --- |

1. Cost of disposal of damaged, unused, or obsolete items
2. Cost to maintain specifications to meet internal and government regulations regarding disposal

**Table 9.3**  *(Continued)*

➤ Prepare an advance interview notice for the interviewee, reserving an hour of his or her time. Send copies of process maps and the activity dictionary beforehand if possible to assist the interviewee in preparation.

➤ Prepare an interview plan and worksheet. Shown on pages 216 and 217 is a completed interview template.

➤ The Office Products Team used the template to account for all activities related to the material/service as well as to document cost savings ideas that surface from the interview.

➤ Write up the interview and call the interviewee for any clarifying information needed.

## INTERVIEW TEMPLATE

### Cost Model Interview Template

| Cost Model Area | Office Products | | |
|---|---|---|---|
| Interview Date | 10/15/97 | Interviewed By | Team Member #1Name |
| Location | Company HQ | | |
| Interviewee Name | Job Title | No. of People | Pay Rate | Dept. | Manager |

| Interviewee Name | Job Title | No. of People | Pay Rate | Dept. | Manager |
|---|---|---|---|---|---|
| 1) Sue Stanton | Sr. Buyer | 1 | $19.23 | Purch. | Mike Moyle |
| 2) | | | | | |
| 3) | | | | | |

### Time Analysis

Sourcing Team / Commodity / Service
Office Products

| | Time Units/Week | | % of Total |
|---|---|---|---|
| | Hours | Days | Time Spent |
| | 16 | 2 | 40% |

### Activity Breakdown

| Activity | Ordering | Receiving & Stocking | Delivery & Shipping | Invoice & Payments | Mailing | Coord. Copiers | Supplier Contacts | Total Time |
|---|---|---|---|---|---|---|---|---|
| | 30% | 10% | 11% | 5% | 4% | 20% | 20% | 100% |
| | | | | | | | | Must = 100% |

**Transaction Information**
Sue works with 116 office products companies currently and accounts for 20% of annual spending. Currently handles 162 POs for the 116 suppliers.

**Additional Comments/Process Suggestions**
Says that everybody has a "favorite" supplier and she buys redundant product from multiple suppliers.

**Interviewee Approval Confirmation**
Date

➤ Revise process maps to reflect data gathered in interviews.

### Step 3

Develop activity costs upon completion of the interviews. The activities are costed out and extrapolated from the sample to account for all people, equipment, and facilities included in the process.

➤ Gather cost data (e.g., wages, overhead rates, facilities allocations, benefit loads).

## EXAMPLE OF ACTIVITY COST CALCULATION

**Process**
*Labor*

**Example**

1. Calculate direct labor costs as determined through the interview process.
2. Extrapolate labor costs to all people who were involved with similar job titles.
3. Calculate labor costs by activity and by job title. Total labor identified in *% of time allocated per interview.

1. Buyer @ ($19.23/hr + 48% load) *2,080 hr/yr = $59,197 year
   Time allocated to office supplies = 40%
   Allocated costs = $59,197 × 40% = $23,679
2. Two buyers @ $23,679/yr = $47,358

3. Ordering = 30% × $47,358 = $14,207
   Receiving & stocking = 10% × $47,358 = $4,736
   Delivery & shipping = 11% × $47,358 = $5,209
   Invoice & payments = 5% × $47,358 = $2,368
   Mailing = 4% × $47,358 = $1,894
   Coord. copiers = 20% × $47,358 = $9,472
   Supplier contacts = 20% × $47,358 = $9,472

**Process**
*Fixed Costs*

**Example**

4. Calculate square footage and facilities costs.
5. Calculate equipment costs.

4. 27 storerooms 700 avg/sq ft.
   $14.75 lease rate = $278,775/yr
5. 1 delivery truck @ $9,000/yr lease
   + maintenance & gas = $13,600/yr

➤ Cost out all interview sheets by assigning appropriate loaded pay rates to the time, assigning facilities expenses to all of the real property, and costing out the repair and maintenance of all equipment.

➤ Once the information is gathered, transfer it onto spreadsheets. The spreadsheets are designed to accumulate the information by activity, so that each activity can be accounted for throughout the organization. The spreadsheets should also be used to extrapolate the activity to all the people who perform similar work. This step will identify budget accountability by defining activities in each organization.

➤ As a rule of thumb, any given team should perform between 20 and 40 activities to achieve the appropriate level of analysis.

## *Step 4*

Ensure that all of the activity descriptions are unique. Develop a spreadsheet that accumulates the sum of costs by organization for each activity. Table 9.4 shows the Office Products Team's summary.

This spreadsheet was useful in identifying both activities and organizations that were substantial cost drivers. For example, *Receiving and stocking* represents the labor, facilities, and equipment associated with 27 storerooms company-wide. Business Unit 3 had a total cost of $680,485, which reflected the

| Activity Organization | Accounts Payable | Business Unit 1 | Business Unit 2 | Business Unit 3 | Procurement and Material Management |
|---|---|---|---|---|---|
| Ordering | $569 | $23,340 | $5,199 | $143,109 | $30,817 |
| Receiving and stocking | $935 | $13,168 | $1,700 | $680,485 | $41,096 |
| Invoices and payments | $23,379 | $11,894 | $13,412 | $173,518 | $5,304 |
| Printing/copying | $405 | $5,730 | $81,943 | $25,174 | $7,801 |

**Table 9.4** Office Products Total Cost by Activity

level of activity associated with local supply rooms and high-lighted the opportunity to pursue process improvements with the suppliers.

### *Step 5*

Summarize the internal and external costs by department to calculate total costs. Table 9.5 is from the Office Products Team.

*External costs* represents price, the amounts paid for office products. *Total internal costs* represents the sum of all activity costs calculated on the previous spreadsheets. *Total costs* is the sum of both the external and internal costs.

The total cost analysis revealed that the internal costs associated with office products exceeded the value of the external expenditure. This cost model gives visibility to the often unseen internal costs and reinforces the value of using the total cost model.

➤ Review the completed information with the team to determine that the cost model is complete. It is a good practice at this point to trace the model back to the process maps to make sure that all people and activities have been included.

➤ Review the process maps and activity costs with the cost center manager and/or interviewee.

| Organization | Office Products External Costs | Total Internal Costs | Total Costs |
|---|---|---|---|
| Accounts payable | $143,604 | $41,322 | $184,926 |
| Business unit 1 | $226,955 | $66,027 | $292,982 |
| Business unit 2 | $22,595 | $172,390 | $194,985 |
| Business unit 3 | $145,609 | $1,170,079 | $1,315,688 |
| Procurement and material management | $93,393 | $180,969 | $274,089 |

**Table 9.5** Office Products Total Cost by Department

### *Step 6*

Identify soft costs. These are costs that represent partial utilization factors (people, facilities, and equipment) and, as a result, cannot be eliminated without changing either the work process or where the work is performed (e.g., centralization). Soft costs should be captured and retained for consideration in the continuous improvement phase.

An example of a soft cost occurred when there were 12 people with similar job classifications, all spending 30 percent of their time on office products, and none of their functions could be combined and/or eliminated due to the fact that these employees worked in different locations and had other job responsibilities. However, in continuous improvement, by changing processes and centralizing functions, cost reductions could be achieved.

In the same example, there were 27 supply rooms throughout the company that were dedicated to office products. However, this was considered a hard cost because local supply rooms could be converted to usable office space.

### *Step 7*

Translate data developed through the total cost model into a summary of opportunities for cost reduction. Once the baseline information is understood, both the sourcing team and the suppliers can more accurately assess the savings opportunity by addressing these activities. Enabling the sourcing team as well as the suppliers to focus on total costs, rather than just the supplier's profit margin, exponentially increases the opportunity for savings.

These opportunities should be captured for consideration when the request for proposal is prepared in Phase E. Total cost opportunity identification includes the sum of the internal and external costs. Opportunities for internal cost reduction are found in areas of high activity and process redundancy.

## TIPS

➤ Processes and activities may vary significantly between operations in various locations. Interviewing representatives of additional locations will add validity to cost extrapolations.

➤ The total cost model is the key to being able to trace projected savings to the appropriate budget responsibility (e.g., if inventory carrying costs are carried at the corporate level, reductions in inventory may not affect business unit budgets).

➤ Whenever possible, allow suppliers to bid against cost models to identify ways they can reduce total costs.

➤ Remember that not all savings are equal. Differentiate between those that have direct budget impact and those that may need to be accounted for as soft savings.

➤ Scope the cycle time of the set of activities that makes up the process. Cutting cycle time can cut costs and better serve the internal customer.

➤ Be consistent in applying overheads and calculating other costs, such as facilities and equipment, throughout the model. For example, when calculating labor time, be consistent in using hours/quarter hours or minutes.

This concludes the assessment phase of the team activity. The outcome of this phase prepares the sourcing team to begin developing its strategy. The team has a sense of the type of supplier relationship that will fulfill the expectations of the stakeholders and reap the cost-saving opportunities identified through the total cost model. The next phase will take the team through the development of a supplier relationship strategy.

*Chapter*

# Sourcing Team Strategy

Preparation and
Design Phases

**Team Activity
Phases**

Business requirements and unique commodity/ market characteristics drive differentiated procurement approaches. The clear picture that the sourcing team has developed through the internal and external assessment, initial supplier screening, and cost model development now serves as the basis for defining a strategy. Sourcing team strategy is how the sourcing team articulates its desired relationship with a supplier. Crafting the sourcing strategy involves integrating all of the work performed to date.

Phase E (see Figure 10.1) is the first instance in the sourcing process in which the sourcing team begins to formulate strategy, although refinement of the strategy continues throughout the process. The sourcing team finalizes its scope and develops criteria for supplier selection. By determining the potential impact various strategies can have on costs and internal stakeholders, the team develops a clearer picture of what the strategy should be.

---

*Activity in this module:*
*Determine desired relationship, develop selection criteria and weightings, develop performance measure categories, determine impact on internal stakeholders, develop request for proposal, conduct supplier rollout meeting*

---

223

In Strategic Sourcing, the goal of the sourcing team is to determine which type of supplier relationship will best deliver the expected results. The sourcing teams typically use four labels to differentiate the various types of supplier relationships. Phase E.2 will take the sourcing team through the deter-

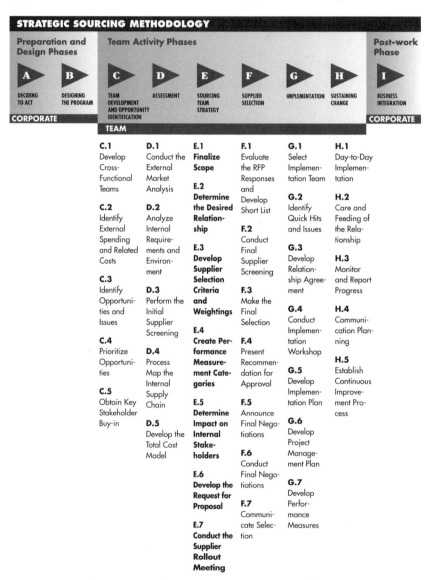

**Figure 10.1** Phase Map—Team Activity Phases.

mination of the appropriate relationship. This phase is designed to take the team through finalizing the scope of the team, developing the appropriate selection criteria, and developing the Request for Proposal (RFP) document. The work of this phase culminates in presenting the RFP to suppliers at a rollout meeting.

The sourcing team will use the methodology to determine the type of relationship that would best serve the scope of its material or service. The outcome of this determination will place the material/service into one of the four following categories:

➤ Alliance
➤ Managed business relationship
➤ General procurement
➤ Bulk purchasing

The first two categories are based on relationships and the second two are based on transactions. Since general procurement and bulk purchasing rely on traditional procurement activity, there is no need for Strategic Sourcing in those cases. If a sourcing team comes to the conclusion that its material/service is best served by general procurement or bulk purchasing, the team should recommend that the company continue with its routine procurement activities.

The two relationship models sought in Strategic Sourcing are alliances and managed business relationships. Through the Strategic Sourcing process the team will determine which relationship will best serve the company. Remember, not all relationships are intended to be alliances.

A brief description of the two Strategic Sourcing relationships may prove useful at this time. Both relationships share a total cost focus, seek mutual benefit, and rely on performance measures. An alliance, however, requires the highest degree of business integration. While the difference between a managed business relationship and an alliance is largely a matter of degree, it can be described by the characteristics shown in Table 10.1.

While companies use many different labels to describe many types of supplier relationships, the Strategic Sourcing methodology seeks to establish relationships that have a number of the characteristics noted in Table 10.1.

## PURPOSE

The objective of the sourcing team strategy phase is to integrate the information gathered in the assessment phase and apply a comprehensive approach to determine the relationship that will be desired with future suppliers.

## DELIVERABLES

By performing the steps within the sourcing strategy phase, the sourcing team will develop the following work products:

| Alliance | Managed Business Relationship |
| --- | --- |
| ➤ High degree of business alignment and process integration | ➤ Selective areas of business alignment and process integration |
| ➤ Relationships established at all levels in both companies | ➤ Relationships primarily at implementation team level |
| ➤ Continual renewal of contract | ➤ Specified contract term (3–5 years) |
| ➤ Seeking of innovative breakthroughs | ➤ Continuous improvement |
| ➤ Possible sharing of employees and facilities | ➤ Performance-based contracting |
| ➤ Incentive-based contracting | ➤ Supply chain information system access |
| ➤ Supply chain information system integration | ➤ Periodic meetings |
| ➤ Face-to-face daily/weekly meetings | |

**Table 10.1** Alliances versus Managed Business Relationships

➤ Finalized scope of work

➤ Selection criteria and weightings for supplier selection

➤ Performance measure categories for supplier performance analysis

➤ Documentation of how internal stakeholders are affected

➤ Selected sourcing strategy to meet objectives

➤ An RFP for suppliers that reflects the sourcing strategy

➤ A supplier rollout session, which is the venue for distributing the RFP to suppliers and for creating understanding of the changes envisioned by the sourcing team

### TRAINING

Plan and implement the following training workshops for sourcing team members when appropriate during this phase:

➤ Designing your supplier relationship

➤ Presentation skills

## E.1 FINALIZE SCOPE

### Description

Work performed in Phase E.1 will be used to determine the materials and services to be included in the scope of the Request for Proposal (RFP). The scope may still change based upon new information provided by the suppliers.

The scope will be determined largely by:

➤ Requirements defined by internal and external customers

➤ Ideas learned from the external market analysis

➤ Suppliers' capabilities learned from the RFI process in Phase D, "Assessment"

➤ Cost savings ideas generated from the total cost analysis

➤ Synergy now recognized among materials/services that was not apparent originally to the sourcing team

## Method

### Step 1

Review the scope of the materials/services to ensure their appropriateness. In reviewing, the sourcing team should address the following questions:

➤ *Should the company consider outsourcing some of the work to a third party?*
If so, that area may be excluded from the sourcing team's scope and assigned to a new sourcing team whose purpose is to analyze outsourcing opportunities.

➤ *Is the current scope too broad?*
The RFP needs to be focused sufficiently so that there is a common supplier base. If suppliers cannot reasonably be expected to provide most of the materials/services requested, the scope is probably too broad.

Generally teams need to be encouraged to think more broadly about possible synergy among materials/services. However, there is a risk of a scope becoming too broad. If the scope is too broad, determine whether the time and resources of the sourcing team would be optimized by dropping the additional groupings at this time. Also, consider whether the sourcing team can handle the additional work without compromise to the integrity of the process.

➤ *Has the sourcing team's work to date uncovered areas that should be added to the original scope?*
New areas appropriate to the original scope could result from reengineering a process or asking suppliers to do

more. Examples include engineering design, product development, or product testing.

### Step 2

Validate the scope with the program management team to ensure support. The program management team is the best place to test for missing materials/services or synergies that may have been overlooked by the sourcing team.

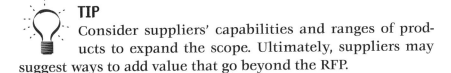 **TIP**
Consider suppliers' capabilities and ranges of products to expand the scope. Ultimately, suppliers may suggest ways to add value that go beyond the RFP.

## 🖳 DETERMINE THE DESIRED RELATIONSHIP

### Description

The purpose of defining the relationship at this stage is to enable a sourcing team to develop RFP questions targeted toward the strategy selected. On the basis of supplier responses, the sourcing team can then determine whether the material/service is best supported in an alliance or managed business relationship framework.

### Method

### Step 1

Analyze expenditures to determine where the material/service falls within the sourcing square shown in Figure 10.2. The sourcing square is a tool that categorizes expenditures on two dimensions: critical/complex and value/cost. Analyzing these

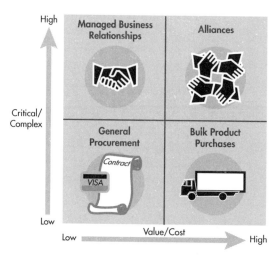

**Figure 10.2** Sourcing Square.

dimensions of a material/service reveals the first indication of possible relationship scenarios. For example, material that is both low in value to the company and not complex (in design, distribution, or utilization) would seem like a candidate for a general procurement strategy.

## Step 2

The sourcing square placement may change based on supplier capability and innovation. Consider the RFI responses to test the sourcing team's assumption regarding the initial placement of a material/service in the sourcing square.

A material/service may become complex or may increase in value to a company through the Strategic Sourcing process. For example, at SCE, office products first appeared to be both low in value and complexity, thereby indicating a general procurement strategy. However, the sourcing team was able to aggregate its office product purchases, totaling millions of dollars per year, across the company. Through the assessment process, the sourcing team found a supplier that would be able to distribute office products to the desktops of thousands of employees, at locations spread over a 50,000-square-mile area.

This innovative view moved office products from the general procurement category to the alliance category.

The sourcing squares in Figure 10.3 contrast the initial placement of materials/services at SCE with the redefined Strategic Sourcing placement based on supplier input.

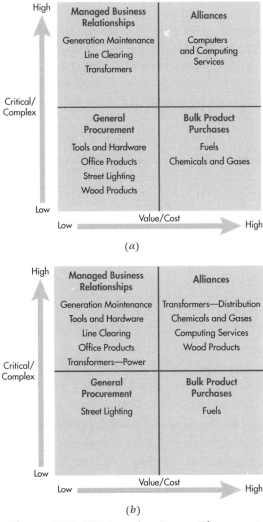

**Figure 10.3** SCE Sourcing Square Placement (*a*) before Strategic Sourcing; (*b*) after Strategic Sourcing.

## *Step 3*

The degree of business integration between the company and the supplier in each of the sourcing squares brings with it different expectations regarding the relationship. The sourcing team's next step will be determined based upon the sourcing square analysis.

> **Outcome 1**—If the sourcing team has placed the material/service on the sourcing square and determined that it falls into the general procurement or bulk product purchases squares, the team should make a recommendation to the program management team to utilize existing procurement practices.

> **Outcome 2**—If the material/service falls into the alliance or managed business relationship squares, pursue the development of an RFP. The RFP will aid in determining the appropriate relationship by validating assumptions about supplier capabilities.

## TIPS

➤ This step will test the sourcing team's tolerance for new ideas. The sourcing team needs to think in terms of "where we need to be" rather than "where we are today."

➤ Many supplier relationship labels are used interchangeably. For example, the term *alliance* is used broadly, and it is used in many different ways. Be clear in defining the intentions and expectations for the desired supplier relationship. Clarity will benefit both parties.

➤ Keep an open mind about what the RFP may reveal regarding how a material/service can move from one sourcing square to another.

➤ The sourcing square is a useful tool that can be used at the corporate level to determine which teams to launch.

# E.3 DEVELOP SUPPLIER SELECTION CRITERIA AND WEIGHTINGS

## Description

In this phase, the sourcing team develops the criteria on which suppliers will be rated, assigning weighting to reflect the relative importance of each criterion. There are two major elements to consider in the development of selection criteria: The first is the pricing of the material/service and the second is the other aspects of total value.

This will require the sourcing team to overcome the traditional mind-set of using price comparison to evaluate suppliers. It also goes beyond supplier evaluations based on just price and quality. The Strategic Sourcing methodology recognizes price, quality, and many other areas when making a total cost evaluation. The criteria and weightings should reflect the opportunities identified in the sourcing strategy selection. These criteria and weightings will guide the team as to what kinds of questions to ask in the RFP.

## Method

### Step 1

Finalize the criteria categories from the strategy. Typically, selection criteria are built around the sourcing strategy. Cost reduction estimates or pricing may be included as well. Typical categories that may be considered in Strategic Sourcing include:

➤ Background of the supplier
➤ Cost management/financial capability
➤ Customer service experience
➤ Subsupplier/subcontractor relationships
➤ Operational capabilities

➤ Quality assurance programs
➤ Technology capability
➤ Materials management programs
➤ Past performance

## *Step 2*

Determine whether there is a threshold screen for all suppliers before they are considered for further evaluation. For example, a first screen for each supplier may be a pass/fail on demonstrated technical competence or capability.

## *Step 3*

Develop the relative category weights. The sourcing team assigns a percentage to each of the categories based on importance or criticality. Weightings for the pricing plus other categories total 100 percent and reflect the importance of each of the criteria to the sourcing team's strategy.

It is important not to put too much emphasis on price at this point in supplier evaluation. Many sourcing teams do a first-round evaluation with a weighting of less than 50 percent on price. Since this evaluation is intended to identify a short list of suppliers, not to determine a final selection, there will be other opportunities to put additional emphasis on price. By setting aside price in this round of the screening process, a sourcing team can address other areas where the supplier can add value.

Percentages can be assigned by having sourcing team members individually assess the categories and then share their reasoning with the sourcing team. The sourcing team may also opt to develop the relative weighting through discussion and consensus.

Discuss any large variances that occur when the sourcing team is determining weighting. The cross-functional nature of the sourcing team will lend insight into the relative importance of the categories. Allow for adequate discussion and allow sourcing team members to change their weightings based on discussion. It is important for the sourcing team to understand that once the criteria are set, they cannot be changed during the RFP evaluation process.

## TIPS

➤ It is preferable to have the relative weights assigned prior to issuing the RFP, but it's essential to have the weightings established before the RFP responses are received and opened.

➤ Selection criteria link the supplier strategy to business objectives. Reviewing opportunities identified in the total cost model provides a valuable cross-check of the criteria and weighting.

➤ The cross-functional representation of the sourcing teams ensures that all pertinent perspectives are considered when establishing criteria and weighting. Encourage every team member to participate fully in the discussion.

## E.4 CREATE PERFORMANCE MEASUREMENT CATEGORIES

### Description

The sourcing team will determine the initial categories of performance measures that should be developed and identify any specific performance levels that constitute minimum requirements.

It is important at this point to begin identifying those performance measures that support a successful implementation. Ultimately, performance measures and targets will be established jointly with the selected supplier(s) during the implementation phase.

Performance measures quantify how well activities or outputs of a process achieve a specified goal. Use of performance measures achieves the following:

➤ Identifies common goals for the company and its suppliers

➤ Allows judgment to be based on data versus perception

➤ Identifies trends that can indicate progress or problems

➤ Forms the basis for ongoing continuous improvement with suppliers (if you don't measure it, you can't demonstrate improvement)

➤ Can become the basis for incentives or penalties

Just as objectives serve as the map for the supplier relationship, the performance measures serve as mileposts to gauge progress toward your goals.

## Method

### Step 1

Develop overall performance measures for cost, quality, and service.

➤ Cost performance measures should quantify price and other total cost elements.

➤ Service and quality measures should track areas that are most important to the customer.

### Step 2

Develop a balanced set of performance measures.

➤ When developing performance measures, focus on key measures that are clearly linked to the strategy. Too many measures will diffuse attention.

➤ Set up measures of administrative processes such as order entry, invoicing, quality, and cycle time.

➤ Examples of performance measures are:

—*Total cost* performance measures:
  Number of purchase orders (POs) and invoices
  Product specification
  Overall cost per unit (i.e., cost per employee)
  Price of materials/services
  Transportation and distribution cost targets
  Inventory levels and turns
  Maintenance and operating costs

—*Service* performance measures:
  On-time deliveries
  PO cycle time
  Responsiveness of supplier
  Delivery locations and frequency
  Supplier diversity participation
  Supplier lead time
  Emergency response time

—*Quality* performance measures:
  Rejection rates
  Damage claims
  Order completeness
  Warranty utilization
  Inspection and testing requirements
  Process capabilities
  Mean time to failure
  Supplier audit results

The performance elements of cost, quality, and service exist in dynamic tension. It is important to recognize that overemphasis on one element may affect the others. The greatest value is achieved when all three elements are in balance. The sourcing team should strive to create a balanced set of measures that addresses all three areas (see Figure 10.4).

## *Step 3*

Assess your existing capabilities in measuring performance. Consider the following:

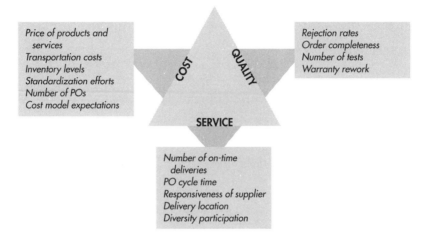

**Figure 10.4** Balanced Performance Measures.

➤ How the data will be collected, and by whom.

➤ How the data will be employed to drive corrective action.

➤ The baseline—it is important to know this before setting performance measures. If the baseline is not readily known, it should be tracked before performance expectations for the supplier or customer are set.

## TIPS

➤ Performance measures should capture data about activities or outputs that can be affected by the sourcing teams and suppliers.

➤ Specific performance measures identified by the team as requirements should be communicated in the RFP.

➤ An alternative resource for collecting performance data may be to look to the supplier's systems/capabilities.

➤ When possible, performance measures should be expressed in units so they can indicate trends regardless of usage-volume fluctuations. For example: A unit-based measure for the cost of office supplies may be "average cost per employee" versus "total office supply spending."

# E.5 DETERMINE IMPACT ON INTERNAL STAKEHOLDERS

## Description

The purpose of this phase is to develop an understanding of how internal behaviors, attitudes, and operations may be impacted or need to change in order for the recommended sourcing strategy to be successfully implemented.

Affected stakeholders are those internal groups or individuals who may be impacted by the changes resulting from the new sourcing strategy.

## Method

### Step 1

Brainstorm the list of stakeholders who will be affected by the potential changes. Start with the earlier stakeholder assessment prepared in Phase C, "Team Development and Opportunity Identification." With an understanding of the sourcing team's current direction, expand or amend the list as appropriate.

### Step 2

Assess the general impact of these changes on these stakeholders. *How would they have to behave differently? What significant operations changes may have to take place? What new roles and responsibilities would these stakeholders be required to assume? What long-held attitudes and beliefs would need to change in order for the strategy to be implemented successfully?*

### Step 3

The assessment will be used in future communication. It is also used at this point to check in with the resource team and the program management team to understand how their broader corporate perspectives support the proposed changes.

## TIPS

➤ Don't make decisions in a vacuum. It is important to understand the impact the sourcing strategy will have on stakeholders.

➤ Early communication of potential changes can help to create a cooperative environment with stakeholders who will likely play critical roles in implementation.

➤ At this point, be sure the sourcing team has sufficiently documented its research, analysis, process, and conclusions before moving to the next phase.

➤ The assessment of potential impact is a useful tool in identifying potential roadblocks.

## E.6 DEVELOP THE REQUEST FOR PROPOSAL

### Description

The sourcing team develops a formal Request for Proposal.

There is a difference between an RFI and an RFP. The RFI prepared in an earlier phase requests generic information from the supplier. The RFP asks the supplier to respond directly to the requirements, standards, and terms and conditions of the company. Additionally, the RFP invites suppliers to demonstrate their ability to impact total costs and to share their ideas for creating value.

The RFP asks suppliers for:

➤ Specific proposals for helping meet business objectives

➤ Information about their products, services, standards, and other capabilities

➤ Description of their quality systems, quality control, and process capability as these relate to meeting the company's quality standards

➤ Experience in other long-term strategic relationships

➤ Description of their performance tracking systems

➤ Information about their companies, financial status, growth potential, background, and performance history

➤ Information about pricing

➤ Suggested terms and conditions

➤ Operational capabilities

➤ Lists of key customer references that sourcing team members can contact for feedback on a prospective supplier's performance

The intent of the RFP is to provide further information about a supplier's capabilities, strengths, and cost-saving ideas. It is designed to give the sourcing team a clearer view of what potential suppliers can do to contribute to the company's competitiveness and is the tool used to screen suppliers to a short list for continued evaluation.

The RFP should serve as a two-way communication vehicle. The RFP should not only ask questions of the supplier, it should also provide suppliers with information about the company to aid them in their response. For example, it is common to share information about warehouse locations, process maps, internal costs, forecasts and spending trends, company vision, and strategic direction. Information such as this will allow the supplier to respond realistically and provide detailed proposals. This represents the third filter applied in the supplier screening process, as illustrated in Figure 10.5.

## Method

### *Step 1*

Prepare the RFP document to ensure that it clearly reflects the business objectives. Be specific in the RFP about the communication required from the suppliers, including some or all of the following:

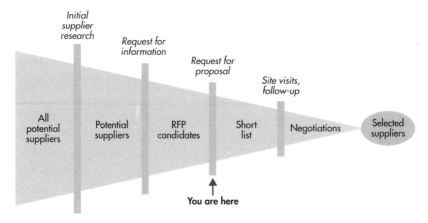

**Figure 10.5** Supplier Screening Process.

➤ A narrative section on how the supplier proposes to meet your objectives.

➤ A matrix listing the materials, services, and value-added activities the supplier might provide.

➤ A pricing template based on the team's total cost model. This will ensure that an accurate "apples-to-apples" comparison of cost savings can be made among suppliers and against the current cost scenario.

➤ A section addressing additional changes that the supplier recommends to enhance value.

➤ Terms and conditions essential to the company.

## *Step 2*

Prepare a detailed questionnaire structured to elicit information about qualitative aspects of the proposal such as relationship potential and capability. This questionnaire provides comparability of suppliers around value alignment, innovativeness, and relationship experience.

Align these questions into the categories that were created previously. Make sure each category asks enough questions for sourcing team members to make an accurate assessment of the suppliers. Here are examples of the types of questions often asked of suppliers in Strategic Sourcing RFPs:

➤ What is your company's vision statement? How is this vision interpreted on your manufacturing floor? How do you ensure that your employees know your vision and understand it?

➤ How many alliances do you currently have? What percentage of your business (dollar value and number) does this represent?

➤ What is your company's alliance development process?

➤ What would you recommend we change in our specifications?

➤ Where do you see process improvement possibilities?

➤ What demonstrated success have you had in alliances?

➤ How do you describe an alliance?

➤ What criteria would you use to measure us as a good customer?

➤ How many alliances can your company handle? What limits you in handling more?

### Step 3

Prior to issuing the RFP, the sourcing team should check in with the program management team and executive steering council to present the impact analysis and the RFP format and content.

## TIPS

➤ One of the biggest challenges of RFP development is to create a pricing framework that allows for apples-to-apples comparisons among the suppliers. Rely on the total cost model for comparisons beyond price.

➤ When bidding services, a method that makes comparability possible is to create a sample "job" or series of "jobs" for the contractor to bid on, with the stated assumption that all future jobs will be priced using the same cost structure.

➤ The questionnaire is designed to enable a comparison of suppliers around qualitative information. It is also used to convey that the company is doing business differently.

## E.7 CONDUCT SUPPLIER ROLLOUT MEETING

### Description

Distribute the RFP to potential suppliers in a group setting. At SCE this process was called the *supplier rollout meeting*. The purpose of the meeting is to explain the components of the RFP, how supplier evaluation will take place, and what specifically is needed from the suppliers. Preparation for this meeting includes the development of a presentation about the changing direction of the company and the sourcing team's vision of the future.

### Method

#### Step 1

Develop the supplier rollout meeting agenda (see Figure 10.6); determine date, time, and logistics.

#### Step 2

Invite selected suppliers and members of the program management team and executive steering council as well as internal stakeholders to the rollout meeting. This is the first opportunity to demonstrate to suppliers broad-based support for the strategy. Select presenters from the team who represent respective stakeholder groups and who are viewed by suppliers as the decision makers on the team. Due to the interactive nature of the meeting and the critical messages discussed, it is

# AGENDA
### May 12, 1995

- **Welcome / Introduction / Desired Outcomes**　　　**Generation Manager**

- **Strategic Sourcing**
  *A Corporate Perspective*　　　**Strategic Sourcing Champion**

- **SCE Business**
  *Today and Tomorrow*　　　**Logistics Analyst**

- **Chemicals And Gases Sourcing Team Scope**　　　**Maintenance Foreman**

- **Request For Proposal**　　　**Procurement Manager**
  *Contents / Expectations / Bid List Scenarios*

- **Evaluation and Schedule**　　　**Division Chemical Manager**

**BREAK**

- **Supplier Diversity**　　　**Supplier Diversity Manager**

- **Question And Answer**　　　**C&G Team**

- **Closing Remarks**　　　**Generation Manager**

**Figure 10.6** Supplier Rollout Meeting Agenda.
*(Source: Chemicals and Gases Team)*

recommended that each supplier be represented at the RFP rollout meeting in order to continue in the selection process.

➤ The rollout meeting is the first opportunity to demonstrate internal alignment. It is critical that all internal stakeholders attend the rollout to provide visible support for the new way of doing business. This unified front will ward off divide-and-conquer tactics by suppliers.

➤ Since it is impossible to fully convey the changes sought in Strategic Sourcing in a written RFP, supplier attendance was mandatory at SCE.

➤ Select the right team members to deliver the key messages. Suppliers will have preconceived notions that decisions are made by the team member with expertise in a specific discipline. For example, if the message to suppliers is to challenge technical specifications, the credible presenter would be from the engineering organization.

➤ Emphasize in your communication to suppliers that what you are seeking is a business strategy, not a typical bid response. Therefore, encourage suppliers to bring decision makers of the appropriate level to hear the business strategy firsthand.

### Step 3

Develop presentation material and prepare bid packages for distribution. The presentation material/packet should include:

➤ Information about what is driving change at your company (e.g., competition, market forces)

➤ The background of the Strategic Sourcing program

➤ An overview of the sourcing team process being used as well as the team's objectives in terms of quality, service, cycle times, and total cost

➤ Pertinent information that may offer insight into current processes or cost drivers, such as process maps, total cost models, and baseline performance levels

➤ The RFP document specifying what is required of the suppliers in the form of responses

➤ A summary of how RFP responses will be evaluated

➤ A summary of the timeline regarding evaluation and selection

➤ Instructions on how questions and answers will be shared during the evaluation process

➤ Information about company programs that suppliers are asked to take into consideration (e.g., diversity, labor relations, environmental issues)

➤ Logistics: when the responses are due back, how many copies, in what format, and to whom

➤ Prepared response diskettes, if you are requesting electronic submittal of questionnaire responses, pricing scenarios, or other information

## TIPS

➤ An electronic submittal format will typically require additional team time to design; however, it expedites the compilation and analysis process upon receipt of the proposals. A standardized response format also enhances the team's ability to make comparisons of competing offers.

➤ It is important to communicate your baseline data for cost, quality, and service. The sourcing team will have conceptualized minimum levels of performance requirements. Now is the time for suppliers to start thinking in terms of the trade-offs of cost, quality, and service to achieve the highest overall value.

➤ This is a different process from typical bid proposals. Be clear as to how Strategic Sourcing is different. Ensure that the suppliers understand the process and the selection criteria for evaluating their proposals. The sourcing team needs to consider the pros and cons and to decide whether it wants to communicate the weighting factors assigned to selection criteria.

### Step 4

Conduct the supplier rollout meeting:

➤ Give suppliers a copy of the RFP and presentation materials. State your boundaries to the suppliers. Let them know if anything is off limits.

➤ Don't be overly prescriptive. Give suppliers data and describe your expected objectives and outcomes—for example, cost reduction and best value options. Listen to suppliers. Be open to their questions or ideas concerning the accuracy and clarity of technical and bid requirements.

➤ Encourage suppliers to work with each other if a combined group could better meet the company's objectives. Such groups should present a joint response that clearly describes the legal, operating, and administrative nature of their relationships.

The presentation slides in Figure 10.7 are from the SCE supplier rollout meeting for suppliers of chemicals and gases. Slides 1, 2, and 3 provide the context for the meeting and business change. Slides 4 through 10 introduce the Strategic Sourcing vision and value concepts. Slides 11 through 14 offer direction to suppliers regarding the proposal package.

## TIPS

➤ Suppliers will often choose to submit a joint response. In these instances, it is essential that suppliers forge a relationship and explore how they will integrate their offering to the company.

➤ It is important that suppliers hear directly from business leaders about the new supply chain strategy and expected changes. Do not send RFP packages before the meeting. The rollout meeting is a dynamic exchange between suppliers, company executives, and business unit leaders. The exchange of ideas that takes place is better served if suppliers don't have preconceived ideas from reading the RFP in advance.

➤ Anticipate a range of supplier reactions, from surprise to denial, even anxiety. Strategic Sourcing is a learning process for both suppliers and the company.

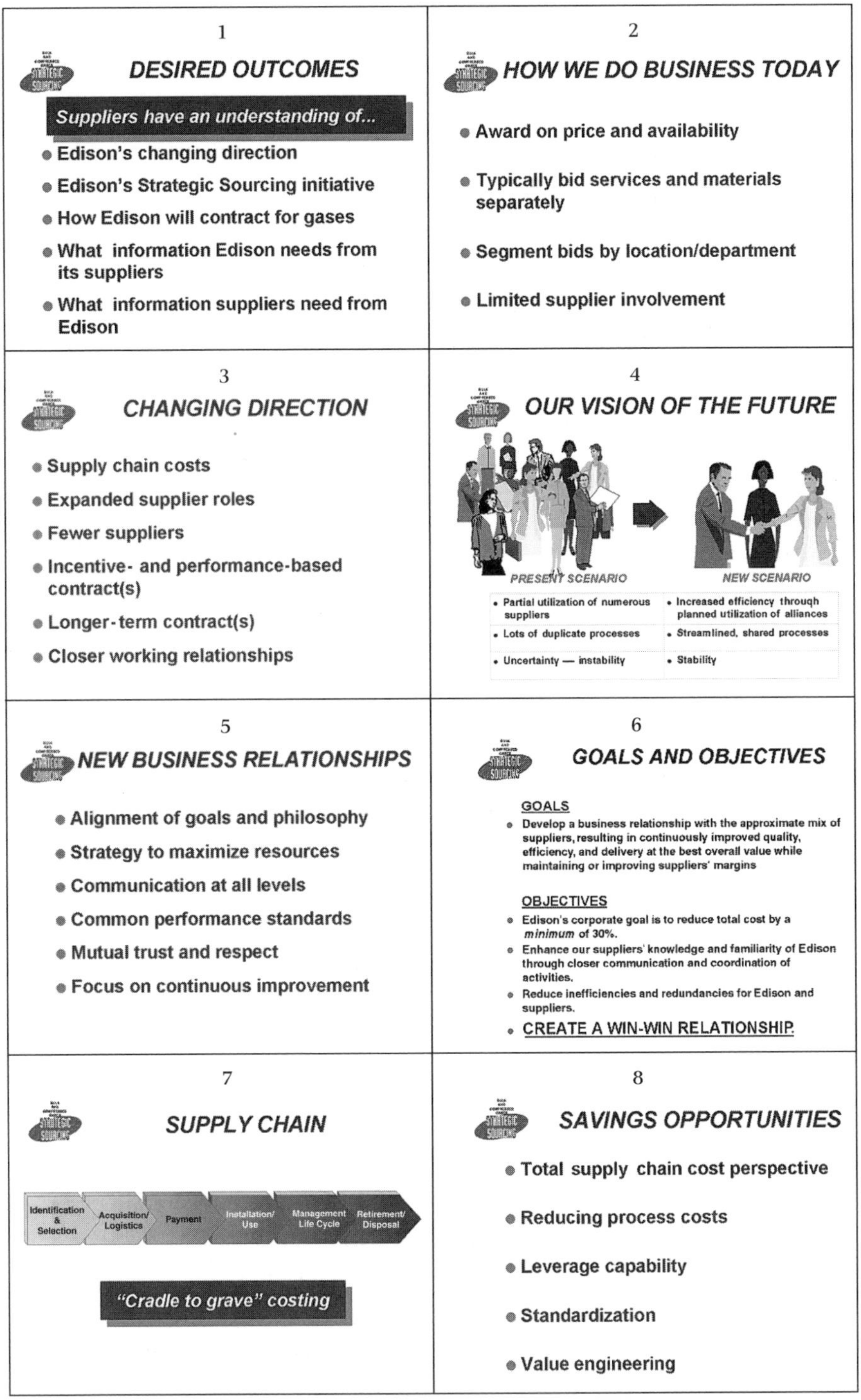


**Figure 10.7** Supplier Rollout Presentation Slides.

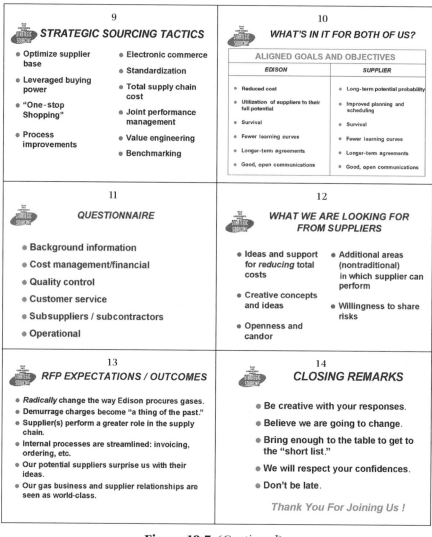

**Figure 10.7** (*Continued*).

## Step 5

Communicate the protocol for questions and answers during the bid process. Share all questions and answers with participating suppliers. It is advisable to require questions to be sent to a single location and to share responses with all suppliers to keep everyone equally informed.

A policy regarding conversations between suppliers and members of the sourcing team should be established. A strong Strategic Sourcing program creates a level playing field among participating suppliers. Therefore, the substance of all follow-up conversations should be documented and shared with all suppliers.

Because the responses to questions may alter a supplier's proposal, a cutoff date for questions should be enforced. Allow the suppliers sufficient time—usually four to seven weeks—to complete the RFP response.

## TIPS

➤ Suppliers inexperienced with Strategic Sourcing may be reluctant to ask questions publicly during the RFP rollout. Explaining that all questions and answers will be shared with all suppliers will serve to encourage questions at the meeting.

➤ There are circumstances that warrant hosting suppliers with tours of facilities to foster their understanding of current processes. Make the tours available to all suppliers on an equal basis.

➤ The question and answer process provides data that suppliers may use to refine their bids. Therefore, the more time the team allows suppliers to send questions, the more time suppliers will want to submit their proposal responses. Establish a cutoff date for questions and answers.

➤ Expect requests for extensions. Don't automatically grant them. Time is part of the value equation: Suppliers need to share your sense of urgency. Be firm with your response due date.

This concludes Phase E, "Sourcing Team Strategy," of the Strategic Sourcing methodology. By now the sourcing team will have formed an opinion about the relationship best suited for the materials or services in question and will have prepared an RFP designed to evaluate potential suppliers. The focus of the strategy development and analysis now shifts to the suppliers. A supplier rollout meeting has been conducted to invite suppliers into the process. The sourcing team is now ready for the next phase: supplier selection.

$\mathscr{C}hapter$

# 11

# Supplier Selection

Preparation and
Design Phases

**Team Activity
Phases**

A   B   C   D   E   F

Supplier selection is the single most important outcome of the Strategic Sourcing process. Selecting the supplier with whom you can build the right relationship is the foundation upon which all value is created. Selecting the supplier(s) who can share your company's vision, have commitment to the relationship, and deliver what they promise is the critical work of this phase.

---

*Activity in this module:*
*Evaluate RFP responses, conduct final supplier screening,*
*make final selection, present recommendation for*
*approval, announce final negotiations, conduct final*
*negotiations, communicate selection*

---

It is during this phase that the sourcing team evaluates RFP responses and develops a short list of suppliers (see Figure 11.1). From this short list, initial negotiations are held, supplier presentations are evaluated, and site visits are conducted. The final selection of supplier(s) is presented to the program management team and the executive steering council for approval. Upon executive steering council approval, a final contract is

253

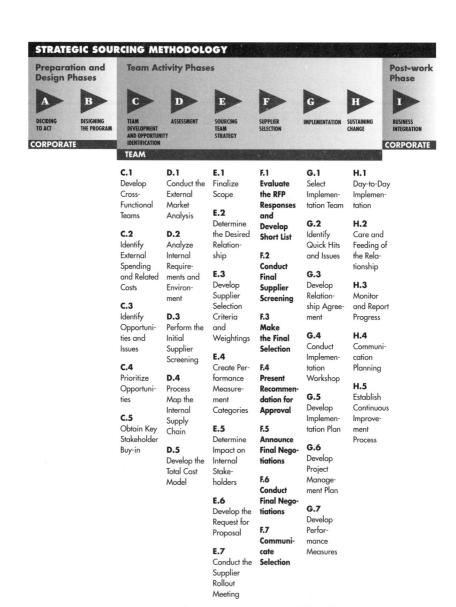

**Figure 11.1** Phase Map—Team Activity Phases.

negotiated. The phase culminates with the announcement of the selected suppliers.

The selection process used in Strategic Sourcing is very different from traditional procurement. It involves a series of steps that serve to screen the number of suppliers and ultimately determine which supplier or supplier networks best serve to meet the sourcing team's strategy. Figure 11.2 illustrates the process for final supplier selection.

Data contained in this phase are used for illustrative purposes and are fictitious to protect supplier confidentiality.

## Supplier Selection Process

Figure 11.2 depicts the typical scope of work from the point when RFP responses are received until final supplier selection. The first set of activities are completed by the sourcing team. The second set of activities are interactive between the team and suppliers. The sources of information used to perform analysis, as well as the relative weighting assigned to these major components, are shown. This chapter describes these steps in detail.

### PURPOSE

The objective of this phase is to select the right suppliers. Through a rigorous analytical process, the team

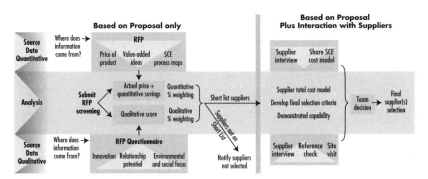

**Figure 11.2** Supplier Selection Process.

will match the company's requirements with the supplier's capabilities. The outcome will be the selection of those suppliers that best demonstrate the potential for developing the relationship necessary to achieve the highest overall business value.

**DELIVERABLES**

By performing the steps within the supplier selection phase, the sourcing team will develop the following work products:

➤ Short list of supplier(s) for further evaluation

➤ Comprehensive evaluation of short-listed supplier(s) based on site visits, interviews, presentations, and negotiations

➤ Final selection of supplier(s) that best meet the sourcing team's objectives

➤ Presentation to management for approval of the strategy and selection of supplier(s)

➤ Finalized contract with negotiated pricing and terms

**TRAINING**

Plan and implement the following training workshops for sourcing team members when appropriate during this phase:

➤ Negotiations training
➤ How to conduct site visits

## ⬛ EVALUATE RFP RESPONSES AND DEVELOP A SHORT LIST

### Description

There are two discrete components to the RFP proposal: quantitative and qualitative. The *quantitative* evaluation considers price and proposals to reduce total cost. The *qualitative* evaluation reviews questionnaire responses to assess future innovation and alliance potential. Evaluate RFP responses according to the criteria and weightings developed by the team. Ultimately, the process will identify a short list of suppliers that will undergo in-depth evaluation.

The short-listed suppliers should represent the best in class in terms of meeting the sourcing team's objectives. This group of suppliers will be further evaluated to determine which supplier, or combination of suppliers, will best deliver the lowest total cost and the highest overall value to the company in the future.

To develop the short list, the suppliers may first be required to pass through a minimum qualification screen to have their RFP responses evaluated (see Figure 11.3). The responses that qualify are then subject to full evaluation based on the selection criteria developed in Phase E.

## ■ F.1.1 REVIEW PROPOSALS FOR MINIMUM REQUIREMENTS

### Description

Evaluate each of the suppliers regarding any issues the sourcing team deems to be minimum thresholds that must be met in order to be considered further in the evaluation process.

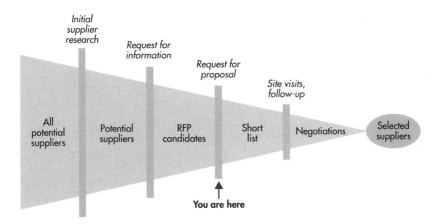

**Figure 11.3** Supplier Screening Process.

## Method

### *Step 1*

Determine the minimum qualifications the team considers necessary for a supplier to be considered in the evaluation process.

Some teams may decide that there is not a minimum qualification. Teams may feel that their earlier survey screening is sufficient and may decide to evaluate all RFP responses.

Examples of some minimum thresholds include:

➤ The supplier must be able to demonstrate a certain level of acceptable technical/engineering support.

➤ Engineering designs must be deemed acceptable from a technical competence review.

➤ The supplier may need to supply a certain percentage of the items requested in the RFP, or a discrete set of items.

➤ The operations people may be required to speak the local language.

➤ The supplier must have expertise/experience in a certain discipline.

➤ The financial stability of the supplier must be judged to be strong enough to handle the size of the proposed contract.

### *Step 2*

Determine which team members will have the responsibility of performing the review. It may be necessary to supplement the team's expertise with that of others within the company.

For example, a financial subteam may need to draw from the accounting department, the treasurers, or the audit organization in order to make a financial evaluation. The financial evaluation may look at the anticipated requirements of the award and how it may affect the financial status of the suppliers. This type of information should be assessed by the subteam and the subteam's documented decision should be presented to the sourcing team. Engineered items may need to be prescreened by the technically qualified team members to be sure they meet the technical needs of the company.

### Step 3

Based on the review performed in Step 2, determine whether any suppliers are to be removed from the process at this point.

**TIPS**

➤ It is important that the team not eliminate suppliers without careful consideration of the criteria. For example, a supplier may be new in the industry and may not have a long track record. In this case, the supplier may not have had alliance experience but the supplier's culture may support alliance behavior.

➤ If the team has a minimum coverage requirement, it must take care not to screen out niche suppliers. These suppliers may need to be further evaluated if there are limited sources for the materials and services they provide.

## ■ F.1.2 PERFORM QUALITATIVE ASSESSMENT

### Description

Review the responses to the RFP questionnaire to perform a qualitative assessment. The RFP includes a questionnaire to elicit qualitative information in a variety of areas such as alliance experience, research and development (R&D) focus, innovation, operational capabilities, and quality assurance.

### Method

### Step 1

Review the questionnaire responses and rate each supplier based on the selection criteria and weightings identified in Phase E.

The scores given to each selection criteria of the RFP questionnaire are multiplied by the percentage weighting allocated to that item by the team. It is recommended that team members set aside sufficient time to review all proposals in the same time frame. Schedule adequate time so that each team member may read the RFP responses and rate each supplier against the screening criteria. It is recommended that the team members review the proposal responses independently. Table 11.1 shows a sample scoring matrix.

### *Step 2*

Prepare a matrix that summarizes each of the sourcing team members' ratings of each of the suppliers as recorded in Step 1.

Table 11.2 illustrates a typical supplier evaluation matrix that should be prepared by the team and the method of calculating the relative rankings of each supplier's qualitative scores.

### *Step 3*

Post the matrix for review and discussion by the entire team. Any area that has large differences in scores should be discussed by the team. It is helpful for sourcing team members to express the thinking that led to supplier scores.

Due to the cross-functional nature of the team, different experience levels and knowledge will often yield insightful interpretations of the supplier's proposals. It is important not to defer automatically to the "expert," but rather to broaden the perspective and interpretation of the entire team through dialogue.

New insights based on discussions may emerge. Team members should be allowed to modify their scores and the matrix should be adjusted accordingly.

Calculate the overall ranking. The average weighted score is used to calculate the overall ranking of each supplier for discussion purposes.

Table 11.3 is a completed matrix. This matrix highlights areas for team discussion. For example, the 65 percent vari-

| Description | % Weight | ABC Corp. Score | ABC Weighted Score | Excellent Supply Score | Excellent Supply Weighted Score | YZ Power Systems Score | YZ Power Systems Weighted Score | USA Electric Score | USA Electric Weighted Score | Jones Mfr. Score | Jones Mfr. Weighted Score |
|---|---|---|---|---|---|---|---|---|---|---|---|
| **Team member: Tom A.** | | | | | | | | | | | |
| *Background information* | 10 | 7.00 | 0.7 | 5.00 | 0.5 | 9.00 | 0.9 | 6.00 | 0.6 | 7.00 | 0.7 |
| *Cost management/financial* | 10 | 6.00 | 0.6 | 5.00 | 0.5 | 9.00 | 0.9 | 7.00 | 0.7 | 8.00 | 0.8 |
| *Customer service* | 15 | 6.00 | 0.9 | 3.00 | 0.45 | 8.00 | 1.2 | 6.00 | 0.9 | 8.00 | 1.2 |
| *Operational capabilities* | 15 | 6.00 | 0.9 | 5.00 | 0.75 | 9.00 | 1.35 | 6.00 | 0.8 | 7.00 | 1.05 |
| *Logistic strategies* | 15 | 5.00 | 0.75 | 5.00 | 0.75 | 8.00 | 1.2 | 5.00 | 0.75 | 8.00 | 1.2 |
| *Subsuppliers / subcontractors* | 10 | 5.00 | 0.5 | 3.00 | 0.3 | 7.00 | 0.7 | 6.00 | 0.6 | 7.00 | 0.7 |
| *Manufacturing / product QC* | 12.5 | 8.00 | 1.0 | 3.00 | 0.375 | 7.00 | 0.875 | 7.00 | 0.875 | 7.00 | 0.875 |
| *Innovation* | 12.5 | 9.00 | 1.125 | 3.00 | 0.775 | 9.00 | 1.125 | 7.00 | 0.875 | 9.00 | 1.125 |
| TOTAL WEIGHTED SCORE: | | | 6.475 | | 4.00 | | 8.25 | | 6.20 | | 7.65 |
| **Team member: Ed B.** | | | | | | | | | | | |
| *Background information* | 10 | 7.00 | | 4.00 | | 9.00 | | 6.00 | | 8.00 | |
| *Cost management/financial* | 10 | 7.00 | | 1.00 | | 9.00 | | 5.00 | | 7.00 | |
| *Customer service* | 15 | 8.00 | | 2.00 | | 9.00 | | 5.00 | | 7.00 | |
| *Operational capabilities* | 15 | 9.00 | | 3.00 | | 10.00 | | 5.00 | | 7.00 | |
| *Logistic strategies* | 15 | 7.00 | | 3.00 | | 9.00 | | 4.00 | | 7.00 | |
| *Subsuppliers / subcontractors* | 10 | 5.00 | | 1.00 | | 9.00 | | 5.00 | | 6.00 | |
| *Manufacturing / product QC* | 12.5 | 7.00 | | 2.00 | | 9.00 | | 5.00 | | 7.00 | |
| *Innovation* | 12.5 | 8.00 | | 2.00 | | 10.00 | | 4.00 | | 7.00 | |
| TOTAL WEIGHTED SCORE: | | | 7.375 | | 2.30 | | 9.275 | | 4.825 | | 7.00 |
| **Team member: Brett C.** | | | | | | | | | | | |
| *Background information* | 10 | 6.00 | | 5.00 | | 9.00 | | 5.00 | | 7.00 | |
| *Cost management/financial* | 10 | 7.00 | | 3.00 | | 8.00 | | 5.00 | | 9.00 | |

**Table 11.1** Supplier Evaluation Matrix

| Description | % Weight | ABC Corp. Score | ABC Weighted Score | Excellent Supply Score | Excellent Supply Weighted Score | YZ Power Systems Score | YZ Power Systems Weighted Score | USA Electric Score | USA Electric Weighted Score | Jones Mfr. Score | Jones Mfr. Weighted Score |
|---|---|---|---|---|---|---|---|---|---|---|---|
| Customer service | 15 | 6.00 | | 3.00 | | 9.00 | | 4.00 | | 7.00 | |
| Operational capabilities | 15 | 6.00 | | 3.00 | | 10.00 | | 5.00 | | 7.00 | |
| Logistic strategies | 15 | 6.00 | | 3.00 | | 9.00 | | 4.00 | | 7.00 | |
| Subsuppliers / subcontractors | 10 | 6.00 | | 1.00 | | 8.00 | | 4.00 | | 7.00 | |
| Manufacturing / product QC | 12.5 | 8.00 | | 3.00 | | 7.00 | | 5.00 | | 7.00 | |
| Innovation | 12.5 | 10.00 | | 3.00 | | 10.00 | | 4.00 | | 9.00 | |
| TOTAL WEIGHTED SCORE: | | | 6.85 | | 3.00 | | 8.825 | | 4.475 | | 7.45 |
| Team member: Daniel D. | | | | | | | | | | | |
| Background information | 10 | 10.00 | | 5.00 | | 10.00 | | 8.00 | | 7.00 | |
| Cost management/financial | 10 | 10.00 | | 5.00 | | 10.00 | | 8.00 | | 7.00 | |
| Customer service | 15 | 7.00 | | 5.00 | | 10.00 | | 7.00 | | 9.00 | |
| Operational capabilities | 15 | 9.00 | | 5.00 | | 10.00 | | 8.00 | | 7.00 | |
| Logistic strategies | 15 | 9.00 | | 3.00 | | 9.00 | | 7.00 | | 8.00 | |
| Subsuppliers / subcontractors | 10 | 7.00 | | 3.00 | | 9.00 | | 7.00 | | 7.00 | |
| Manufacturing / product QC | 12.5 | 9.00 | | 1.00 | | 10.00 | | 8.00 | | 7.00 | |
| Innovation | 12.5 | 10.00 | | 1.00 | | 10.00 | | 9.00 | | 8.00 | |
| TOTAL WEIGHTED SCORE: | | | 8.83 | | 3.50 | | 9.75 | | 7.73 | | 7.58 |

**Table 11.1**  (Continued)

| Description | ABC Weighted Score | Excellent Supply Weighted Score | YZ Power Systems Weighted Score | USA Electric Weighted Score | Jones Mfr. Weighted Score |
|---|---|---|---|---|---|
| Team member: Tom A. | 6.48 | 4.00 | 8.25 | 6.20 | 7.65 |
| Team member: Ed B. | 7.38 | 2.30 | 9.28 | 4.83 | 7.00 |
| Team member: Brett C. | 6.85 | 3.00 | 8.83 | 4.48 | 7.45 |
| Team member: Daniel D. | 8.83 | 3.50 | 9.75 | 7.73 | 7.58 |
| AVERAGE QUALITATIVE SCORE: | 7.38 | 3.20 | 9.03 | 5.81 | 7.42 |
| RELATIVE QUALITATIVE RANKING: | 3 | 5 | 1 | 4 | 2 |

**Table 11.2** Supplier Evaluation Matrix with Relative Rankings

ance of Excellent Supply from the base case of YZ Power Systems should cause the team to explore the individual scores in order to confirm that the ranking is appropriate.

**TIPS**

➤ The more time that elapses between reading of the proposals, the more difficult it is to make a comparison. Keep this in mind when establishing the review schedule.

| Description | ABC Weighted Score | Excellent Supply Weighted Score | YZ Power Systems Weighted Score | USA Electric Weighted Score | Jones Mfr. Weighted Score |
|---|---|---|---|---|---|
| Team member: Tom A. | 6.48 | 4.00 | 8.25 | 6.20 | 7.65 |
| Team member: Ed B. | 7.38 | 2.30 | 9.28 | 4.83 | 7.00 |
| Team member: Brett C. | 6.85 | 3.00 | 8.83 | 4.48 | 7.45 |
| Team member: Daniel D. | 8.83 | 3.50 | 9.75 | 7.73 | 7.58 |
| AVERAGE QUALITATIVE SCORE: | 7.38 | 3.20 | 9.03 | 5.81 | 7.42 |
| # DIFFERENCE FROM BASE (HIGHEST) SCORE: | 1.64 | 5.83 | BASE | 3.22 | 1.61 |
| % DIFFERENCE FROM BASE (HIGHEST) SCORE: | 18% | 65% | BASE | 36% | 18% |
| RELATIVE QUALITATIVE RANKING: | 3 | 5 | 1 | 4 | 2 |

**Table 11.3** Completed Supplier Evaluation Matrix

➤ If a large number of responses are received, team members should be requested to go back over the responses they evaluated early in the process, since their level of expectation tends to mature during a lengthy review process.

➤ Consider requiring sourcing teams to use mandatory silence regarding their opinions about responses until all team members have completed their review.

➤ Encourage the team members to take notes regarding their individual ratings of each proposal. This will enable detailed discussions to occur before the final short list is completed.

➤ A significant degree of judgment is involved in developing qualitative supplier ratings. Each sourcing team member has a responsibility to explain his or her scoring fully and listen carefully to the ideas of others.

## ■ F.1.3 PERFORM QUANTITATIVE ASSESSMENT

### Description

Evaluate each supplier proposal to develop the quantitative assessment of the total cost of the submittal.

### Method

#### Step 1

Review each proposal for any value-added services or process changes. For example, a supplier may propose access to its online product catalogue. This would be an example of both a value-added service and a process change that would affect the total cost of that supplier's proposal.

#### Step 2

Review the total cost model to assess the financial impact of the value-added services and process changes.

## Step 3

Calculate the total price of the bid. For the initial total cost assessment, the team must create scenarios that equal 100 percent coverage of line items requested. If a particular material or service is not bid by the supplier, the team can either use the price it is paying currently for that item, or combine the present bid with that of another supplier that is offering those particular items. This will allow the team to assess a scenario that delivers all of the requested materials or services.

## Step 4

Combine the cost savings from Step 2 with the extended bid price from Step 3 to assess the total cost. Rank the suppliers relative to each other to assign a score. The supplier with the greatest savings receives a 10 and becomes the base against which each supplier is scored.

Assign a score that reflects the relative magnitude of savings. Assume Supplier A's proposal yields a savings of $2 million and Supplier B's proposal yields a savings of $1 million. Scoring should reflect the relative magnitude of the savings—for example, assign a 10 for Supplier A and a 5 for Supplier B. To calculate quantitative score relative to base, divide savings identified for the base case into savings identified for each of the other suppliers.

Table 11.4 shows a sample of quantitative scoring based on cost savings identified.

| Description | ABC Corp. Score | Excellent Supply Score | YZ Power Systems Score | USA Electric Score | Jones Mfr. Score |
|---|---|---|---|---|---|
| SAVINGS IDENTIFIED IN MILLIONS $: | 1.23 | 0.12 | 6.2 | 6.5 | 4.8 |
| $ DIFFERENCE FROM BASE (HIGHEST SAVINGS): | 5.27 | 6.38 | 0.3 | BASE | 1.7 |
| QUANTITATIVE SCORE RELATIVE TO BASE (HIGHEST SAVINGS): | 1.89 | 0.18 | 9.54 | 10.00 | 7.38 |
| RELATIVE QUANTITATIVE RANKING: | 4 | 5 | 2 | 1 | 3 |

**Table 11.4** Supplier Evaluation Matrix with Quantitative Scoring Based on Cost Savings

## TIPS

➤ Cost savings may be found throughout a supplier proposal. Therefore, it is helpful to ask team members to flag pages that should be considered by the subteam preparing the total cost analysis.

➤ Keep in mind that the total cost component of the evaluation is typically less than 50 percent of the short-list evaluation. In the final evaluation, there will be ample opportunity to develop the total cost analysis jointly with the short-listed suppliers.

➤ In both the quantitative and qualitative evaluations, the scores are reduced to a value on a scale. At SCE, teams typically used a scale of 1 through 10. While a team may choose a different rating scale, the important thing is that the scale is consistently applied on both the qualitative and quantitative evaluation.

## ■ F.1.4 CREATE THE SHORT LIST OF SUPPLIERS

### Description

Determine which suppliers should be considered for final evaluation. The short-listed suppliers are those that the team determines have the potential to be considered for final selection and recommendation.

### Method

#### Step 1

Record average qualitative score for each supplier and multiply by weighting factor assigned to qualitative elements. Repeat for quantitative elements.

## *Step 2*

Combine the weighted qualitative analysis and the weighted quantitative total cost analysis to determine the short-listed suppliers.

## *Step 3*

Select the short-listed suppliers. Generally, there is a natural break in the scoring to indicate suppliers to consider for final selection. Review the combined scores to determine where the cutoff is. Often there is a cluster of suppliers that have high scores. Conversely, teams also may consider screening out any supplier that does not reach a minimum total score.

Table 11.5 demonstrates how a break in score may occur to indicate which suppliers should be considered for the short list.

### TIPS

➤ The objective is to produce a manageable number of suppliers to further evaluate; the selection may include combinations of suppliers. There is no predetermined number of suppliers for a short list.

➤ The activities involved with screening suppliers on the short list drive costs for both the company and suppliers (e.g., site visits, refinement of bids, negotiations). Be mindful of these costs when making the final short-list determination.

➤ If you are planning to use a professional negotiator to develop the contract, invite him or her to observe during team discussions of supplier scores. This will provide valuable education for the negotiator.

## **F.2 CONDUCT THE FINAL SUPPLIER SCREENING**

### **Description**

Meet with the suppliers on the short list to obtain RFP response clarification, assess facilities, collaboratively revise

| Description | ABC Weighted Score | Excellent Supply Weighted Score | YZ Power Systems Weighted Score | USA Electric Weighted Score | Jones Mfr. Weighted Score |
|---|---|---|---|---|---|
| Apply Weighting Factors: | | | | | |
| Average Qualitative Score: | 7.38 | 3.20 | 9.03 | 5.81 | 7.42 |
| Weighted Qualitative Score— 60% Weight: | 4.43 | 1.92 | 5.42 | 3.48 | 4.45 |
| Average Quantitative Score: | 1.89 | 0.18 | 9.54 | 10.00 | 7.38 |
| Weighted Quantitative Score— 40% Weight: | 0.76 | 0.07 | 3.82 | 4.00 | 2.95 |
| COMBINED QUALITATIVE AND QUANTITATIVE SCORE: | 5.19 | 1.99 | 9.23 | 7.48 | 7.41 |
| OVERALL RANKING: | 4 | 5 | 1 | 2 | 3 |
| SHORT LIST SUPPLIERS: | | | X | X | X |

**Table 11.5** Supplier Evaluation Matrix Showing Break in Score

the total cost model analysis, and conduct in-depth interviews. Perform final screening of the suppliers based on the outcomes of these sessions.

By this stage of evaluation, the sourcing team has learned a lot about suppliers' capabilities, total cost saving ideas, and commitment to the new relationship. However, up to this point all the information has been interpreted without interaction with the supplier. This step brings the supplier into the process and is the final filter in the supplier screening process (see Figure 11.4). The outcome of this phase is the selection of the supplier(s) with whom final negotiations are held. All of the activities of the final screen are intended to provide data to support the team's judgment and decision.

## ■ F.2.1 CLARIFY SUPPLIER RESPONSES

### Description

Prepare clarification questions. It is common at this stage to ask suppliers to demonstrate their answers to the RFP questions to help the team refine its evaluation.

For example, you may need to clarify when value-added services or cost savings ideas can be implemented. Suppliers may propose to perform a service for you, but may not be completely capable of following through at the present time.

## Method

### *Step 1*

Assign team members to follow up with short-listed supplier candidates to clarify any ambiguous responses and verify questionable or unexpected information. At this point, adequate information has been submitted to allow the team to move the supplier into this stage of evaluation. The team is now requesting supplier-specific information to assist in preparation for interviews and site visits.

### *Step 2*

Conduct reference checks to determine whether there are any areas of concern that the sourcing team may want to consider in its interview or site visit.

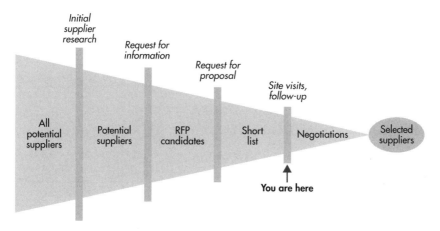

**Figure 11.4** Supplier Screening Process.

**TIP**
Timing for implementation is part of the value equation. Suppliers' innovative ideas may need to be tested with stakeholders to determine their viability as well as timing for utilization.

## ■ F.2.2 DETERMINE FINAL SELECTION CRITERIA

### Description

Determine the final selection criteria to be used to differentiate the short-listed suppliers and the process for determining which one(s) to select for recommendation to the executive steering council. The sourcing team's expectations have matured. The sourcing team can build on what has been learned during the process to develop final selection criteria. Criteria will be applied in each of the final evaluation activities: interviews, site visits, and total cost model development.

### Method

#### *Step 1*

Establish final selection criteria.

#### *Step 2*

Determine the information to be learned through the use of supplier interviews, reference checks, site visits, and total cost evaluation. The purpose is to enable a comparison among suppliers on all identified criteria. The information requirements may differ.

In this stage, teams often use a scoring mechanism to document whether the supplier demonstrates an acceptable level of understanding for each criterion. The team needs to determine how the scoring mechanisms will be used. For example, suppliers may need to maintain a certain minimum or average score during each stage of evaluation to remain on the short list.

# ■ F.2.3 CONDUCT INTERVIEWS WITH SUPPLIERS

## Description

Invite each supplier on the short list to meet with the team to present RFP responses, answer further questions, and explore innovative and cost-saving ideas.

## Method

### *Step 1*

On the basis of the final selection criteria, develop an interview scoring template. Typically, suppliers are asked to present their RFP responses in detail and to be prepared to answer questions. Additionally, they should be requested to further develop any cost-saving ideas so the team can complete the total cost model analysis. Table 11.6 shows an example of an interview template used in a sourcing team.

Teams at SCE used a 0-3-6-9 scoring range to force a higher degree of discrimination in judging suppliers' responses. Team members' individual interview scorings were aggregated to create a team averaged total score for each supplier. Suppliers that didn't achieve an average total score of 4.5 were eliminated from further consideration.

### *Step 2*

Meet with suppliers. Invite operational people from the supplier who will be involved on a day-to-day basis as well as the supplier contact who will be responsible for the account.

This step has three major areas of emphasis:

➤ To make sure the sourcing team can properly compare competing offers ("apples to apples")

➤ To test the suppliers for their ability to deliver according to their RFP responses

➤ To jointly assess the information in the cost model

This meeting serves as the first round of formal negotiations. There will be discussions regarding expectations and deliverables. The sourcing team should understand that this interview will set the stage for final negotiations.

| Supplier Name: | Date of Interview: | Team Member: | | | | |
|---|---|---|---|---|---|---|
| 1. The supplier demonstrates their understanding of the content in their RFP response. | | | 0 | 3 | 6 | 9 |
| 2. The supplier is capable of addressing the technical questions posed by the team. | | | 0 | 3 | 6 | 9 |
| 3. The supplier can articulate their understanding of an alliance. | | | 0 | 3 | 6 | 9 |
| 4. The supplier has demonstrated experience with alliances. | | | 0 | 3 | 6 | 9 |
| 5. The supplier is willing to openly address cost savings opportunities. | | | 0 | 3 | 6 | 9 |
| 6. The supplier recognizes how resource intensive alliance implementation is. | | | 0 | 3 | 6 | 9 |
| 7. The operations people are fluent in the inventory methods suggested in their proposal. | | | 0 | 3 | 6 | 9 |
| 8. The operations people demonstrate an understanding of their quality assurance procedures. | | | 0 | 3 | 6 | 9 |
| 9. The supplier has demonstrated experience in obtaining cost savings for their customers. | | | 0 | 3 | 6 | 9 |
| 10. The supplier can cite specific examples of cost reductions ($ and %) from other alliances. | | | 0 | 3 | 6 | 9 |
| 11. The supplier can demonstrate how they will provide all of the products specified in the RFP. | | | 0 | 3 | 6 | 9 |
| 12. The supplier proposes unique ideas and/or innovations. | | | 0 | 3 | 6 | 9 |
| TOTAL SCORE: | AVERAGED TOTAL SCORE: | | | | | |

**Table 11.6** Supplier Interview Template

This meeting will also test whether operational people from the supplier understand the depth of what your company is requiring and the details of the offer. Many RFP responses are prepared by the supplier's marketing department and need to be understood by people in the field who will have to deliver on the expectations and develop the desired relationships.

## ■ F.2.4 CONDUCT SITE VISITS

### Description

The purpose of the site visit is to confirm that the supplier can live up to its proposal. The outcome of the site visit is either confidence in the supplier's capabilities or the determination that the supplier should be dropped from further consideration. Any supplier that makes it through the site visit is judged to be a viable partner.

### Method

#### *Step 1*

Determine the locations to be included on the site visit and how the visit will be scored. This determination must take into account which facilities will serve you as a customer, as well as ask whether a visit to the supplier's corporate center to observe that company's research and development efforts or technology capabilities is warranted.

#### *Step 2*

Develop a site visit evaluation template. An example of a site visit assessment guide is shown on the following pages.

#### *Step 3*

Conduct site visits to the short-listed suppliers' facilities as appropriate. These visits are an essential tool in narrowing the field during the supplier selection process. A site visit allows you to:

➤ Observe the supplier's production capabilities and practices for adherence to generally accepted standards and the capability to meet the company's requirements

➤ Perform audits to ensure that all the quality criteria have been met

➤ Check for proper levels of compliance (for example, permits and licenses, certifications)

➤ Test whether the supplier's employees understand the relationship for which you are striving

---

## OFFICE PRODUCTS SUPPLIER VISIT ASSESSMENT GUIDE

Company: _____

Evaluator: _____

Date: _____          Circle one number per comment*

**Background**

| | |
|---|---|
| Has experience in working with clients in similar relationships | 0 3 6 9 |
| Has experience in being a sole or lead supplier to other customers | 0 3 6 9 |
| Has experience in working in a non-traditional role with other customers, i.e. direct shipments, supplier managed inventory, usage reports, etc. | 0 3 6 9 |
| Has experience providing other value added services such as electronic catalogs, standardization programs, easy order forms, desktop delivery, etc. | 0 3 6 9 |

Has experience in similar
geographically diverse areas                    0 3 6 9

Comments _____

_____

**Cost Management/Financial**

Has experience in creating systems
which help customers to standardize
products                                        0 3 6 9

Has experience in creating systems
which help customers to standardize
processes                                       0 3 6 9

Has significant experience in internal
continuous improvement processes and
TQM                                             0 3 6 9

Obtains significant volume leverage
with manufacturers/producers                    0 3 6 9

Obtains high percentage of products
directly from manufacturer                      0 3 6 9

Post (or keep readily available) visuals
of their own performance measures,
cost savings initiatives and process
control data                                    0 3 6 9

Can converse easily about the tools
they use in continuous improvement
programs                                        0 3 6 9

Comments _____

_____

**Quality Control/Safety**

Has a well documented QC policy and procedures
Has up to date safety records, procedures,
equipment, injury logs, etc.

Comments _____

_____

*Guide to scoring: 0 no capabilities, 3 below average, 6 above average, 9 very
high capabilities

## OFFICE PRODUCTS SUPPLIER VISIT ASSESSMENT GUIDE

**Customer Service**

Has operations people (not sales) who can
communicate/interpret customer needs      0   3   6   9

Has a sound customer service policy and
procedures, complaint handling, documenting
calls, expedition of orders      0   3   6   9
Comments _____

_____

**Sub-suppliers**

Has measurement records      0   3   6   9

Program to develop sub-suppliers      0   3   6   9
Comments _____

_____

**Operations**

Has computerized inventory tracking system,
full data requirements met      0   3   6   9

Has flexibility and in-house capabilities to
create specialized reports and system changes      0   3   6   9
Effective layout of storage, shipping and
receiving areas      0   3   6   9
Has an effective logistics infrastructure in place      0   3   6   9
Comments _____

_____

Suggestions:

Ask supplier to walk through how one item on the Edison specification (a key one) is met, ask to see how checks are made at all steps of the process that could impact whether the specification is met. Ask to see examples of documentation, schedules, QC records, and any piece of paper that is mentioned during the discussions.

Ask supplier to discuss their "superior logistics efforts", how scheduling is planned, delivery schedules, delivery personnel and tracking systems. Ask for real examples, i.e. routing sheets, delivery/time reports. Observe the condition and organization of the facilities and equipment.

Ask supplier to describe ad hoc how they may envision teaming/partnering with other suppliers to take a lead role in supplying the full complement of products.

*Guide to scoring: 0 no capabilities, 3 below average, 6 above average, 9 very high capabilities

*(Source: SCE Office Products Team)*

➤ Validate commitment to continuous improvement

➤ See the problem-solving capability of the supplier

➤ Observe employee competence, involvement, and morale

➤ Validate whether operational competence supports the supplier's RFP response

➤ Test emergency response capability

➤ Test for evidence of quality principles and practices

➤ Validate accuracy and completeness of paperwork and documentation

➤ Test compatibility of information systems

➤ Investigate general issues regarding the supplier's methodology, philosophy, and corporate culture

The site visit is also a time to meet key participants in preparation for the long-term relationship that will result from successful negotiation and contracting. The opportunity to set the tone for this relationship is advantageous to both parties. Some of the departments a sourcing team may wish to visit include:

➤ Billing/accounts receivable

➤ Customer service

➤ Manufacturing

➤ Pricing/sales and marketing

➤ Quality control

➤ Order processing

➤ Materials shipping and handling

If a service is under evaluation, it is helpful to call and/or visit the supplier's customers to check the quality of the work being performed.

 **TIPS**

➤ Caution: the larger the supplier organization, the greater the likelihood of communication breakdowns between those who write the proposal and those who must implement it.

➤ If a site visit demonstrates that the supplier does not have the capabilities to perform as proposed, this is sufficient basis for eliminating the supplier from consideration.

➤ Talk to and listen to everyone. Many new insights come from informal conversations.

➤ Sourcing teams may be diverted from their purpose by the prospect of making site visits. The team needs to make a determination of the expected benefits of the site visits. Using a site visit evaluation template is recommended to keep the team focused.

➤ The site visit team may be the entire team or a subteam that represents critical expertise. The membership of the site visit team must remain constant for all of the supplier evaluations.

## ■ F.2.5 DETERMINE THE TOTAL COST OF THE SUPPLIER PROPOSAL

**Description**

Work with the supplier to determine the total cost impact of the supplier's proposal. The purpose of this activity is to clarify and explore the supplier's specific proposals and refine the estimate of cost savings.

## Method

### *Step 1*

Review with the supplier the cost model, process maps, and calculations used in determining the estimated financial impacts of the proposal.

Up to this point, the savings calculations have been made by the sourcing team based on its interpretation of the supplier's ideas. Using the supplier input, make adjustments to the financial impact calculations.

### *Step 2*

Create a new cost model that reflects the supplier's proposals. Calculate the timing of the savings based on a proposed implementation schedule and the feasibility of the cost-saving ideas. This cost model is the basis from which contractual commitments may be made, so it is important to schedule adequate discussion time with the suppliers. Table 11.7 is a completed cost model sample.

The team has refined the quantitative and qualitative supplier evaluation that took place in Phases F.1 and F.2. Drawing on all the evaluation performed to date, the team is prepared to make a final selection.

### TIP
➤ A technique that has proven effective in comparing suppliers is to prepare a scenario that matches how your company does business for the targeted material or service. Ask each short-listed supplier to explain how its offer would be priced, delivered, and invoiced under these prescribed conditions. A sensitivity analysis can be run by asking how the supplier's price and service would change with changes to key parameters like quantity and timing.

| | Current Totals | Total Savings | Bid Options—Cost Driver |
|---|---|---|---|
| **Cost of Material** | $13,245,500 | $397,365 | 3% due to volume of contract |
| **Activity costs** | | | |
| Accounts receivable | $1,867 | $433 | Reduced number of invoices |
| Approval | $11,375 | 0 | Not affectable |
| Bid evaluation | $37,022 | $27,766 | 5-year PO |
| Receipting online | $93,631 | $47,520 | Deliver to job site |
| Receive and put away | $30,694 | $15,347 | Included in pricing |
| Rework | $14,100 | $14,100 | Guaranteed by supplier |
| Return to district yard | $8,350 | $8,350 | Backhaul included |
| Requisition | $159,036 | $79,518 | Online requisitioning |
| Request for proposal management | $33,511 | $23,870 | 5-year PO on 90% of line items |
| Update real-time system | $256,174 | $207,300 | Alliance |
| Specification development | $44,941 | $21,277 | On-site engineering assistance |
| Spec revised/material coding | $20,516 | $16,412 | 5-year PO |
| Surplus | $14,829 | $8,173 | Forecast assistance |
| ACTIVITY SUBTOTAL | $726,046 | $470,066 | |
| Vehicle expenses | $2,201,344 | $1,150,000 | Use supplier fleet for 50% of deliveries |
| Inventory carrying costs | $1,080,554 | $864,443 | Reduced inventory |
| Inbound freight | $308,112 | $308,112 | Freight on board (FOB) delivered |
| Salvage recovery credit | ($1,500,000) | 0 | |
| TOTAL | $16,061,556 | $3,189,986 | Total committed savings by supplier |

**Table 11.7** Completed Cost Model (Fictitious Data)

# ⬛ MAKE THE FINAL SELECTION

## Description

Choose the supplier or network of suppliers that offers the best total value proposal to move into negotiation. Pending successful negotiations, the supplier(s) will be recommended to the executive steering council for selection.

This is very different from traditional procurement because the sourcing team may ultimately choose a supplier that has higher pricing than other suppliers, but that offers the best overall value and total cost savings.

## Method

### *Step 1*

Determine which suppliers best meet the company's needs based on the results of the interview, site visits, and total cost analysis. The team will make a determination of each supplier's alliance potential expressed as a capability for joint value creation, innovation, and business value alignment. This decision must also factor in the risk assessment and implementation issues. Any supplier that reaches this point is acceptable to the team. Therefore, in the final selection the team is making a judgment of overall value.

### TIP
➤ Given the complexity of the decision and the amount of information to be considered, it is recommended that a facilitated session be held to determine the selected supplier based on all information the team members have learned to date. This final decision is sometimes self-evident to the team because a single supplier may stand apart from the rest and be judged the best business partner.

### *Step 2*

Create a comparison of short-list suppliers' proposals. Include only those suppliers that were advanced through Step 1.

Figure 11.5 is an example of how the final short-list suppliers compared in the quantitative analysis. Figures 11.5 and 11.6 are samples of the type of information included in the recommendation packages to demonstrate the cost savings of var-

| | SCE Current Suppliers Edison Spec Current Costs 3-Year Contract | **A** Supplier A and B ANSI Spec Proposed Costs 3-Year Contract | **B** Supplier A and C ANSI Spec Proposed Costs 3-Year Contract | **C** Supplier A and C SYP Proposed Costs 3-Year Contract |
|---|---|---|---|---|
| Total Cost | $12,240,000 | $10,920,000 | $9,100,000 | $11,900,000 |
| Projected Spending | $9,670,000 | | | |
| Savings over 3-Year Contract Period | | $1,320,000 | $3,140,000 | $1,340,000 |
| % Savings over Contract Period | | 14% | 32% | 14% |
| One-Time Savings | | $240,000 | $240,000 | $240,000 |
| Ongoing Annual Savings | | 11% | 30% | 11% |

**Figure 11.5** Summary of Alternatives. *(Source: SCE training template)*

ious alternatives proposed by short-listed suppliers. Figure 11.6 is an example of how the savings would be captured over the first three years of the contract.

## Step 3

Identify successful suppliers. Meet with the suppliers before making the final presentation to the executive steering council. The purpose of this meeting is to continue to define the elements of the strategy and cost savings and to confirm the cost model and its implications. The suppliers help the team focus on greatest savings opportunities and specific implementation strategies.

## Step 4

When crafting your recommendation, anticipate concerns and document options that were considered. Address risk assessment and implementation issues and incorporate that information into the overall best value scenarios.

## TIPS

➤ At SCE, final supplier selection was a consensus decision. It is important that every team member support the recommendation.

| SCE Current Suppliers Edison Spec | **A** Supplier A and B | **B** Supplier A and C | **C** Supplier A and C SYP |
|---|---|---|---|
| Current Costs 3-Year Contract | Proposed Costs 3-Year Contract | Proposed Costs 3-Year Contract | Proposed Costs 3-Year Contract |
| Contract Year 1 | $600,000 | $1,210,000 | $610,000 |
| YEAR REALIZED — Contract Year 2 | $360,000 | $970,000 | $370,000 |
| Contract Year 3 | $360,000 | $970,000 | $370,000 |
| TOTAL SAVINGS OVER THREE YEARS | $1,320,000 | $3,140,000 | $1,340,000 |

**Figure 11.6** Savings by Year. *(Source: SCE training template)*

➤ Hold the team members individually and collectively accountable for the selection decision.

➤ To this point there have been three discrete phases of supplier screening. The selection criteria will change as the process advances. The sourcing team has the responsibility of documenting criteria at each phase and applying them consistently among all suppliers.

Additionally, it is recommended that the team keep a record of the suppliers removed from consideration in each phase, and the basis for the decision.

## F.4 PRESENT THE RECOMMENDATION FOR APPROVAL

### Description

Present to management the team's sourcing strategy and recommended supplier(s), and receive approval for the recommendation.

### Method

### *Step 1*

Develop a presentation of the team's recommendation to the executive steering council. A standard presentation format for all sourcing teams assists the council by providing consistency.

A standardized format may contain the following elements:

➤ Background
  —Team composition
  —Scope and external spending
➤ Analysis
  —Total cost (internal and external)
  —Sourcing strategy
➤ Recommendation
  —Recommended supplier(s)
  —Option scenarios
  —Supplier evaluation criteria
  —Savings analysis: hard versus soft (by year)
  —Performance indicators
➤ Next steps
  —Continuous improvement opportunities
  —Changes required of internal stakeholders
  —Suggested implementation team members

### TIPS

➤ The program management team should take responsibility for developing a presentation template, taking into account the level of detail that the executive steering council will need to make its decision.

➤ Even though there have been many milestone check-in points with the executive steering council, each team member should take responsibility to inform his or her executive steering council representative prior to the final presentation.

➤ Be conversant in areas that are not being recommended. The executive steering council will ask questions regarding other alternatives to ensure that the team has considered competing possibilities.

➤ A message to the executive steering council—speak now or forever hold your peace. Peers and employees will hold you accountable for acting on the decision. This is the ultimate test of your commitment.

## F.5 ANNOUNCE FINAL NEGOTIATIONS

### Description

Communicate which supplier(s) were selected for final negotiations.

### Method

#### *Step 1*

Once the program management team and executive steering council have approved the recommendation, the team needs to notify non-selected suppliers.

In early communications during this phase, it is important to emphasize that "selection" at this stage means that the selected supplier or suppliers have been chosen to proceed with final negotiations, not that the contract award has been completed.

#### *Step 2*

Send a communication package to those suppliers not selected, explaining that they were not chosen for the final round of negotiations. This communication should state that if negotiations with the other supplier(s) are not successful, the nonselected suppliers might be reconsidered.

Be sensitive to the tone of the communication. Experience has shown that nonselected suppliers can misinterpret this to mean that they still have an opportunity to secure the business for themselves, and they often go into active selling mode. It is important to stress that the team is confident that the negotiations will proceed as expected and that the selected supplier(s) will be awarded the contract.

### TIPS

➤ Suppliers should be notified as to their selection status as soon as is practical. Often it is difficult to keep selection status confidential. You don't want word to get out before you have had the chance to notify unsuccessful suppliers.

➤ Strategic Sourcing is designed as a learning process. Therefore, it is recommended that a debriefing session be offered to nonselected suppliers to allow them to receive and give feedback. Offer to conduct these sessions after final negotiations are completed and supplier selection is announced.

## F.6 CONDUCT FINAL NEGOTIATIONS

### Description

Conduct final negotiation meetings with the selected supplier(s) to create a contract that will formalize the commitments made in the recommendation to the executive steering council.

This is the beginning of a relationship. It is very important to conduct negotiations in a manner that is consistent with the values and principles of an alliance.

### Method

#### Step 1

Review and document all commitments and discussions with the supplier throughout the Strategic Sourcing process. These points need to be included in your final negotiation goals (i.e., minimum performance levels for cost, quality, and service).

### *Step 2*

Develop a detailed list of items that need further clarification in final negotiations.

### *Step 3*

Jointly prepare an agenda for the final negotiation meeting to complete the contract with the selected supplier(s). The agenda should include the following topics:

- ➤ Outstanding issues
- ➤ Review of the implementation process
- ➤ Outline of the next steps

### *Step 4*

Conduct the final negotiation meeting. Typically, this involves finalizing details such as the scope of the contract, timing, terms and conditions, charges for value-added services, initial performance measures, and continuous improvement activities.

During the actual negotiation meeting, the recorder needs to display agreements on a flip chart as each issue is agreed upon. Recording provides visibility for the many issues to be negotiated and traded off.

Summarize at the end of the meeting so that final conclusions can be documented. Arrange for each person to leave with a list of agreements. Most of the negotiation with the supplier(s) has already occurred during the process. The final negotiation meeting basically wraps up the negotiations and ensures that the contract constitutes a win-win situation for both parties.

### *Step 5*

Prepare and sign a contract.

➤ The more sourcing team direct experience that is brought to bear in negotiations on both sides, the greater the likelihood of win-win outcomes.

➤ Think forward to implementation. Involving implementers in contract development is important because they are the ones who need to deliver on the commitments being made. This builds a sense of personal accountability. Encourage suppliers to bring implementers to the table.

➤ Now that there is a true handoff from the sourcing team to the implementation team, it is a good time to celebrate the sourcing team's success. At SCE, celebrations took many inventive forms and were highly participative. Executives and managers throughout the company took team members to dinners and exchanged fun mementos to commemorate their time spent together.

## F.7 COMMUNICATE THE SELECTION

### Description

Communicate the supplier selection to all stakeholders.

➤ Notify suppliers whose contracts will be terminated.

➤ Notify users of the material or service of the new suppliers, and of any product or specification changes.

➤ Notify anyone involved in the supply chain who will be impacted by process changes.

### Method

The sequence of communication that should take place includes:

1. Notification to suppliers
   - Unsuccessful suppliers
   - Terminated suppliers

2. Presentation to company employees
   —Users of material or service
   —Supply chain
3. General announcement
   —Company-internal
   —Public

**TIP**

Recognize that it will take time to define the details of implementation. When notifying existing suppliers whose contracts will be terminated, establish a termination date that allows time to transition to the new suppliers.

The supplier has been selected and a formal contract has been signed. During this phase, suppliers first became active participants in the Strategic Sourcing process. Short-list suppliers collaborated with the sourcing team to complete the final in-depth evaluation of their proposals. With the successful suppliers identified, from this point forward in the Strategic Sourcing process, suppliers will be full participants. The model for working together introduced in the implementation team launch will become the norm for the company-supplier relationship into the future.

# Chapter 12

# Implementation

Preparation and
Design Phases

Team Activity
Phases

Up to this point, most of the work has been preparatory—developing strategies, analyzing proposals, making recommendations, and selecting a supplier. It is at this point that recommendations are converted into action. Specific actions have been identified by the sourcing team, and the implementation phase (see Figure 12.1) brings the team's work to fruition. Taking immediate action on recommendations serves to demonstrate commitment to the strategy selected by the sourcing team and sends the message that change is here.

*Activity in this module:*
*Select the implementation team, develop the relationship agreement, conduct the implementation, develop the workshop implementation plan, develop the project management plan, develop performance measures*

The implementation process is intended to lay the foundation and serve as a road map for creating an alliance. Simply using the term *alliance* does not change the relationships and attitudes that have existed over years. Therefore, it is critical to spend time engaging the implementation team in a structured process. The implementation phase is also designed to assist in the initial transition to the selected supplier and phase out the current supplier, if the two are different. The process is designed as a series of events that over time introduce changes and build collaborative behaviors. Additionally, it teaches the

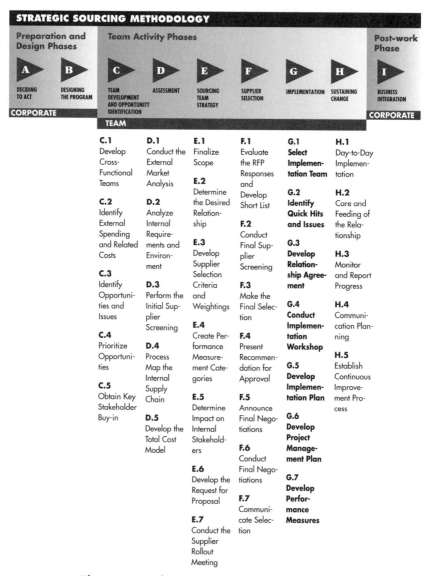

**Figure 12.1** Phase Map—Team Activity Phases.

cross-functional customer-supplier team how to enhance those relationships into the future.

The ultimate goal of an alliance is to create a relationship between a supplier and the company that sustains high-level supplier performance as measured by established targets and fosters continuous improvement to achieve tangible, positive results for both companies.

## PURPOSE

The objective of the implementation phase is to transform projected savings into real savings by establishing the new supplier relationship(s) and managing the changes. The team will develop an implementation strategy and specific action plans.

## DELIVERABLES

By performing the steps within the implementation phase, the implementation team will develop the following work products:

➤ Communication plan for stakeholders describing the new supplier agreement

➤ Termination of existing supplier agreements

➤ Implementation workshop with the company and supplier implementors

➤ Plan for implementing the sourcing strategy

➤ Formal relationship agreement

➤ Jointly developed company/supplier performance measures

## TRAINING

Plan and implement the following training workshops for implementation team members when appropriate during this phase:

➤ Team development—see Phase C

➤ Designing performance measures

In a typical purchasing model, once the agreement is negotiated and signed, future activities would be governed by the contract. Because of the dynamic nature of sourcing relationships, additional dialogue is necessary to develop a plan of action for implementation. As a result, a transition period is required. This transition period is unique to Strategic Sourcing. Phases G.1, G.2, and G.3 are the transition work.

## G.1 SELECT THE IMPLEMENTATION TEAM

### Description

Establish an implementation team. This is a critical component for the success of the relationship.

The implementors become the "face" of the relationship, guiding it, making key decisions, and ultimately being responsible for its success. This team expands the definition of *cross-functional* to include representatives from the affected line organization(s), the supply management organization, and the supplier organization.

The company and the supplier should strive to select implementors who are technically competent and respected within their organizations. Additionally, it is desirable to have implementors who are strong communicators, responsive to new ideas, and in tune with the need to develop the relationship to achieve its goals and objectives. The sourcing team becomes the foundation for the implementation team. Team composition should be tailored to the operational requirements for the materials or services being provided. The work of the implementation team includes relationship building, development of joint objectives, design and implementation of performance measures, communication, and, ultimately, implementation of the program.

## Method

### *Step 1*

Form the company's team of implementors. Review the existing sourcing team to determine whether you have the appropriate team makeup. The implementation team should include at least one member from the original sourcing team. This is important because it provides the implementation team with continuity from the selection process and will aid that team in understanding why the selection was made the way it was. Implementation team members who were not on the original team often have questions about the evaluation process and wish to pursue areas that may have already been researched and documented. Having original team members involved allows new members to gain the benefit of the original members' experience.

### *Step 2*

Identify team sponsors from key operational areas within the company. The implementation team may recommend sponsors.

Roles for sponsors include:

➤ Removing implementation roadblocks

➤ Driving change and dealing with resistance

➤ Monitoring savings progress, performance measures, and continuous improvement

➤ Serving as liaisons to the executive steering council to report progress and accomplishments

### *Step 3*

Obtain a list of implementation team members from the suppliers, along with a list of identified sponsors within their organizations.

## Step 4

Establish time commitments from both the company and supplier team members. For example, are they expected to commit one day a week for the first six months? It is important that the time commitment be discussed and communicated to implementors.

## Step 5

Conduct Strategic Sourcing training for new team members. Review the training needs for implementation team members. New members should take the initial workshops provided for sourcing team members, covering the following topics:

- ➤ Charter development
- ➤ Team skills
- ➤ Effective meetings
- ➤ Consensus building
- ➤ Effective communication
- ➤ Continuous improvement techniques

## Step 6

Conduct a transition meeting between the sourcing team and the new implementation team (although several sourcing team members may continue into the implementation phase).

This meeting excludes the new supplier(s). Its purpose is to transfer knowledge gained through the sourcing process to new team members and address potential roadblocks. Transition items include:

➤ Overview of the sourcing team's findings

➤ Overview of the total cost model to gain an understanding of expected cost savings and the process improvement opportunities within the supply chain

➤ Overview of the rationale for supply strategy and selected supplier(s)

➤ Specifics of recommendations and vision for the future

➤ High-level recommendations for an implementation plan

### *Step 7*

Establish an alliance steering committee, if appropriate. An alliance steering committee consists of senior management from both the company and the supplier. This committee provides for continuing contact among top leaders to discuss broad goals or changes in each company. The importance of the material or service makes it critical that the top executives be supportive and involved. If you are forming an alliance with your supplier, a greater degree of integration is required because of the high value and complexity of the material or service.

The frequency with which the alliance steering committee meets evolves over time. During initial stages of the alliance, it is important that these meetings be held on a regular basis. This should occur at least until the alliance is well under way and both companies have learned to work well together operationally.

**TIP**
Organizations are often aligned by function. It is inevitable that a cross-functional implementation team will not align naturally. This will create tension for team members. The cross-functional executive council will help to bridge the gap between team structure and organizational structure.

## G.2 IDENTIFY QUICK HITS AND ISSUES

### Description

Identify a comprehensive list of quick hit opportunities and issues that will need to be resolved during the implementation phase.

This comprehensive list of issues forms the basis for continuous improvement, the task list for the implementation team, and the road map for project completion.

## Method

### *Step 1*

Review the presentation given to the executive steering council and identify issues the council may have raised for implementation.

### *Step 2*

Identify all current purchase orders with those suppliers being phased out. Review documentation regarding cancellation charges and other penalties and transition issues.

### *Step 3*

List quick hit opportunities identified through the sourcing process. This list should include those immediate changes that can be implemented to reduce total costs and demonstrate the new sources of value derived from the relationship.

 **TIP**
At SCE, the transition plan was called the 30-day hit list (see Figure 12.2). It served to jump-start action and act as a tool to bring the company's implementors together.

## G.3 DEVELOP THE RELATIONSHIP AGREEMENT

## Description

Finalize the relationship agreement. This agreement contains the guiding principles and commitment to a collaborative working relationship between companies (see Figure 12.3). It is signed by the responsible executives.

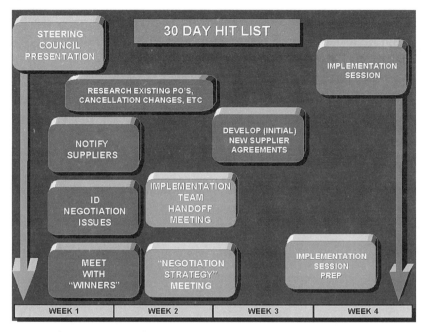

**Figure 12.2** 30-day Hit List. *(Source: SCE Training Template)*

## Method

### *Step 1*

Develop the relationship agreement with the supplier(s). This document contains the agreement about the relationship and details how the company and the supplier(s) will work together. The relationship agreement complements the contract and describes the spirit and intent of the relationship.

The relationship agreement addresses various aspects of the relationship between the company and the supplier. It usually contains the following elements:

➤ Mission statement
➤ Statement of commitment
➤ Expectations

Whereas, Through Edison's Strategic Sourcing efforts the undersigned contractors have been selected to provide line clearing services to Edison for a period of three years, and longer if the contracting parties agree;

Whereas, The purchase order documents contain the essence of the agreements, this document sets forth the spirit in which our companies and the implementors (Green Team) will strive to conduct our new relationship, which will include establishing and maintaining a Managed Business Relationship (MBR) that fosters open communications, sharing of information, cost reductions, and continuous improvement in such areas as customer relations, tree listings, tree trimming and/or replacement, emergency response, administrative processes, green waste, and the development and utilization of women, minority and disabled veteran owned business enterprises (WMDVBEs) subcontractors;

Whereas, The Green Team will identify areas of opportunity and mutual benefit, obtain and analyze cost information, develop recommendations, and implement improvements, which will result in more efficient operations, improved profitability for our respective shareholders and/or customers, and contribute to the communities we serve;

Resolved, That to achieve the MBR benefits described above, we the undersigned hereby acknowledge our commitment to the Green Team and the spirit of this agreement on this _____ day of _____, Nineteen Hundred and Ninety Five.

| | | |
|---|---|---|
| Dave Stall | Jim Lewandowski | Rhonda Mowbray |
| Vice President | President | General Manager |
| Asplundh Tree Expert Company | Tip Top Arborists | Mowbray's Tree Service |

| | | |
|---|---|---|
| Larry Abernathy | Dennis Eastman | Emiko Banfield |
| Vice President | Division Vice President, EDBL | Manager of PAMM |
| Davey Tree Surgery Company, Ltd. | Southern California Edison Company | Southern California Edison Company |

**Figure 12.3** Managed Business Relationship Resolution.
*(Source: Vegetation Management Team)*

➤ Goals and mutual objectives
➤ Performance indicators

### Step 2

Conduct a formal signing ceremony with executives from both companies. The agreement serves to symbolize commitment to the new relationship. The ceremony brings together senior management from the supplier and the company, along with the implementation and sourcing teams. It also marks the closure of the sourcing team's activities and the start of the implementors' activities.

## G.4 CONDUCT THE IMPLEMENTATION WORKSHOP

### Description

Conduct an implementation workshop with the supplier(s). By conducting this session with the implementors from both companies, the joint team will lay the foundation for the new relationship.

Objectives of the workshop include:

➤ Jump-starting the implementation process

➤ Achieving a common understanding of the alliance and the team's role in this relationship

➤ Developing mechanisms for solving problems, resolving conflicts, and implementing continuous improvement

➤ Developing reciprocal performance measures

➤ Developing a comprehensive road map for achieving the savings identified by the sourcing team

➤ Choosing team leader(s)

An example of the three-day agenda for SCE's Office Products Implementation Workshop is shown on the following pages.

## G.5 DEVELOP THE IMPLEMENTATION PLAN

### Description

Determine the scope and timing of implementation and prepare the formal change plan.

Adoption of the plan represents agreement between the company and the supplier(s), as well as management's support for the upcoming tasks. Necessary resources for both the company and the supplier(s) are identified as part of the plan. The purpose of a formal implementation plan is to develop commitment to and alignment regarding the specific course of action.

## OFFICE PRODUCTS IMPLEMENTATION TEAM AGENDA OCTOBER 5, 1995

KICK-OFF (Launching of company-to-company partnership).

Purpose is to celebrate the signing of the Relationship Agreement.

Dinner

Who: Invite executive leadership from all companies and all implementation team members; key stakeholders may also be invited.

What: Formal signing ceremony for Relationship Agreement; celebration.

DAY ONE

➤ Continental Breakfast

➤ Welcome and Introductions (Susanne Wagner)

Set the tone for collaboration. It is important that the "people-to-people" connection be emphasized. Team members introduce themselves—their role in their company, number of years with the company, prior experience with sourcing, tell a story about a successful team experience (what they enjoyed, what was accomplished). The agenda is built around interactive discussion and facilitated group work.

➤ Team Orientation

—What "Sourcing" means to Edison (Gary Myers)
An overview outlining why SCE chose to do this and what it hopes to accomplish through the initiative. Review of teams launched to date. What has been learned.

➤ Office Products Team History
A review of the work of the sourcing team.

➤ Rigor of the Sourcing Process (Jim Shivertaker)
Presentation of cost model emphasizing the rigor of the process.

Break

➤ Report Card (Debbie Avila)

Review of preliminary work on performance measures.

➤ Introduction of Suppliers

—Xerox (Scott Minshall)
—Office Depot (Andy Wolf)

Each person from the supplier team will share their views on their company, what they do well, the operating culture, prior experience with partnerships with other companies, and any issues with the current contract.

➤ Open Issues (Debbie Avila)

Questions from the sourcing team which need to be addressed; additional items are added by the implementation team. These issues tend to be operational and are resolved during the workshop. Revisit 30-day hit list.

Lunch

➤ Forms and Printing

This is a subset of Office Products.
—Champion Kickoff—Statement of expectations
—Work Done to Date (Debbie Avila)—Review of the sourcing team's work
—Implementation Overview—Statement of scope
—Adjourn

Dinner

➤ Continue relationship building and planning for implementation

DAY TWO

➤ Implementation Planning—See Charter Development, Phase C.

➤ Implementation Team Ground Rules and Mission Statement

➤ Road Map Development

DAY THREE

➤ Communication Plan Development—Identify stakeholders and potential issues.

➤ Performance Measures—Determine availability of baseline data. Refer to sourcing team input.

➤ Lunch

➤ Discussion on Remaining Open Issues

➤ Review Commitments/Evaluation

Adjourn

*(Source: Office Products Team)*

## Method

### *Step 1*

Make a list of tasks that need to be accomplished in order to implement the strategy. These tasks will include the required changes in processes, products, and suppliers. Examples include:

➤ **Supplier cutovers**—changing from existing suppliers to new suppliers.

➤ **Product cutovers**—changing from existing products to new products.

➤ **Inventory transitions**—reducing existing inventories to lower levels or, in some cases, to zero, or having suppliers agree to minimum stocking levels.

➤ **Specification changes**—changing internal specification documents and procedures, such as new product testing and training related to specification changes.

➤ **New process design**—designing and installing the specific new processes. Examples might include electronic ordering, job site delivery, or electronic funds transfer.

### *Step 2*

Develop specific action plans to achieve changes and to monitor progress, including:

➤ A list of operational changes that identifies each person's responsibilities and the completion dates necessary to make the project successful

➤ A detailed implementation plan for achieving operational changes

➤ A plan for communication to all stakeholders that ensures awareness and buy-in to changes

➤ A review process and monitoring tools

➤ A road map to guide implementation

# G.6 DEVELOP THE PROJECT MANAGEMENT PLAN

## Description

Complete a project management chart that defines all tasks and identified barriers. Identify targeted beginning dates, completion dates, and assigned responsibility, leading to the successful implementation of the Strategic Sourcing changes.

## Method

### Step 1

Develop a specific plan that details key actions required for the successful implementation and institutionalization of the Strategic Sourcing changes.

➤ In this phase, the implementation plan is expanded into a set of specific actions that are assigned to responsible individuals. Completion of these actions is key to achieving the identified goals and cost savings.

### Step 2

Create a project management chart that details these tasks. Include identified responsible parties and time frames with expected start and completion dates.

➤ Establish milestones for each action and management checkpoint. Check the plan against the high-level implementation plan to ensure that those timelines will be met.

➤ If discrepancies are found in timing, accelerate specific actions or readjust the implementation plan.

### Step 3

Establish a schedule for the specific actions and milestones for which each person has responsibility, and, on a regular basis, take action to ensure that the implementation plan is staying on schedule.

Make sure each person periodically reports the outcome of these actions to the implementation team to ensure the coordination and accomplishment of timelines. Immediately raise and deal with issues and barriers encountered during implementation.

### *Step 4*

Keep a list of tasks requiring completion by both the company and the supplier, along with due dates. Communicate this list to the program management team.

➤ Action plans are living documents. Continuously update the plan as implementation progresses. Actions may be added or deleted and timing may change.

### TIPS

➤ Effective implementation planning must be flexible. An overaggressive and inflexible plan can result in costly failures.

➤ Assume that nothing will happen unless it's written on the task list and followed up regularly.

➤ The list of changes required of internal stakeholders should be maintained during the implementation phase. Make sure that specified activities and tasks are identified in the implementation plan. Visibility will facilitate required changes.

➤ Be vigilant in monitoring the progress of the implementation effort. Slip-ups or problems will inevitably occur, especially during the early stages of implementation. Regular monitoring will minimize the effect.

## G.7 DEVELOP PERFORMANCE MEASURES

### Description

Identify performance measures for cost, quality, and service.

### Method

#### *Step 1*

Review performance measure categories prepared by the sourcing team in Phase E.4. Review the contract, relationship agreement, and cost model to specifically identify objectives and priorities.

#### *Step 2*

Develop performance measures that link to the business objectives and drive the right behaviors.

Test performance measures against the six criteria for effective measures:

➤ **Validity**—Does the measure track the true customer requirements or real productivity?

➤ **Coverage**—Does the measure (or group of measures) track all relevant factors?

➤ **Comparability**—Can the measure be compared across time or in different locations?

➤ **Usefulness**—Does the measure guide action?

➤ **Compatibility**—Is the measure compatible with existing data and information available?

➤ **Cost effectiveness**—What are the trade-offs between the cost of measurement and the potential benefits to be gained?

### Step 3

Select and agree to performance measures for both the company and the supplier.

In a typical relationship, the company measures the supplier's performance. In Strategic Sourcing, performance measurement is a two-way street. To achieve the level of cooperation and ownership of results needed, the company must understand its part of the performance bargain and establish measurable targets for its performance. Monitoring and reporting company performance is fundamental to collaboration.

### Step 4

Identify how and by whom data will be collected. Define how and when performance data are reported.

Considerations that may affect your ability to immediately implement measures include:

| Area | Cost | Quality | Service |
|---|---|---|---|
| Overall | ➤ Total cost per employee | ➤ Customer satisfaction rating | ➤ Customer satisfaction rating |
| Office supplies | ➤ Same (cost per employee) | ➤ >10% per quantity from baseline for 1st year<br>➤ Error rate<br> —Invoicing<br> —Products<br> —Ordering | ➤ % On-time delivery<br>99.8% next day<br>➤ % Order completeness<br>98.6% fill rate |
| Printing | ➤ Cost per employee (internal printing)<br>➤ Cost per customer (external printing) | ➤ 1% error rate | ➤ Forms and printing: Same as for supplies |
| Copiers/ documents | ➤ Cost per copy | | ➤ % Uptime<br>95% uptime |

**Table 12.1** Sample Performance Measures

➤ Availability of data

➤ Lack of baseline information

➤ Inadequacies of systems

A sample of performance measures for the Office Products Team is shown in Table 12.1.

**TIP**

Don't let limitations become an excuse for not measuring performance. Put in place whatever measures are practical and plan to develop the capabilities needed to support your optimal metrics.

The transition from sourcing team to implementation team is now complete. The implementation team, composed of members from the company and the supplier, has been established. The implementation team now has the responsibility to make the changes that will optimize value in the supply chain.

# Chapter 13

# Sustaining Change

A  B  C  D  E  F  G  H

The implementation team has a plan in place and is prepared to begin work. At this point, the company needs to put in place an infrastructure, processes, and systems to support the teams in their task of managing organizational change (see Figure 13.1).

---

*Activity in this module:*
*Proceed with day-to-day implementation and care and feeding of relationship; monitor and report progress, communication planning, and continuous improvement*

---

There needs to be clear assignment of responsibility for day-to-day management of team activities and specific attention to building the relationship between company and supplier. The team will develop formal mechanisms for monitoring and reporting progress and ongoing communication. A key element of this infrastructure is a formal process for continuous improvement.

At some point there will be a shift in the relationship from achieving initial implementation results to a focus on

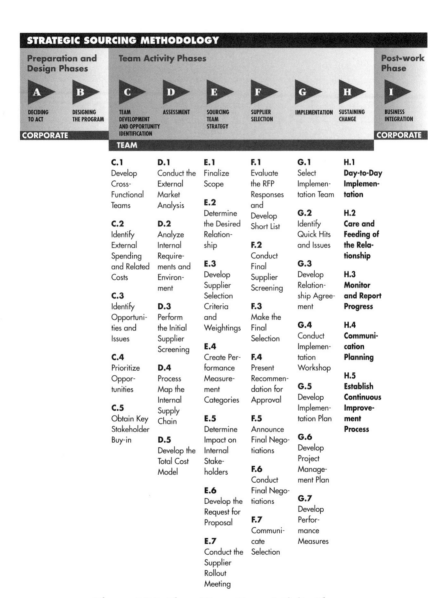

**Figure 13.1** Phase Map—Team Activity Phases.

continuous improvement. This transition occurs between 6 and 12 months into the relationship, and when it does the team is likely to lose momentum. A way to reenergize the team is to focus it on developing continuous improvement initiatives.

A word of caution: The first commitment of the team is to establish the level of performance proposed by the supplier in the contract and to assure that basic targets are being met. Don't let teams get distracted by continuous improvement pursuits to the detriment of existing performance commitments.

The intent of an alliance is to foster a long-term relationship that delivers total cost savings and contributes to operational excellence. Therefore, it is essential to create an environment, processes, and mechanisms within the relationship to enable continuous improvement initiatives. Prerequisites for valuing continuous improvement are baseline performance data and tools for monitoring progress.

In the course of undertaking improvement efforts, something important occurs. The relationship between the company and its suppliers evolves into one that is aligned toward common goals—achieving cost reduction and operational excellence through integrating business processes and strategies. If optimum results are to be achieved, improvement efforts must be a joint program between the company and the supplier.

### PURPOSE

➤ In this phase, structures and systems are put in place that will support implementation teams as they pursue making changes.

➤ The company will establish structures and systems that will encourage and enable ongoing relationship building and progress toward goals.

➤ Also, the implementation team will build the capabilities to constantly create new value and manage the focus of continuous improvement to yield the highest mutual benefit.

**DELIVERABLES**
By performing the steps within the sustaining change phase, the implementation team will develop the following work products:

➤ An infrastructure appropriate for the strategy
➤ Formal structures for supporting team progress
➤ A performance tracking and reporting system
➤ A plan for ongoing communication

**TRAINING**
Plan and implement the following training workshops for implementation team members when appropriate during this phase:

➤ Continuous improvement process and tools
➤ Refresher training on strategic sourcing skills and tools

## H.1 DAY-TO-DAY IMPLEMENTATION

### Description

Establish responsibility for day-to-day management of implementation activities.

Follow-up and attention to detail are key to successful implementation. Planning and project management will enable progress, but the responsibility for keeping the actions moving falls to the implementation team.

### Method

#### Step 1

Assign specific responsibility for overall management of implementation plan activities. This role typically is performed by the team leader, but may be performed by another team member.

This responsibility includes convening team meetings on a regular and ad hoc basis, enlisting management help for the team when needed, keeping the team sponsor informed, and monitoring progress against the project management plan.

## *Step 2*

Identify the official "single point of contact" representative for the company and the supplier. Establishing identified point responsibility will help break through bureaucratic road-blocks and expedite day-to-day decision making. The relationship between company and supplier will be built at many levels. However, those on the implementation team must have clear authority and accountability to speak for their company. This will facilitate the development of personal relationships and trust building.

## *Step 3*

Establish a structured approach for early problem resolution.

When problems arise, deal with them immediately. Search for the root cause, and communicate the cause and the proposed solution to those involved as soon as possible. Immediate response and communication can head off damaging speculation and rumors that undermine the health of the alliance.

# H.2 CARE AND FEEDING OF THE RELATIONSHIP

## Description

Establish mechanisms to support ongoing relationship development and sustain progress toward continuous improvement.

## Method

### *Step 1*

Establish structures to ensure the team stays focused on achieving results aligned with the sourcing strategy. These can range from formal structures, such as regular progress and management review meetings, to informal opportunities, such as team mentoring sessions conducted by business leaders.

### *Step 2*

Assess the company-supplier relationship and devise ways to build it. Examples of ways to create new links between the company and the supplier are reciprocal site visits at all levels from front-line worker to executives and colocation or exchange of employees for periods of time.

### *Step 3*

Design and implement programs to support the team's ability to achieve continuous improvement. Joint training of all team members in a specific skill area will both strengthen that capability and create a common basis for working together. A program to jointly assess best practices and develop competitive benchmarks will encourage innovation and alignment.

### TIPS

➤ The teamwork that occurs on the implementation team is a major contributor to successful outcomes. Pay attention to the dynamics of the team and support and encourage its ongoing development. Occasional team-building events, recognition of accomplishments, and celebrations will sustain enthusiasm and morale.

➤ Recognize that the real work of the implementation team is creating organizational change. Regardless of the specific scope of the team's focus, the team is changing the relationship with suppliers and, in many areas, the way the company operates. The team must develop specific strategies to support and manage change: training, communication, relationship building, recognition, and celebration.

# H.3 MONITOR AND REPORT PROGRESS

## Description

Establish a structure and formal process for obtaining updates and status reports on the team's progress—to keep management informed of issues, barriers, and successes and to provide a mechanism for regular dialogue between the teams and management.

## Method

### *Step 1*

Establish a *projected cost savings matrix* listing all of the savings categories, both hard and soft. Divide the matrix into time periods, with the projected savings depicted in each period. Add two blank columns within each period in order to record the actual results and the variance to projected savings. This matrix may utilize either monthly or quarterly time periods.

Categories of hard and soft savings include:

➤ Hard savings
   —Price reduction
   —Scope/quantity reduction
   —Reduced inventory
   —Head count reduction (full)
   —Product standardization
➤ Soft savings
   —Lead time reduction
   —Internal process cost
   —Rework reduction

–Head count reduction (partial)

–Improved quality

## Step 2

The implementation team sets a regular meeting schedule to review actions being taken and ensure that actions are coordinated in relation to the implementation plan.

On a quarterly basis, review the projected cost savings matrix and the action list. Establish a time frame for achieving targets. If targets are not being met, involve the team sponsor for guidance.

## Step 3

The program management team should set up a regular schedule to review all implementation teams and their performance relative to goals and cost reduction targets.

## Step 4

The executive steering council should schedule meetings at key milestones to review the overall Strategic Sourcing effort and to lend support where needed in order to ensure successful achievement of the project's goals and savings.

**TIP**

➤ Instill a results orientation in the implementation team. Make performance measurement a focal point of team meetings.

## H.4 COMMUNICATION PLANNING

### Description

Develop and implement a detailed plan of communication in order to inform and enroll stakeholders in the ongoing changes.

It is important to remember that during the implementation phase, the desired outcome of your communication efforts is behavior change; therefore, the methods for communicating need to be even more participatory than during the sourcing phases.

## Method

### *Step 1*

Prepare a communication plan.

Follow the steps for building a communication plan outlined in Phase C.1, "Develop Cross-functional Teams", and develop a specific plan for communicating to stakeholders throughout implementation.

### TIPS

➤ In delivering messages, take the time to set the stage and create the context or bigger picture for why these changes are taking place. Use every opportunity, both formal and informal, to communicate the progress and successes of the implementation process.

➤ Encourage feedback. Be alert for information from stakeholders that may cause you to alter implementation tasks and/or timing.

### *Step 2*

Implement the communication plan.

Communicating during implementation is a primary means for creating visibility and enrollment for the Strategic Sourcing changes the team is pursuing.

Implementation requires people throughout the company to make changes that challenge their habits and work identities. Without an effective communication process, the employees will not be engaged fully in the changes required to obtain benefits.

**TIPS**

➤ Publicize your successes and respond to failures (real or perceived). Look for, collect, and incorporate data and anecdotes into your communication. Be clear, consistent, and persistent.

➤ Each communicator has a unique style. This variety of styles allows for greater diversity in how key changes resulting from the Strategic Sourcing project are communicated. Be thoughtful in placing communicators with audiences that will respond to their particular styles. Matching communicator and audience will facilitate effective communication.

## H.5 ESTABLISH THE CONTINUOUS IMPROVEMENT PROCESS

### Description

Establish a shared point of view and a process through which feedback gained from performance monitoring is to be utilized, within the company, within the supplier's organization, or between the two organizations, to drive new value and operational excellence.

### Method

#### Step 1

Using performance measures established in Phase G, set new stretch goals. Goal setting is best done after team members feel the metrics previously chosen accurately represent the process being measured and provide timely data.

#### Step 2

Scan existing sources of ideas to evaluate priorities and focus continuous improvement efforts.

➤ Explore the continuous improvement ideas that were identified during Phases C through F.

➤ Review the earlier work performed in Phase C, "Team Development and Opportunity Identification," and Phase D, "Assessment," to identify areas that were set aside as future savings possibilities. Because process maps have been developed, the team can quickly develop improvement ideas and calculate the expected savings using the total cost model.

### *Step 3*

Brainstorm new ideas to explore. Encourage "out of the box" thinking. Invite people from the user community and the supplier community to participate.

For example, if it is determined that an improvement in the payment process is necessary, then knowledgeable representatives from the company's accounts payable department, as well as the supplier's billing department, will need to be involved.

### *Step 4*

Establish a review process that evaluates the potential of new ideas and weighs their value relative to other identified continuous improvement ideas. This will ensure that the opportunities with the highest value receive priority attention.

### *Step 5*

Install formal mechanisms within both the supplier and the company to generate new ideas that can be tried and implemented by the people involved with the material or services on a timely basis.

Once formal mechanisms are being used, you will have a continuous-improvement-oriented relationship. Examples of some mechanisms include:

➤ Continuous improvement subteams

—Supplier-specific teams

—Commodity-specific teams (multiple suppliers)

➤ Suggestion systems

—Supplier-specific and commodity-specific system

—Guidelines for making it work and keeping it consistent

➤ Application of the total cost model methodology to identify suppliers' cost drivers

—Identify suppliers' infrastructure and process issues that adversely affect cost

—Identify company process changes that reduce supplier costs

➤ Continuous improvement training

—Problem-solving skills

—Quality improvement methodology

—Performance management concepts

—Concept of waste reduction

—Statistical process control

➤ Recognition programs

—For suppliers

—For individual employees

—For teams

➤ Project feedback meetings/two-way reporting

—Use project feedback meetings to give suppliers specific feedback from their customers on how they performed, and vice versa

## TIPS

➤ Formalize continuous improvement mechanisms whenever possible. Typically, continuous improvement does not "just happen" unless formal mechanisms are in place to enable and encourage it.

➤ Don't be seduced by process. Process is a means to an end. Maintain a results focus so that the opportunities with the highest value are given priority.

Phase H concludes the team activity component of the Strategic Sourcing methodology.

Initial implementation will focus on putting in place those recommendations made by the supplier in the proposal. Once this is successfully accomplished, the team will pursue continuous improvement opportunities. As each team implements change, the Strategic Sourcing methodology and principles become institutionalized. Supply chain activities are managed collaboratively between the company and supplier partner. Creating a relationship of mutual respect and trust is the cornerstone. Collaborating to create new value and achieve mutual benefit is the charter.

# Business Integration

Preparation and    Team Activity                                    Post-work
Design Phases      Phases                                           Phase

A   B   C   D   E   F   G   H   I

Strategic Sourcing was a reinvention of the supply chain business practice at SCE. The starting place was a well-defined and
institutionalized business process. The Strategic Sourcing
methodology was the organizational intervention that redefined how every aspect of the process worked. The change in
business practice ultimately needed to be institutionalized
and embedded in the company's operation.

With the initial teams nearing completion and their success evident, it was time to redesign the organizational systems and structures to support Strategic Sourcing as a new way
of doing business. Specific tools were developed to accomplish
the organizational change strategy.

Systems required to support sourcing included performance management, supplier recognition, communications
vehicles, and electronic commerce. Structures such as organizational design, new roles and job definitions, and formal relationship guidelines needed to be created or adapted to sourcing
work.

Due to the complexity of integrating all of these changes, a
business integration tool kit and master plan were developed.
The tool kit consists of the following:

Supplier and team performance measures

Strategic sourcing organizational assessment and design

Competencies and job design

Staffing tools

Supplier recognition program

Sourcing multimedia communications

This phase (see Figure 14.1) describes the elements of business integration.

### PURPOSE

The objective of this phase is to integrate new supply chain processes and practices with company operations as a new way of doing business. The company will establish structures and systems to support the new work of Strategic Sourcing.

### DELIVERABLES

During the business integration phase, the following are put into place:

➤ New organization structure

➤ Redesigned supply chain roles and jobs

➤ Supplier performance management and recognition program

➤ Systems for supporting information and communication

## 🔲 EXPANDING RELATIONSHIPS

As implementation progressed, relationships were being built between the company and supplier team members. These relationships were core to the Strategic Sourcing partnership.

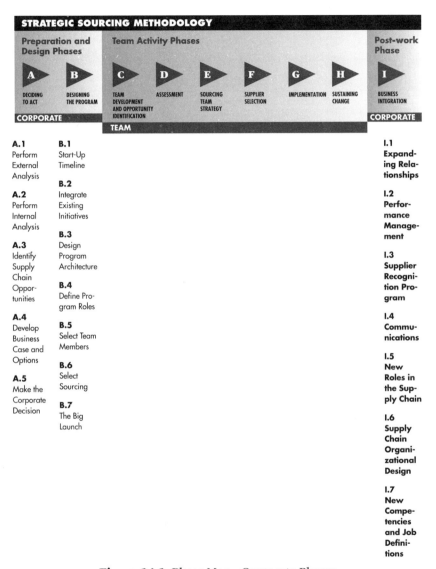

**Figure 14.1** Phase Map—Corporate Phases.

With the magnitude of change occurring and the growing interdependence between suppliers and SCE, we recognized that relationships needed to be built at all levels. Programs specifically aimed at building relationships and confidence between partners were put in place.

## Company to Company

The Executive Liaison Group was formed to establish and nurture relationships at the executive and operating manager levels. This group is composed of key managers from SCE and selected supplier partners, and meets semiannually to discuss operational business issues that have an effect on the working relationship. Members use their experience to recommend how Strategic Sourcing at SCE can be improved, as well as working to refine and enhance the sourcing process and build communication links between suppliers and SCE at all levels. The recently introduced supplier performance program was developed with participation from the executive liaisons.

Reciprocal site visits for technical personnel and line managers constitute another dimension of building company-to-company bonds. Personal visits contribute to a sense of working together. People can put faces with names, understand the working environment, and build acquaintances. Site visits deepen the knowledge level to stimulate innovative thinking, thereby creating opportunity beyond the original scope of the team.

## Crew to Crew

Perhaps the most innovative relationship-building program is what we call *crew to crew*. In fact, some of the most effective and extraordinary breakthroughs in sourcing came through building relationships at the front-line working levels. In the crew-to-crew program, suppliers' employees involved in manufacturing a product came to see their product installed by SCE field employees. In turn, SCE field employees went to see the products manufactured at the supplier's facility. These two groups identified thousands of dollars' worth of continuous improvement ideas—ideas that could only have come from the crews.

An example of the personal impact of these visits was seen when a supplier's quality assurance manager, the person in charge of ensuring electrical equipment was safe when it was energized, commented that the crew-to-crew relationship changed the way he viewed his job. He said that in the past he had viewed his job as checking the quality of the product. After this trip, he said his new job was to make sure his quality check allowed his SCE friend to go home safely to his children. No dollar amount can be placed on this kind of personal insight.

## I.2 PERFORMANCE MANAGEMENT

A system of evaluating performance in Strategic Sourcing contracts was developed. It encompassed regular monitoring and reporting, as well as periodic meetings to discuss progress, outstanding issues, and new opportunities for continuous improvement.

### Performance Measurement

Each sourcing team maintains a report card that addresses cost, quality, service, and other measures of performance. The unique aspects of each team and supplier require individually tailored performance measures.

Each measure is developed and mutually agreed upon by the supplier and SCE. Performance data is updated monthly. Performance targets are established for each measure selected for the report card. Minimally acceptable performance should be identified, as should the maximum performance for point award. Point values are assigned based on the importance of the parameter. The performance point system forms the basis for the supplier recognition program.

### Annual Critique Schedule

Sourcing team progress is monitored on a regular basis. Figure 14.2 shows the schedule used by all sourcing teams for the life cycle of the contract.

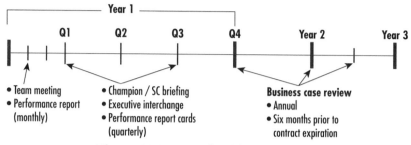

**Figure 14.2** Annual Critique Schedule.

At a minimum, the target audience for scheduled critique events will include:

Steering council

Team champions

Key business unit managers

Sourcing personnel

Suppliers

## Annual Business Case Review

An annual business case review is conducted for each supplier on each sourcing team. The business case will be developed by the sourcing team, evaluating the performance of suppliers as well as SCE. The business case is reviewed by the sourcing manager, the appropriate business unit managers, and the Executive Steering Council. A review of team performance should cover the following subject matter.

### *Total Cost*

The entire supply chain cost for providing the sourced material and services will be addressed, including a high-level review and update of the cost model as well as a review of the supplier product prices.

The sourcing team, including the supplier, should revisit the base assumptions of the cost model (originally presented to the Executive Steering Council) to determine what has been achieved. The process flow charts should be verified and updated as required.

## Quality

The agreed-upon quality goals should be reviewed and compared to actual performance by the supplier.

## Delivery

The annual business case should address the supplier's on-time delivery performance and logistics strategy. The sourcing team sets goals by product type and compares the supplier's performance to the goals.

## Alliance Behavior

The annual business case should address the supplier's performance in areas such as support of emergencies, major storm coverage, service orientation, efforts to improve the alliance, and any other pertinent issues. The report should also address the performance of SCE as an alliance partner from the supplier's perspective.

## Continuous Improvement

Team continuous improvement goals and project plans should be reviewed on an ongoing basis. Continuous improvement progress is a factor in overall team/supplier performance.

## New Technology

Changes in technology and supplier capability are assessed as part of the annual business case review. A supplier's ability to continue to produce leading-edge technology in the market, as well as its ability to keep pace with electronic commerce, are critical elements to the success of the alliance and should not be overlooked.

### Commercial Guidelines

Strategic Sourcing relationship guidelines institutionalize traditional commercial considerations in the Strategic Sourcing program. These complement the sourcing team process and serve as a consistent commercial framework for all teams.

These guidelines are necessary to maintain the integrity of the Strategic Sourcing program and provide direction for ongoing sourcing activities. The guidelines are categorized into the following subjects:

- ➤ Infrastructure
- ➤ Sourcing contract—annual review
- ➤ Contract renewal/extension
- ➤ Contract cancellation—full/partial
- ➤ Problem resolution
- ➤ Documentation requirements

## I.3 SUPPLIER RECOGNITION PROGRAM

At SCE, a supplier performance program was established. This program is designed to monitor and recognize superior performance by suppliers. Working together through this program, we strengthen goal alignment between companies and improve product and service quality.

The performance of our suppliers directly impacts our ability to meet Edison business unit goals. Key goals supplier performance can affect are:

- ➤ Average minutes of customer interruption
- ➤ Number of circuit interruptions

➤ Outage time

➤ Financial performance

➤ Customer satisfaction levels

## Program Design

Data on cost, quality, service, and other factors are combined into an overall supplier performance rating. SCE issues quarterly report cards to each supplier.

The reporting process includes a preliminary report card and a final report card. The preliminary report card is submitted to suppliers for a 30-day reconciliation period. During the reconciliation period, suppliers are encouraged to review the accuracy of the data contained in the preliminary report card. An adjustment is made for data discrepancies and the final report card is issued to the supplier.

Suppliers whose total scores fall within a defined performance range, and meet all established minimum acceptable levels, are formally recognized. Supplier performance that falls below the acceptable range or fails to meet minimum levels is subject to probation.

The performance rating categories are as follows:

Gold

Silver

Bronze

Improvement expected

Unacceptable

Annually, a celebration event is held to recognize suppliers whose quarterly scores qualify them as having achieved gold, silver, or bronze performance levels for the year. The event includes dinner and awards commensurate with annual performance.

## I.4 COMMUNICATIONS

A communication infrastructure needed to be built. Communication within the teams received a great deal of attention. The teams developed stakeholder lists and communicated about the specific changes within the scope of their material or service. At the corporate level, we knew that the teams' efforts were only part of the communication needed. Field personnel were interested not only in a single material or service, but the entire scope of changes affecting them. As a result, we implemented a comprehensive Strategic Sourcing communication strategy. The suppliers participated with us in developing a strategy for communication with both SCE and supplier employees.

### Communication Plan

We created a formal communication plan to provide systematic and ongoing information about Strategic Sourcing. The communication plan took into account the range of communication needs for everyone from executives to people who used and produced the material or service. To develop this broad plan, we identified the target audiences and developed customized media and products.

### Access to Information

The first step was to provide ready access to information about Strategic Sourcing and changes taking place. To this end, we installed and publicized a Strategic Sourcing information hotline for people to call for program updates and to have questions answered. The inquiries on the hotline also provided valuable input that enabled us to better understand communication needs. A Strategic Sourcing Web page was created that allowed people to access more in-depth information on topics of interest to them.

## Brochures

Brochures were used to periodically update employees on the progress and changes created by Strategic Sourcing (see Figure 14.3). This kept Strategic Sourcing visible and enlisted employee support. Brochures targeting specific products that had broad-based interest were sent to employees. The brochures explained how we selected the suppliers and how much SCE would save when employees used the suppliers and recommended products. Brochures that targeted the overall sourcing strategy were also distributed to employees to provide an overview of the sourcing process as well as specifics about team progress.

**Figure 14.3** Strategic Sourcing Update Brochure.

### Videos/CDs

Professional videos and compact discs (CDs) were another form of communication used to explain Strategic Sourcing and its goals. Both SCE and suppliers' employees received these communications targeted at the material or service they used or produced.

At the yearly celebration held for the teams, one team expressed its creativity in a homemade video describing how members had invented a new product to prevent animals from crawling into energized equipment. Stuffed animals were the "actors" used to illustrate the change.

Persistent and personal communication is essential to keep the sourcing process momentum in high gear.

## 1.5 NEW ROLES IN THE SUPPLY CHAIN

The Strategic Sourcing process is composed of several new roles that are uniquely different from traditional procurement. In some companies, the entire corporation is reengineered to align with the supply chain and the new roles become institutionalized. Absent such a company-wide redesign at SCE, we implemented a more dynamic, team-based organizational model in which some roles translated into permanent jobs, others into ad hoc team assignments for a period of time, and still others into assignments performed in addition to job responsibilities. The following overview describes roles at the highest level; a detailed role definition is found in Phase C and Chapter 4, "Critical Success Factors in Strategic Sourcing."

### Executive Steering Council

The corporate steering council is made up of key executives from SCE business units that use the products or services of the sourcing teams and/or have a management or financial interest. The executive steering council is the approving body that authorizes initial sourcing recommendations and subsequent changes (i.e., significant pricing changes, renewal, suspension, termination). The council generally meets quarterly or on an as-needed basis.

## Team Champions

Team champions are key business unit managers closely aligned with sourced products or services and are critical resources to sourcing teams. Champions are responsible for working with teams to determine identified savings projections as well as how identified savings will be accounted for at the business unit level. Champions also help clear roadblocks and provide direction. Champions typically participate in team meetings on an as-needed basis and meet with the executive steering council to provide periodic updates.

## Team Leader

The team leader is the primary point of contact for the sourcing team. Team leaders are responsible for building team cohesiveness around a common charter and demonstrating personal commitment to team goals and objectives. Team leaders coordinate and drive team schedules, support individual team members, actively participate on team activities, and drive the team toward continuous improvement opportunities. Team leaders are also responsible for communicating with stakeholders (business units) and sponsors (champions, executive steering council).

## Project Management Team

Sourcing project managers are responsible for overall project management and coordination, and are assigned as full-time resources to teams. They collect, analyze, and organize cost model, performance measurement, and report card information pertinent to team activities. They provide advice to the team leaders based on their personal experience with Strategic Sourcing. The sourcing project manager coordinates efforts with other resources (i.e., business strategist, logistics analyst, and so on) to ensure timely completion of assignments and to avoid duplication of effort.

### Team Members

Sourcing teams are composed of members from business units and the Procurement and Logistics Department. Members are users of the product or service being sourced and are familiar with the contracting, ordering, and inventorying practices. They typically have decision-making authority. Team members discuss concepts, analyze information, and make recommendations to improve processes. Sourcing teams meet collaboratively with their suppliers on a monthly basis.

## I.6 SUPPLY CHAIN ORGANIZATIONAL DESIGN

The organizational structure needed to be changed to support Strategic Sourcing. Many of the functions of the department changed as we evolved from a transaction-based organization to a collaborative, facilitating organization. A cross-functional redesign team was established to determine the organizational changes needed in procurement and material management functions to support this new work.

Since the initial sourcing teams were supported by procurement and material management personnel on assignment, many of the changes in the work were known before the redesign team was established.

It was critical to understand the functions of the department in order to determine what work was currently being performed, as well as to perform a gap analysis from the current to the new organization. The gap analysis helped to determine what work needed to be eliminated and what work needed to be transitioned to the new organization. Table 14.1 lists and aligns the functions to be performed in the new supply chain organization.

**TIPS**

➤ Since all of the work groups interact with one another, it's essential to think in terms of function and work flow from the start. A function chart was used to focus attention on the critical question of what work needs to be performed in the new organization. By not beginning with an organization chart, we were able to discuss roles and work without being distracted by typical questions of job levels and work group sizes.

➤ The experience of the initial teams guided the organizational design project team, and made the pending organizational changes seem less dramatic to employees in the department.

## Logistics Redesign

The logistics redesign is an example of how this approach of functional analysis without regard to organizational boundaries creates value. SCE had 13 corporate warehouses servicing multiple business units.

A logistics redesign team was established to deliver a comprehensive plan that integrated the efforts of sourcing teams and applied best practices. The logistics redesign team was composed of material management and business unit personnel. Members acted as a coordinating body and as links to sourcing teams, addressing and targeting logistics cost drivers. The scope of the team was to review the material processes from the point of requisition through salvage. The components addressed by the logistics redesign team were requisition, client ordering, storing inventory, issuing, transportation,

| Sourcing | Logistics | Business Strategy and Analysis | Business Support |
|---|---|---|---|
| Supplier relations | Distribution center operations | Client relations | Systems |
| Sourcing expertise | Supply chain optimization | Business opportunity ID | –Electronic commerce |
| Leveraging | Inventory management | Launch of teams | –Business systems |
| Performance management | Logistics strategies | Strategy development/ maintenance | –Systems analysis |
| Results management | Material distribution | Performance metrics | |
| Team staffing | Investment recovery | External communications | Administration |
| Standardization | Hazardous waste management | Business analysis | –Finance/budget |
| Continuous improvement | | –Financial analysis | –Administrative support |
| Facilitation | | –Cost modeling | –Credit card administration |
| Supplier diversity | | –Spending analysis | –Supplier qualification |
| Contract negotiation | | –Risk analysis | |
| Claims resolution | | –Business case | –Graphics |
| Terms & conditions | | Benchmarking | –Management information |
| | | Surveys | –Reporting |
| | | Process mapping | |

**Table 14.1** Function Alignment in the Supply Chain

surplus/salvage, distribution, and receipting of material. The team's redesign efforts resulted in lower client costs and increased customer satisfaction.

Analyses of the current sourcing teams, supplier capability, and overall performance requirements were some of the first steps of the logistics redesign team. Significant total cost reductions were found through logistics reengineering that incorporated both supplier-based logistics management and internal SCE changes. Initial sourcing teams had pursued various supplier-related improvements in logistics areas. However, company-wide coordination in the areas of transportation, job site delivery, and inventory strategies provided greater total cost savings and increased performance. The result of the work done by the logistics redesign team was a $30 million cost reduction to SCE and consolidation of several warehouse locations.

## ⅡⅦ NEW COMPETENCIES AND JOB DEFINITIONS

The functional definitions are the basis for understanding what skills and competencies the organization requires.

A more detailed analysis of the new skills, knowledge, and abilities was important to document what work needed to be done and to create new job descriptions. A matrix listing competencies required for the various positions was developed to ensure proper coverage of the functions in the new department. Table 14.2 shows a list of competencies and how they correspond to four new sourcing jobs of business strategist, business strategist support, logistics analyst, and sourcing analyst. Having clarity at this level of job definition greatly strengthens the staffing process.

### Staffing

To perform the critical task of staffing the new supply chain organization, we developed a performance-based dimension interview. Work done around organization functions was the

| Competency | Business Strategist | Business Strategist Support | Logistics Analyst | Sourcing Analyst |
|---|---|---|---|---|
| Analytical ability | X | X | X | X |
| Business understanding | X | | | X |
| Computer skills | X | X | X | X |
| Conflict resolution | | | | X |
| Customer service orientation/ customer focus | | | X | X |
| Facilitation | | | | X |
| Leadership | | | | X |
| Multiple project management | | X | | |
| Negotiation/persuasion | X | | | X |
| Oral communication skills | X | X | X | X |
| Policies and procedures | X | | | X |
| Presentation skills (verbal) | | | X | X |
| Presentation skills (written) | X | X | | X |
| Risk taking/resilience | X | | | |
| Team building | | | X | |
| Team player | X | X | X | X |
| Written communication skills | X | X | X | X |

**Table 14.2** Skills, Knowledge, and Abilities Matrix

springboard for the questions to be asked in the interviews. In addition, custom performance tests were used to assess individual analytical skills in the areas of total cost model and finance.

In the new organization, the shift was toward job complexity. In a traditional procurement organization, jobs are defined more narrowly. Strategic Sourcing introduced jobs that required a diverse skill set. Since new jobs required both analytical skills and relationship skills, applicants were also asked to demonstrate their facilitation ability as part of the selection process.

## TIPS
➤ Review existing positions to determine whether the current positions contain sourcing skills, knowledge, and abilities. At SCE, with the exception of some

administrative and systems jobs, most positions had changed so significantly that a major redesign was required, which resulted in posting new jobs and selecting employees for those positions on a competitive basis.

➤ Crafting jobs that are more complex and require a range of skills attracted more highly qualified candidates to the sourcing role.

This phase introduced elements of the approach to align organizational structures and systems to support the new business model. However, business integration is an ongoing endeavor. Strategic Sourcing is a dynamic organizational model that assumes continuous improvement not just in the implementation teams, but also in the supply chain practice of the company. As the company learns from its suppliers and from experience, new requirements and opportunities for enhancement will arise. The SCE model for business integration seeks to take full advantage of such opportunities.

## ■ SUMMARY

This concludes Part Two. This section serves as a framework for considering Strategic Sourcing as a corporate supply chain strategy, as well as a practical guidebook to applying Strategic Sourcing.

In Part Two, we have examined in depth the methodology used to implement Strategic Sourcing at SCE. The corporate-level preparation work included an assessment of the opportunity presented by Strategic Sourcing and consideration of the decision to pursue the strategy. The sourcing program design phase defined elements that need to be put in place prior to launching this significant organization change effort. Business integration issues and strategies following sourcing team activity completed the corporate perspective. Phases C through H provided a comprehensive overview of the sourcing team activity, introducing tools and the step-by-step detail methodology for performing the work of Strategic Sourcing.

The book concludes with an epilogue to the story of Strategic Sourcing at SCE. It provides a preview of ways SCE has devised to sustain the business advantage created by Strategic Sourcing and relationships with supplier partners. It looks forward, describing the pursuit to create even greater value through relationships—which brings us to the new supply chain vision of value networks.

# Epilogue–Beyond Strategic Sourcing

When we were preparing to launch Strategic Sourcing at SCE in the fall of 1994, a group of executives attended the Change Acceleration Program at General Electric's Crotonville Center. The invitation to the group was to create a direction for the company to lead us beyond Strategic Sourcing. To begin the working session, I said to my colleagues, "We have devised a solid strategy for implementing what we are calling Strategic Sourcing. It will dramatically change the way we do business in the company and with suppliers. We will kick off two pilot sourcing teams as soon as we return. I know it's a leap of faith, but I would like to suggest we use this opportunity at Crotonville to think beyond Strategic Sourcing to where we can take the company by building on what Strategic Sourcing will do." To which one wry colleague replied, "No, Emiko, it was a leap of faith to come to New York to spend five days to strategize change. I want to make this an opportunity to figure out exactly what we will be doing in the Strategic Sourcing process and what we need to do to lead the change." Of course, he was right and the group ultimately became the Executive Steering Council for Strategic Sourcing. Now it is four years later and we have turned our attention to looking beyond Strategic Sourcing.

---

*After four years of experience in Strategic Sourcing,
SCE is looking ahead.*

---

Strategic Sourcing has transformed the SCE supply chain business practice. A vision of what the principles of Strategic Sourcing could accomplish was the catalyst for change. The Strategic Sourcing methodology was the road map for change. Teams of employees were the vehicle for creating strategies and implementing far-reaching organizational changes. But, Strategic Sourcing is not just a vision or a process or a methodology. Strategic Sourcing is a business model that highlights two values: the soundness of taking a holistic, integrated view in making business decisions for a company, and the power of relationships.

Strategic Sourcing taught us those values and we want to leverage what we have learned. We continue to look for ways to enhance the sourcing strategy and practice. We are also looking for ways to expand upon the strong supplier relationships we have built. We want to weave Strategic Sourcing lessons into the fabric of business at SCE.

---

*The relationship provides a platform for business
alignment beyond materials and services.*

---

This chapter examines how to institutionalize and build on a collaborative company-supplier relationship model. Specifically, the chapter discusses initiatives at SCE in three areas: building company-to-company relationships, extending the supply chain, and creating value networks.

## ■ COMPANY-TO-COMPANY RELATIONSHIPS

The relationships between SCE and its Strategic Sourcing partners provided a platform for achieving business alignment beyond just the provision of materials and services.

The team implementation structure served well to focus the supplier relationship on creating supply chain value, but it also confined the relationship to the sourcing scope. Through the growing acquaintance that took place in implementation, mutual respect and trust was built between companies. People began to appreciate the value of collaborative partnerships. We recognized the potential for expanding value creation through our strong supplier bonds and saw the importance of nurturing company-to-company relationships. Forums were established to ensure executive-level attention to the business relationship and ongoing opportunity for dialogue.

## ■ SUPPLIER EXECUTIVE COUNCIL

The Supplier Executive Council is composed of top-level executives from 10 Strategic Sourcing supplier companies. The purpose of the council is to foster two-way discussion of business issues and identify opportunities to create value through business alignment. The council meets twice a year with the president of SCE and other top SCE executives. The day-long sessions are interactive: Suppliers are updated on current events impacting SCE's business outlook and, in turn, suppliers advise the company about how to most effectively optimize the supplier network. SCE executives also get to hear how the sourcing program is progressing and to surface issues impacting suppliers generally.

## ■ EXECUTIVE-TO-EXECUTIVE SUPPLIER CONFERENCE

An idea that came from the Supplier Executive Council, the Executive-to-Executive Supplier Conference is an annual event that brings together executives from all supplier partner companies to hear SCE executives discuss the current business environment, share SCE strategies and goals, and review the progress of the past year. A panel of line executives present their respective business units' operating plans and then answer questions from the suppliers. The opportunity for suppliers to interact with business leaders has been a source of mutual value. SCE produces a report of the conference and distributes it to all suppliers.

*Convening suppliers strengthens ties and is a source of mutual value.*

## ■ BUSINESS ALIGNMENT

An important dimension of a relationship is alignment that complements each company's business practices and values. This alignment greatly strengthens the company-to-company partnership. SCE convenes special events to bring the company and suppliers together in discussions of how to pursue particular mutual business initiatives.

*Shared corporate values reinforce the relationship.*

### ➤ Business Technology

Suppliers were invited to participate in a day-long conference sponsored by SCE to discuss electronic commerce strategies, share best practices, and identify technology issues. SCE used this forum to solicit input from suppliers in defining an electronic commerce strategy for the company. Recognizing that suppliers would be affected directly by such a strategy, the purpose was to gain an understanding from the suppliers' perspective of value, priorities, and readiness. This information was used to craft a strategy and develop a plan for electronic commerce.

## ➤ Environmental Values

"Greening of the Supply Chain" is a supply chain environmental initiative pursued through a working group of businesses led by Business for Social Responsibility (BSR). We take best practices from the working group to engage our suppliers in examining ways to support environmental values and sustainability through supply chain relationships.

## ➤ Supplier Diversity

Outreach programs provide training to women- and minority-owned small businesses on a variety of business skills and topics. SCE encourages networking opportunities for suppliers to become acquainted and pursue business ventures.

Prior to the launch of the Strategic Sourcing initiative, a widely held misconception that supplier diversity programs would be negatively impacted as a result of the aggregating effect of Strategic Sourcing supplier relationships existed within the supplier community. However, experience at SCE has demonstrated that the sourcing process provides substantially better opportunities to proactively manage supplier diversity results through aligned objectives and collaborative supplier relationships.

Prior to the Strategic Sourcing initiative (1994), supplier diversity spending for commodities now sourced was 19 percent. After 3 years and 22 sourcing teams, supplier diversity spending is now 39.5 percent for sourced commodities, with a 27.5 percent minority spending component (see Table 15.1).

|  | WMBE | Minority | Corporate Total |
|---|---|---|---|
| Before Strategic Sourcing (1994) | 19% | 12% | 25.2% |
| September 1998 | 39.5% | 27.5% | 29% |

**Table 15.1** Sourced Commodities

Year end 1998 is the culmination of a 10-year pledge to achieve a 30 percent expenditure level with women- and minority-owned businesses enterprises (WMBEs). As a result in part of the success of the Strategic Sourcing program, SCE will clearly achieve this comprehensive goal. Recently, SCE was recognized by *Fortune* magazine as the top-performing large corporation in America relative to minority spending.

# ■ VALUE NETWORKS

The foundation for creating value in Strategic Sourcing is the relationship that is formed between the company and suppliers. The initial selection process seeks to identify suppliers who share the values and principles that define Strategic Sourcing: collaboration, openness, and mutual respect and benefit. As the relationship develops through implementation, alignment strengthens, personal relationships grow, trust builds, and business processes become more integrated. Both companies learn together and jointly develop new ideas, insights, and strategies. The outcome of this shared experience base is a strong business relationship that successfully creates mutual value. At SCE, we believe such relationships can become a new foundation for expanding the value proposition in several different directions. Our goal is to build on the supply chain to leverage these business relationships and ultimately create value networks.

> *Supplier relationships are the foundation*
> *for expanding the value propositions.*

## ➤ Extend the Supply Chain

The first push to expand and leverage the company-supplier relationship is to move up and down the supply chain.

> *Leverage the relationship up and down the supply chain.*

We explore ways to link our supplier partners through to our customers. We ask, "How could we leverage our proven suppliers to create value for our customers?" One example would be an offer to give a special discount at Office Depot—a Strategic Sourcing partner—to all SCE customers. This creates value for Office Depot, for SCE, and for SCE's customers. Office Depot increases sales. SCE leverages on behalf of customers and creates goodwill. SCE's customers save money on purchases from Office Depot. This is a simple example to illustrate the value creation opportunity. The concept of customer linkage can be applied in many supply chain areas.

A word of caution: When you become the link between your supplier and your customer, the supplier becomes your company representative in the customer's mind. For that reason, a prerequisite to pursuing such a strategy is confidence that the supplier you are linking to your customer will represent your company well.

Another way to extend Strategic Sourcing upstream along the supply chain is to bring in the companies who are suppliers to your suppliers. This creates an opportunity for suppliers to leverage the methodology, tools, and skills they have learned through Strategic Sourcing. There may also be innovations and efficiencies of business processes that have come out of the implementation team's work that could be applied to subsuppliers. This strategy strengthens alignment along the supply chain, to the benefit of all players.

Another strategy for building on the relationship with suppliers is to explore opportunities to leverage company capabilities to create value for suppliers. This is a role reversal in which suppliers become customers. An example at SCE is an opportunity to leverage the company's fleet services operation. SCE has a fleet of over 6000 vehicles. To maintain that fleet, there are 43 local garage operations with skilled mechanics. Many of the suppliers providing material and services to SCE have fleets as part of their operations. By contracting to maintain and repair the suppliers' vehicles, SCE is able to leverage facilities and expertise in vehicle maintenance to create new revenue. At the same time suppliers can reduce their costs by taking advantage of SCE's capability and geographic proximity (i.e., suppliers' vehicles are typically located at the SCE field locations).

# ■ THINK NETWORK

The next challenge is to think beyond the linear supply chain. How do we build on the foundation of strong relationships to create linkages that become new sources of value? This is a question we are asking at SCE.

---

*The linear supply chain is replaced by value networks.*

---

To date, we are taking the linkages in three directions: linking supplier to SCE employee, linking supplier to supplier, and linking suppliers and the company to an agency that advocates for corporate social responsibility.

## ➤ Supplier to Employee

One strategy is a variation on the model linking suppliers to customers. Only this strategy ties SCE employees to SCE suppliers. This is a leverage opportunity that gives employees the advantage of SCE buying power, increases sales for the supplier, and creates a perk for SCE to offer employees. Everyone wins.

## ➤ Supplier to Supplier

Just as a shared value system and business approach develops between the company and supplier partners, that common denominator exists among suppliers to SCE. The shared experience of doing business in the Strategic Sourcing model creates a basis for relationship building between suppliers. At SCE, we developed a network to give suppliers visibility of fellow suppliers and enable linkages between suppliers. The first step was to have those suppliers that were interested in exploring supplier-to-supplier links submit supplier profiles describing their companies and products. These profiles were compiled and made available online to all suppliers in the network. Suppliers benefited from the business contacts and an awareness of business leverage opportunities. The company gained through increased alignment and connection among suppliers.

## ➤ Supplier Network–Company–BSR

Founded in 1992, Business for Social Responsibility (BSR) is a U.S.-based association of businesses with more than 1500 member companies and affiliated members. BSR provides assistance to companies seeking to implement policies and practices that contribute to the long-term sustained and responsible success of their enterprises and that fairly balance the competing claims of key stakeholders—their investors, employees, customers, business partners, and communities—and the environment.

This network strategy has as its goal strengthening the alignment of the company and its supplier network in support of corporate social responsibility values. One example at SCE is the linking of SCE suppliers to the Greening of the Supply Chain initiative. BSR, which convened the supply chain work group, sponsors initiatives in all aspects of corporate social responsibility. BSR, and groups like it, become valuable partners to establish a network that links companies and promotes and aligns values. Their programs highlight and inform about important social issues. They convene various forums, work groups, conferences, and training sessions. They raise awareness and focus attention on issues in which companies can take a leadership role. Their mission is to stimulate discussion, give visibility to best practices in corporate social responsibility, and act as a catalyst for coordinated action.

*Value networks are the next horizon.*

SCE is just embarking on the strategy to create value networks. The necessary building blocks are in place: company-supplier relationships and understanding of the value potential of linking those relationships broadly to create new opportunities. We have just scratched the surface; the next horizon of creating value networks lies ahead.

## ■ SUMMARY

This chapter has examined strategies for sustaining change created through Strategic Sourcing and expanding the impact of Strategic Sourcing. It has focused on ways SCE was able to strengthen and leverage its strong supplier relationships. The concept of value networks was introduced, along with some examples of how SCE is trying to translate the concept into reality to create even greater supply chain opportunities.

This is not the end of the Strategic Sourcing story. Recall the evolution of Strategic Sourcing over just four years at SCE. Through the original Strategic Sourcing project, the company created a new way of doing business internally: taking a strategic view of the supply chain and introducing a model and process for working collaboratively across the company. The implementation of Strategic Sourcing with supplier partners expanded the Strategic Sourcing impact to create new value by redefining how SCE worked with its suppliers and by building collaborative relationships based on trust and mutual benefit. SCE is now exploring beyond Strategic Sourcing to expand supply chain linkages from a linear value chain to a view of the possibilities created by value networks.

So, I repeat, this is not the end of the Strategic Sourcing story. The possibilities seem endless.

# Index